FEMALE RAGE

FEMALE RAGE

Unlocking Its Secrets, Claiming Its Power

The Medusa Myth retold by Arnold Weinstein

Mary Valentis, Ph.D., and Anne Devane, Ph.D.

CAROL SOUTHERN BOOKS • NEW YORK

From Mary to John, Phillip, and Tom

From Anne to Jimmer and Brendan

Permissions acknowledgments to reprint previously
published material appear on page 256.

Copyright © 1994 by Mary Valentis and Anne Devane.

Published by Carol Southern Books, an imprint of Crown
Publishers, Inc., 201 East 50th Street, New York, New York
10022. Member of the Crown Publishing Group.

Random House, Inc. New York, Toronto, London, Sydney,
Auckland.

Carol Southern Books and colophon are trademarks of
Crown Publishers, Inc.

Manufactured in U.S.A.

Library of Congress Cataloging-in-Publication Data
Valentis, Mary.
Female rage : unlocking its secrets, claiming its power / by
Mary Valentis and Anne Devane.—1st ed.
Includes bibliographical references and index.
1. Anger. 2. Women—Psychology. I. Devane, Anne.
II. Title.
BF575.A5V35 1994
152.4′7′082—dc20   94-18287
                                         CIP

ISBN 0-517-59584-2
10 9 8 7 6 5 4 3 2 1
First Edition

Contents

Acknowledgments

We are grateful to the dozens of women who shared their lives and sometimes painful memories with us. Their honesty, their insights, and their personal stories are the fabric of this book; many are models of how rage can become the foundation for personal change and growth.

We acknowledge the expertise and guidance we received from the psychiatrists, psychologists, social workers, psychiatric nurses, and other healers of mind and body we consulted. Dr. Jeanne Shub, Dr. Susan Britain, Dr. Jilisa Snyder, Sandra Cross, Pearl Mindell, Pam Killen, Carolyn Blackman Miroff, and Ann Waldorf in particular deepened our thinking and discussion by their knowledge and therapeutic experience.

We thank our students at the State University of New York at Albany whose humor, freshness, and approaches to literature, film, and popular culture enhance our classrooms each week and whose viewpoints are well represented in this book.

Our research assistants, Shirley Belden and Margaret Lyons, have provided invaluable research and technical support. Our colleagues in the English Department offered encouragement for the project and shared articles and insights. We especially thank Martha Fleming, Warren Ginsberg, Richard Goldman, Nadia Lawson, John Mason, Rudy Nelson, Iliana Semmler, Tom Smith, and Donald Stauffer.

We thank Maggie Paley for her patience and her editorial and literary skills that brought the manuscript to term. At Crown Publishers, we acknowledge the intelligence and cheerful assistance of Eliza Scott. We are grateful to poet and playwright Arnold Weinstein, who took the scattered material of Medusa's myth and transformed it into contemporary Ovidian poetry. Our agents, Betsy

Amster and Angela Miller, inspired, cajoled, and cheered us on. We are grateful for their assistance and friendship at every stage.

We thank our editor, Carol Southern, who had the courage and vision to support this controversial topic and whose literary sensibilities and remarkable energy have guided this project from the outset. Carol's standards of excellence have stretched us to discover our own possibilities, while her graciousness and wisdom have provided models to follow.

Mary personally thanks her husband, Dr. John Valentis, for his generous sharing of professional knowledge, for answering so many questions, and for his love and support; her mother and sister Barbara, Ira and Helen Mendleson, who proofread the manuscript in various stages, and the following friends, who know how much they contributed to this book: Linda Goodman Pillsbury, Marta Greene, Sara Freifeld, John Gillespie, Xenia, Charles, and Bret Stephens, Judith Frangos, Marcia Alazraki, Judith Baskin, Elizabeth Wilson, Betty Nathan, David Tate, Dina Anthony, Evelyn Zuccardy, Ruth Greenhouse, Carline Davenport, Nancy Thayer, Rosette Lamon, Larissa Kirchner, Kevin Ernst, Barbette Lhersson, Francesco Dominquez, Jeffrey Berman, Nader Uthman, Denise McCoy, and Susan Novotny.

Anne would personally like to acknowledge the help and encouragement of several friends, especially Frances and Michael Harrison, Roberta O'Rourke, Lynn Fisher, Nancy Crutcher Tunnicliffe, Robyn Posson, Jeannie Subik, and her sisters Noreen, Martha, and Julie. Special thanks are due Stephen Herubin for innumerable kindnesses.

M.V.
A.D.

". . . women's anger is a molten pond at the core of me, my most fiercely guarded secret. I know how much of my life as a powerful feeling woman is laced through with this net of rage. It is an electric thread woven into every emotional tapestry upon which I set the essentials of my life—a boiling hot spring likely to erupt at any point, leaping out of my consciousness like a fire on the landscape. How to train that anger with accuracy rather than deny it has been one of the major tasks of my life."

—Audre Lorde, *Sister Outsider*

Introduction: Rage Comes of Age

It was a late summer afternoon. Ellen loved this time of year and was enjoying her ride home from work across the city. Her teenage boys would be out that evening and she was planning to give Don a drink on the patio before dinner. She stopped at the four-way intersection light, checked her lipstick in the mirror, and then shifted her attention to the convertible in front of her. A man and a woman were in the front seat. He was driving; she was beside him, caressing the back of his neck. Ellen looked again; the man was her husband, Don. The woman was his redheaded assistant, and by this time they were kissing. Without hesitation, Ellen backed up her Honda, jammed the shift into drive, and smashed headlong into Don's light blue Le Baron.

Not all women in Ellen's situation would have expressed their rage in the same way. Another woman might have regained her composure, made it home, then asked Don what was going on and how he saw their future together. A third might have absorbed the incriminating scene, called her lawyer, and then at breakfast served her husband notice that she was filing for divorce. Other women might react by popping a few Prozacs, heading for the nearest Dunkin' Donuts, or drowning the memory in a bottle of scotch and continuing without ever confronting the issue head-on.

Rage—like fear, aggression, sexual desire—is a basic instinct and one we share with all animals; it stimulates the production of adrenaline, a natural substance that is used by the body to defend itself against threats to its sense of wholeness or integrity. Ramming the lovers in front of her was a purely instinctual response on Ellen's part. Her natural aggression, combined with an enormous surge of adrenaline, compelled her to take some kind of action on the spot.

If Ellen had taken a few deep breaths, mentally stepped out of the scene, and decided to confront Don at home, she might have saved her valued car, along with her self-respect. In the days and weeks that followed, she might have examined the dynamics of her marriage, what part she had played in provoking her husband's behavior, and then weighed her options for the future. Ellen didn't understand the secret weapon she possessed.

Rage is an emotion no woman can control; what she can learn to control is her behavior and response. The initial rage is merely a physical release of emotion, the beginning of the process by which a woman can later right a wrong, take care of herself, or turn a lethal weapon into an instrument of power.

In Manassas, Virginia, at the end of the twentieth century, Lorena Bobbitt went to the kitchen for a glass of water and instead picked up a knife. Returning to the bedroom and her sleeping husband, John, she cut off his penis and fled with it into the night. Like Lizzie Borden, whose initials match hers, Lorena instantly became a part of popular folklore, the subject of songs, and the source of endless late-night television jokes.

A central topic in the American cultural conversation, the Bobbitt affair soon became an international incident and made front-page news around the world. What had captured the headlines, electrified conversations in diners, classrooms, and fine restaurants was a woman who had literally emasculated her husband and given a name and face to contemporary female rage. Lulled into thinking that this kind of female brutality happens only in Greek myths and tragedies of antiquity, the world woke up with that brutal cut. Yet Lorena's was merely the "final blow" in the long history of women's rage that has smoldered underground for centuries.

In the early thirteenth century B.C., as the invading Hellenes conquered Greece, they destroyed the shrines where goddesses were worshiped, tore the masks off the priestesses, and replaced the female powers with male gods and heroes. Later in their myths, the Greeks represented this moment of male triumph over the powers of female darkness in the image of Perseus holding up the severed head of Medusa. Fifteen centuries later, Medusa is back, and her rage has entered mainstream culture.

Swept to the forefront on a wave of media publicity by such celebrated cases as Anita Hill and Clarence Thomas, Amy Fisher, and the split of Princess Diana and Prince Charles, female rage announced its presence in the results of the 1992 elections and in films like *Fatal Attraction* and *Thelma and Louise*. At the supermarket checkout, in the voting booth, in the bedroom, on the comedy networks, on campus, at pro-choice rallies, over lunch with girlfriends, women of all ages are just beginning to tap into the energy and power of their rage.

Mythology, literature, and popular culture might present stunning images of enraged women, but the behavior of real women has been dictated by powerful proscriptions against expressing any aggressive emotion on that sliding scale registering anger to intense rage. Trained from infancy to be good, women are adept at masking their rage, many times behind mental or physical illness. Unacknowledged female rage expresses itself in phobias and panic attacks. It may disguise itself as manipulation, passive-aggressive behavior, chronic fatigue, control, or suicide threats. An enraged woman may even wear a smile on her face or develop a strategy of pleasing everyone around her—except herself.

Fortunately, a new generation of angry girls and women is emerging, fed up with all ideological perspectives, in touch with their rage, and armed with a sense of humor, sex appeal, and savvy about the media and its hype. Musicians, performance artists, and comedians express rage in creative acts, while political activists join WAC (Women's Action Coalition), with chapters in twenty U.S. cities and in Europe. There are cat-costumed pro-abortion advocates who call themselves Pussies for Choice; Guerrilla Girls conduct street actions against censorship and discrimination in the arts. There's FURY (Feminists United to Represent Youth), a band of high school girls who paint themselves in bright colors to express outrage at rape. Encouraged by the proliferation of talk shows where "rage referees" oversee an endless parade of betrayals and abuses, women's rage has seized the microphone and demanded a hearing.

As professors of literature and popular culture in daily contact with younger women more in touch with their rage than women of our own generation, we decided the subject of female rage was an important one that warranted close examination. We have watched rage emerge on campus, where young women, unwilling to perpetuate the conspiracy of silence, refuse to carry the burden of rage alone and quietly. We have looked around us at friends, colleagues, and neighbors to see what ordinary women were thinking and feeling. Were we all enraged, as one woman suggested? We began to monitor the reactions of our women students during discussions of *Madame Bovary, Anna Karenina,* and *The Awakening.* We wanted to know why women were just now getting in touch with their feelings of rage. What is it about contemporary life that has so strained the emotional lives of women in the United States and elsewhere that our rage is intensified, scary, and still there?

We started to question women between the ages of eighteen and eighty. They came from a broad cross-cultural sampling—young and old, professionals and homemakers, mothers, daughters, grandmothers, single, married, separated, and divorced; most of them were from the middle class. Some were calm, controlled, and reflective; others laughed, whooped, and wept. These were not women from the fringes; we did not seek out women in prison or anyone with a serious mental disorder or an ideological ax to grind.

We asked them when and if they experienced rage, what it felt like, what their particular rage triggers were; we asked whether they could point to particular moments of rage. We asked them if they understood what rage is, how it is different from anger, and, most important, how they deal with it and channel it. Each of these women was at a different stage in her own journey back to the sources of rage. Some were just beginning and were overwhelmed; others, through therapy, had recently discovered the source in their childhoods; others were working their way toward a fuller understanding of their rage step by step. Some women we interviewed were in the last stages of the journey and had transformed their lives in ways they couldn't have imagined. Their stories are funny, unsettling, horrifying, sometimes shocking, and inspiring.

As a whole, they were relieved to tell their stories—but as they began to give a name to their feelings, they often felt fear and confusion about how to deal with the powerful emotions they were evoking. We also began to understand how unacknowledged rage can lead to depression and illness—how unresolved rage leads to paralysis or self-destructive acts.

We found women who experience rage in every area of their lives—at home, on the street, in the workplace, in the bedroom and boardroom. Some are enraged because they no longer feel physically safe—whether they're jogging in the park, driving their cars, or walking around in their apartments. Others feel rage at their wrinkles and the realization that they're growing older. Many experience rage about rapes on campus or gender stereotyping. Still more experience the rage that grows out of dependency on a man. In spite of the passing of the Year of the Woman, many women feel excluded, ignored, discounted, abandoned, or condescended to.

Even as women make inroads in politics, on production lots, in corporations, and on the playing field, the contours of the male-dominated status quo shift only slightly. While menopause, "the silent passage," can easily wipe out the men's movement on the top of the best-seller list, the gap in equality between male and female is still there. A wide breach remains between an ideal world of sexual equality and the realities of women's lives. Female rage is created by this chasm and swirls in the cross fire, between expectations that raise hopes and the real world that makes us see red.

When we asked women what female rage looked like to them, it was always Medusa, the snaky-haired monster of myth, who came to mind. (Glenn Close in *Fatal Attraction,* Roseanne Barr in *She-Devil,* and Lady Macbeth came in as close seconds.) One woman told us that at times her rage feels "mythological." Another psychologist, with a mass of curly hair, said her teenage clients call her "Medusa" because she can see right through them. A third told us her coworkers have dubbed her "Medusa" and address her so, "Because I don't take any shit." When she first experienced her own rage and released it at an anger retreat, she said, "it was like a flood of snakes coming out of me."

We all remember Medusa's head of horror from comic books, old movies like *Clash of the Titans,* or excursions into the world of ancient mythology. Although we might not recognize her, we have seen Medusa in movies like *Alien* and *Fatal Attraction.* We have met her in the giantesses of literature, opera, and history—Clytemnestra, Medea, Shakespeare's "shrew," and the Queen of the Night in *The Magic Flute.* We have read about Medusa in the form of Amy Fisher, shooting her lover's wife. We have seen her, too, in the supermarket, screaming at her toddler, or picketing outside an abortion clinic against patients who try to enter.

Many of us connect the hideous head with feelings that are strangely uncomfortable and vaguely familiar. Face-to-face with the image of Medusa, our inclination is to turn away, to avoid staring directly at her tendrils of coiled, hissing snakes, at her bold, penetrating gaze, her fiery eyes, tusklike teeth, and threatening claws. Her mouth is a gash in stone, her expression twisted in fury. Her gaze turns the male beholder into stone. In one interview after another, we were told that Medusa is "the most horrific woman in the world."

What is it about this figure, we asked ourselves, that still has such impact? Why do so many of the women we've spoken with describe their rage in Medusan terms? We also asked ourselves why so many men, from Freud and his disciples to contemporary male psychoanalysts, have written so extensively about the meaning of Medusa. In their explanations of her place in human consciousness, they project her as ferocious and vengeful, sexless, punishing, relentless, and castrating.

Those who have seen only horror in Medusa's gaze have forgotten that she was once a beautiful woman, her face inspiring poets, artists, and writers. Cellini's great statue of Perseus and Medusa presents a gorgeous female face: classical nose, full lips, well-shaped eyes, smooth skin on a severed head. As we gaze at her in stone, we see not serpents but soft, falling curls resembling Perseus's own. The Romantic poet Shelley was taken by Medusa's beauty, and female poets of our own century, compelled to penetrate her truth, have adopted her as their muse. May Sarton gazes at Medusa to explore her healing powers.[1]

> I turn your face around! It is my face.
> That frozen rage is what I must explore—
> Oh secret, self-enclosed, and ravaged place!
> This is the gift I thank Medusa for.

None of the women we interviewed could remember the details of the myth; none of them knew how Medusa came to be the symbol of female darkness and furious anger. In this male-dominated society, women do not know much about Medusa because her story has always been told from Perseus's point of view. It was time, we felt, to tell Medusa's story as a woman's experience; time to see her not only as a warning but as the gatekeeper of the secret realm of female rage.

Women have also been reluctant to return Medusa's stare, to confront their rage directly. Yet a woman who looks into those eyes will not be turned to stone; rather, she will see in those tortured features a mirror of her own pain. Medusa's story is much more than a parable of horror and frozen rage. In following her transformation from maiden to monster, it is our intention to point a path for modern women to acknowledge their rage and become the women they were born to be.

In recent years, there have been many books about the relevance of Greek and other mythologies to the lives of both men and women. Women are encouraged to find their personal "goddesses within," their "wild woman"; Athena, Aphrodite, and Diana have been written about at length, but Medusa's story had been lost in the rush to present positive ancient models that translate into nineties-style empowerment. With her ghastly face and deadly powers, she didn't even share victim status with Persephone. We concluded that Medusa's story of transformation was a secret and powerful one.

We were fortunate to be conducting our study during a period in which there were several significant books published for women and about their issues. As we surveyed them, we noticed how often the writers seemed on the verge of recognizing rage but either veered away or backed off from naming it. Behind "backlash," behind "self-esteem," behind "loving too much," behind our "erotic silence" and our "foolish choices" is a reservoir of female rage, denied and, yes, repressed.

There have always been women who have refused to collude with the forces of repression, who have used the secret of rage and shared it with others to advance feminist causes. Backlash may occur when women push beyond circumscribed limits and challenge the status quo, but they are able to push and challenge only when utilizing healthy, empowering rage. Those who fear women's full potential would keep rage a secret, but contemporary history suggests that women are ready to reclaim their rage and use it to transform themselves and their society.

Unfocused, undifferentiated rage can contaminate and destroy a woman's entire life. The women we talked with had no trouble discussing the destructive potential of their rage. Some have destroyed personal property, cut or mutilated themselves, and terrified their spouses and children by their outbursts. All feared what they might do if they let their rage explode and never put the brakes on. As we will see, there are many classic models of female violence and revenge, images that are particularly disturbing to women who know the energy and power of this emotion. Free-floating rage is terrifying not only to those who get in its way but also to the woman who experiences it herself.

But a woman who makes the journey back to Medusa by exploring her history and understanding the realities of her rage begins to understand the powerful weapon she possesses. Rage is the gateway to self-assertion, deeper psychological development, and emotional well-being. The power of rage has changed the face of the U.S. Senate and launched art galleries, publishing houses, and accounting firms.

Rage has successfully exposed and fought sexual harassment, the glass ceiling, and a medical establishment that has ignored women's health issues.

After recovering their rage, women we have spoken with are able to leave toxic marriages, to stop eating or dieting compulsively, to pursue dreams, and to discover their real, long-buried selves. The dynamics of rage and revenge are complex and intricate psychological operations that must be recognized, then understood, and finally dealt with in a conscious, careful way. Women are beginning to learn how to use this lethal weapon and train it accurately to channel its aggressive surge. The goal is to achieve authenticity in our lives without hurting others or ourselves.

Understanding and transforming rage is not a process that occurs overnight. Indeed, it would be irresponsible for us to suggest that there is a quick fix for rage. This book does not set out formulas or prescriptions for feeling better. Rage in our culture is far too complicated for a simple solution; knowledge, reflection, and understanding are required to deal with it constructively. Rage is a primal and raw emotion from which civilized people try to dissociate; we want to believe we have progressed far beyond our primitive beginnings and that we act on reason rather than instinct. But rage is normal; it is human; it is real. In our research, we had to move beyond our own fears, squeamishness, and denial to see the truths of our own and other women's lives. We hope the reader will push beyond these barriers as well and confront the Medusa in herself.

In one of the last scenes of Edith Wharton's novel *The Age of Innocence,* the mysterious countess Ellen Olenska is alone in a carriage with her lover, Newland Archer, for the last time. As they speak about their doomed romance, he exclaims that she is "the most honest woman" he has ever met, because she looks "at things as they are." Her reply is the answer of all women who understand rage: "I've looked at the Gorgon," she says. "It's a delusion to say that she blinds people. What she does is just the contrary—she fastens their eyelids open, so that they're never again in that blessed darkness."

1 The Birth of Female Rage

Medusa was Athena's loveliest handmaiden;
golden strands of hair capturing the sunlight
crowned the rare fairness of her face.
She was the human granddaughter of Gaea,
goddess of Earth. Many hopeful young men
*   pursued her.*
But she was wary of their ways.
And when the sea god Poseidon wanted her
she refused him too. Some say
he came to her as a sinewy stallion
and turning her into a mare took her
in Athena's sacred grove.
Others tell simply of the rape of a maiden
by a relentless god, in a goddess's temple.

The Rage of Innocence

The Medusa story begins where all women's stories begin—when they are lovely, young, and innocent. Whether it's a grade school photo, a sweet sixteen birthday snapshot, or a wedding portrait, every woman can look back at a time when her eyes were dewy and she was full of hope about her possibilities and future life.

But for many women, innocence becomes a lifetime condition of suspended development and lack of emotional growth. Like Alices in Wonderland, these women fall into life's rabbit holes still wearing rose-colored glasses, unprepared for its disappointments, betrayals, and mad hatters. Innocence in a girl becomes naïveté in a grown woman: The romantic illusions of teenage women turn into infantile and unrealistic fantasies in the female adult. The infantilizing of women is reinforced throughout the culture and fortified in myth and fairy tale. An innocent woman, with her unrealistic expectations, is set up for rage in both intimate and professional relations.

Betrayal and violation are at the heart of the Medusa story. Before her transformation into a Gorgon (or monster), she honored the goddess Athena and played by her rules; she was a great beauty, admired

American Athena *by Audrey Flack (1989) Audrey Flack's contemporary sculpture* American Athena, *in bronze with gilded ornament, captures the strength and wisdom of the virgin goddess. Outraged by Poseidon's rape of her priestess, Athena transformed Medusa into a hideous monster.*

and pursued by many suitors. Her fall into experience was abrupt and unexpected: Poseidon, the powerful god of the sea, seduced the maiden Medusa in disguised form. Some versions of the myth say he raped her in the guise of a horse; others say he appeared to her as a great bird. Still others tell how he seduced her with his charm. His deceptions are a crucial part of the myth because he represents, in symbolic terms, two important sources of Medusa's rage.

First, Poseidon wears a disguise. In this story, as in many women's, he is a prince on the outside and a "prick" underneath.

Innocent women often feel deceived by the people they trust—not only the men in their lives but their own mothers or best friends, or the coworkers or employers whose loyalty they take for granted. Second, Poseidon is a charmer. Many women, like Medusa, are susceptible to the flattery, deception, and manipulation of men who know how to charm and have a knack for spotting innocence. A naïve woman often lacks the healthy skepticism necessary for realistic evaluation of danger.

Thus, a woman feels the rage of innocence when a traumatic event undermines the viability of her perceptions and alters her expectations about her world. Fundamentally, her trust has been betrayed. She may endure the shock of rape, the most dramatic of violations; she may discover a husband's preference for men or a long-term infidelity. Accompanying her rage at betrayal may come additional anger and fear from the prospect of a bleak future: the breakup of a marriage; an unwanted pregnancy; the relinquishing of custody of her children, a high income, or a crown.

On film and in real life, we are familiar with the untransformed woman whose features and expression seem undisturbed by knowledge of pain and anguish. The wide-eyed wonder of Judy Garland in *The Wizard of Oz,* Doris Day in *Pillow Talk,* or Julia Roberts in *Sleeping with the Enemy* suggests life untouched by betrayals and free from the setbacks and traumas suffered by most men and women as their lives unfold. A woman may, in fact, remain psychologically inviolate into her twenties and thirties, even though she is no longer sexually innocent. Our contemporary mythology, as expressed in film, fiction, and celebrity biography, is filled with images of innocent females whose emotional blinders were the direct cause of their rage.

In the fifties, Debbie Reynolds, star of the "Tammy" movies and partner in an apparently idyllic courtship and marriage with singer Eddie Fisher, epitomized this ingenuous quality. Behind the popular image, according to Reynolds's own story, was a woman frightened about sexuality and passion.[1]

When the press paired her husband in an adulterous affair with "the most beautiful woman in the world," Elizabeth Taylor, Reynolds was in denial: "I'm slow at seeing what I don't want to believe," she writes in her memoirs. Only when she called the Plaza Hotel at three in the morning and found Eddie in Liz's suite did she believe all the rumors. The next day, Fisher told her he had never truly loved her, that he "loved only Elizabeth," says Reynolds. This double-edged betrayal—the infidelity of her husband compounded by the treachery of a close woman friend—was the turning point for Reynolds, and it transformed her in real life as well as on film.

Another icon of feminine innocence is Lady Diana Spencer, the ingenue of the eighties, visibly sparkling with expectation during her engagement to Prince Charles. Although her experiences in childhood had left her emotionally scarred and suffering from bulimia, Diana at the time of her marriage had blossomed from a somewhat gawky schoolgirl into an elegant young woman. When she stepped into that gold carriage on her wedding day, with her went the wishes of the 750 million people watching who wanted to believe in this fairy tale come true. As Andrew Morton, Diana's biographer, notes, "She now speaks of those hours of heady emotion in a voice of wry amusement: 'I had such tremendous hopes in my heart.' "[2]

Whether or not she had any inkling of the hazards that would lie ahead for her as the wife of the future king, Diana was rudely awakened on the honeymoon when two photographs of Charles's lover, Mrs. Camilla Parker-Bowles, slipped from the pages of the diary he was reading. Her rage exploded when she spotted her husband's new pair of cuff links in the shape of two C's—for Camilla and Charles.

From then on, according to Morton's account, Diana's bulimia worsened as she binged and purged four or five times a day. The rest of her story is well known: the continuation of Charles's affair with Camilla; Diana's massive weight loss; constant scrutiny by the press. As rage at her husband increased, the princess turned to self-cutting with a lemon peeler and suicide threats to flag the attention of anyone who would heed her calls for help.

Betrayals, like those experienced by Debbie Reynolds and Princess Diana, happen every day to ordinary women who listen to a culture that tells them they will live happily ever after—if they find the right relationship and the right job, the right clothes, hair, apartment. With their eyes closed, women living by this belief system inevitably take a fall, but as we will learn, these falls from innocence are fortunate and necessary. Innocence is dangerous and blinds women to reality; experience and consciousness clear the path for real growth.

Sandra, a professional woman in her mid-forties, is still incredulous about her own naïveté when she married nearly twenty-five years ago. She began by showing us her wedding pictures. The binding of the album is broken, she explained, because during the last days of her marriage she hurled it at her then husband, hitting the wall, and then threw it in the wastebasket, where it was retrieved by her housekeeper. But the pictures are colorful and clear as ever: Sandra with her father, a portrait of girlish innocence in a white dress; her husband, Michael, handsome in tails, signing papers over the rabbi's desk. But the last photograph in the album is most telling: As the happy couple is pulling out of the driveway at the country club, Michael's expression is sly; he looks very much like the fox at the door of the henhouse.

"My family had tried to stop me from marrying Mike from the beginning," Sandra told us, "but I wouldn't listen. I thought he was a great catch. He was good-looking and seductive; he had just finished law school. I was very young and he was very ardent. I was so flattered by his attention that I shut my eyes to certain things that bothered me. Other people didn't like him—unless they were women he chose to charm. He was smooth; he told me he was in love with me on the second date, and I was swept away. I was so attracted to him. In retrospect, I can recognize his arrogance; I remember he always helped himself to my father's most expensive scotch. He told me he was going to be governor someday and I'd be the one to decorate the mansion."

As it turned out, Michael was less a handsome prince than what psychiatrists call a psychopathic personality. Sandra, in love, saw what she wanted to see. "I'd been married five years," Sandra told us, "when I discovered my engagement ring was missing. Later, I learned he had hocked it for cash, and then he'd reported it stolen to the insurance company and collected on it once again."

That was just the beginning of her journey into the underworld of rage and disillusion. "We separated three times and kept getting back together. I kept trusting him—I didn't want to believe I had made such an error in judgment." Ten years into the marriage, Michael's aunt told Sandra that he had been stealing municipal bonds from her husband's living trust. "Even when the IRS called and asked me questions about the tax returns, I still believed *his* version of the story. I believed what he told me even after my father saw him leaving his office holding hands with his female bookkeeper.

"But despite my naïveté and denial, I could not ignore the telephone call from his mistress's husband. He told me all about my husband's affair with his wife. He had even hired a detective to follow them. He said to me, 'Your husband has ruined my life, my child's life, and my marriage. Will you help me get the son of a bitch?' I was dumbstruck, not only by Michael's huge deception and his double life but particularly by the depth of my own illusions. I felt ashamed that I could be such an idiot. I believe I have finally worked through my rage at him and understand the sources of his behavior, but it has taken much longer to work through the shame and anger at myself."

Eventually, with her eyes wide open, Sandra married a man with less surface charm but whose depth of character enabled her to form a real relationship. Wiser and feeling that she could trust herself again, she found a husband whom she can also trust.

Anguish turned to shame is a root cause of female rage. Simultaneously simmering with rage at her betrayer and castigating herself for her own stupidity, a woman experiences an inversion of basic truths. Once she felt authentic, filled with purpose, and loved; now purpose turns to doubt, love to disgust, and self-worth to lowered self-esteem.

As with all elements in myths, Medusa's "rape" is symbolic and may represent the actual penetration of the female body or the violation of a woman's psychological health and spirit. Western mythology and poetry are filled with female falls from innocence. But where are the roots of female rage, and when does it first show itself in a woman's life? We discovered answers in women's basic training, their conditioning in relation to their bodies, their sexuality, and their families.

The Rage That Rocks the Cradle

> *Remind me how we loved our*
> *mother's body*
> *our mouths drawing the first*
> *this sweetness from her*
> *nipples . . .*
>   —Adrienne Rich

All babies, male and female, experience something like rage at birth. We hear it in the birth cry, the so-called primal scream, and we see it on their contorted faces as they emerge from the sanctuary of the mother's body. Infants in the birth pangs look like miniature Medusas. Their birth rage is their signature—all infants seem to know at an instinctive level the profundity of this first loss: separation from the warmth and security of the mother's womb.

Most researchers now agree that the emotion of anger develops when the infant is four to six months old, emerging simultaneously with its apprehension of cause and effect. Observable in the infant's facial expressions and motor movements such as kicking and waving of arms, anger ". . . is the emotional response typically associated with the blockage of activity toward an expected goal," according to Dr. Michael Lewis.[3] An infant uses anger to try to change its circumstances, with the goal of feeling warm, secure, fed.

Current research suggests that real rage makes its first appearance only when an infant becomes conscious of itself as distinct from its mother, usually at age eighteen to twenty-four months. This is the time when babies begin to experience a clear sense of their individuality and their separateness. It is this sense of separation that creates the climate for feelings of deprivation and loss—those psychologically deeper wounds that engender rage. In his studies of rage and small children, Dr. Henri Parens has observed that rage is not taught; "it is not a learned reaction." Rather, it is an "experience-dependent" response to those "unpleasurable" events that cause children mild to intense psychic pain.[4] Rage, along with fear, aggression, and sexual desire, is a basic instinct, carried deep within the human genetic program. Rage is the simplest, most natural form of defense against a threat to the self and its sense of wholeness and integrity. If we are enraged, we naturally feel aggressive and seek retribution.

Until now, researchers studying the brain and its systems have linked rage with two centers or emotional regulators: these are the hypothalamus and the amygdala. Both parts of the oldest and most primitive system of the human brain, the limbic system, these rage centers are essentially control panels that regulate our emotional lives. Located in the brain stem, they are the body's holding areas for rage. When a fuse blows and rage combines with an act of aggression to produce a vengeful result, more evolved parts of the brain located in the neocortex may come into play.

Psychologist Carol Tavris in her book *Anger: The Misunderstood Emotion* argues that these two brain centers, the limbic system and the neocortex, do not work independently, but in combination with other parts of the brain, as well as with social and environmental factors. All interact to produce an individual's emotional life: her "affect." Depending on her upbringing, her life experiences, her memories, one woman can blow a fuse over infidelity or rape, while another may exercise her rage circuit over seemingly minor slights such as being excluded from a cocktail party.

Rage is a total mind and body experience. Women report that they feel rage throughout their entire bodies: "it's like an intense pressure," "a burning in my insides," "a swirling surge of energy," "a lethal explosion in my head," "a dark helmet of turmoil" are just a few of the descriptions of women's rage we have collected. The good news about rage is that when it explodes, it is the ultimate emotional wake-up call. Depression and repression lead to psychic numbness and blurred vision. Rage, when it explodes, is the psyche's reality check on existence: If we can feel it, we know we are alive.

Rage is literally a mind-blowing experience; when all the circuits go haywire, it blocks out all other emotions. Once in motion, rage takes over the entire psyche, so that it's difficult for an enraged woman to access any thought processes; she disconnects from anything that's happening outside her experience of rage. When rage overpowers a woman's system, unconscious memories of key humiliating experiences may come flooding back. Her painful memories flash before her eyes, overloading her brain circuits, dulling her cognitive powers, and shutting down the entire system.

Some children, because of inborn differences in physiological and psychological makeup, have lower tolerance levels for pain and distress. What is well tolerated by one child is excessive psychic distress for another. With each new unpleasant experience, the rage of susceptible babies is constantly reinforced. Dr. Parens believes that individual "vulnerabilities, tolerances, and coping abilities children are born with," as well as their interaction with their environment, "determine how much rage and hostility is generated." Once the pattern of rage triggering and hostility is played out in infancy, it becomes ingrained as part of an individual's personality. By the middle of an infant's second year, Parens claims, earlier reactions to distress—neglect, no bottle or no breast, isolation, or physical pain—grow more intense; they "stabilize into hate" and feelings of hostile destructiveness. This is when children start saying, "I hate you, Mommy."

Even more than physical deprivation, narcissistic wounds—injuries, either actual or perceived, that diminish or invalidate autonomy and self-esteem—are the principal triggers of childhood rage. Rage in response to primary wounds is embedded in the tissues of the self, says Nantucket-based psychotherapist Pam Killen, and never really heals unless properly addressed. These primary wounds include neglect, abandonment, psychological or actual incest, and sexual or physical abuse. The deepest wounds are inflicted, Killen believes, "when a child is disregarded or not recognized as a distinct human being." When her autonomy is not recognized, she internalizes a belief that her selfhood is invalid and unworthy and that she is somehow to be blamed for her own inadequacy.

When the primary wound is irritated over and over again, it becomes infected with rage, and many times it is covered and sealed, Killen says, with an "overcoating of shame." Girls are well trained to contain their slights, to stifle their fury at a parent's neglect or lack of recognition, and to repress intense feelings connected with the violation of their bodies and souls. The work of therapy in a woman's later life is gently to excavate the site of the primary wound until the hurt is finally acknowledged and released.

When the infection is severe and painful, a young woman's emotional growth cannot progress beyond those moments of trauma in her early development. Her behavior, her appearance, and her survival mechanisms are defined and stunted by rage. Without professional help, she rehearses her rage endlessly, expressing it in passive-aggressive behavior, or unpredictable aggressive outbursts, or illnesses, or a perpetual aura of personal injury. Women caught up in childhood rage find it difficult to step out of this self-destructive, addictive cycle, and their relationships suffer.

Buried in the subconscious, the rage response is primed to operate according to these early patterns. When a person's sense of self-worth is threatened in later life, rage rushes in to shield the psyche. This rage is rooted in a young child's earliest experiences and causes her to replay those primitive dramas.

Mothers and the Rage of Separation

I held her tight for one long moment in our unseeing embrace.
                              —Sue Miller, *The Good Mother*

To recover the feeling of security and pleasure experienced in relation to the mother's body is a natural quest for both sexes. At times, we all want to come in from the cold and duplicate that first safety and warm fusion with the mother's womb and with her loving arms. The thwarted desire for intimacy with the mother is a source of rage for girls and boys. An adult heterosexual male will compensate for this loss: In his lovemaking with women, he will suck at the breast again and reexperience the engulfing warmth of female flesh. His early rage at the lost mother will be assuaged in a relatively straight-forward manner. He gives up the mother, but he can still get the girl.

But a heterosexual woman is expelled forever from union with her mother, the first love of her life. Her psychosexual course is more difficult and complex than her brother's and its underlying theme is not substitution, but shame. Between eighteen months and three years, when both sexes are engaged in the dance of closeness and separation from the mother, the little girl begins to notice physical differences between her mother and father and their respective roles and to identify with her mother. At the same time, she begins to explore her body. She is aware at some level that certain sensations arise from a part of her body that she can't see. Her curiosity about where her urine comes from is matched by her intrigue concerning the pleasurable sensations she feels when she rubs herself between her legs. According to psychologists, she is likely to decide that some-thing is missing that could be there. As she moves out into the world, her male playmates will show her, with great delight, their handy "out there" equipment. Even if she never actually sees male genitalia, she has most likely already internalized physical differences between her mother and father, and if she has a brother, she has additional evidence that he's got something she hasn't. Along with his equip-ment, he's given privileges she's often denied. The resulting rage and shame she experiences with this perception of being different or of an absent penis, according to Dr. Lucy Lafarge, "triggers a reverberat-ing cycle of loss and anger" that she brings into her sexuality and her idea of self.[5]

Freud, of course, called this particular female phenomenon "penis envy" and believed that all little girls were angry at being "have-nots." Certainly Western culture idealizes the male genitals. The

Greeks, for example, considered the male body the ideal and the female body inferior both in terms of strength and beauty. In Greek sculpture from the classical period, the female body is usually clothed. In *Sexual Personae*, Camille Paglia describes the ancient Greeks' fixation on the idealized form of what she calls "the beautiful boy."

> The beautiful boy was the focus of Apollonian space. All eyes were upon him. His broad-shouldered, narrow-waisted body was a masterwork of Apollonian articulation, every muscle group edged and contoured. There was even a ropy new muscle, looping the hips and genitals. Classic Athens found the fatty female body unbeautiful, because it was not a visible instrument of action.[6]

In the modern vernacular, courage, bravery, and power are linked with testicles and the penis. It is only a small leap for the girl to internalize the perception that without the equipment, she lacks these personal traits. Mythology, literature, advertising, and movies underscore her status. Today the "beautiful boy" is an anorectic model like Kate Moss.

If her mother has not dealt with her own feelings of inferiority about being a woman, the little girl also becomes the receptor of another generation's shame. Mommy refers to her entire genital region as "down there." Girls learn that this "secret garden" should not be touched, even if it feels good to rub her clitoris against the bar of her brother's bicycle or touch herself before she goes to sleep. When her mother draws the line between her and her genitals, the girl comes to believe that her sexuality is not only inferior and hidden but untouchable and unmentionable. Many women have never heard the words *vagina*, *vulva*, or *uterus* from their mother.

At the time of her first discoveries of differences and lack, the girl's psyche and fantasy worlds are still evolving; she puts ideas and images together in ways that make sense to a child focused on getting pleasure and avoiding pain. She doesn't have a penis and neither does her mother, a perception that she equates with lack of power for all women. With this knowledge, the girl suffers a narcissistic wound, feeling the shame of her perceived inferiority and powerlessness. These notions may appear consciously in the child's questions, explorations, and furtive observations, or she may deal with them on a more subconscious level.

"Some days the fury the girl feels is like a dark cloud that envelops them both," observes psychoanalyst Louise Kaplan, describing the wild and destructive rages of the two-year-old female confronting her mother.[7] This confused, unfocused infantile fury, Kaplan says, is "not yet clearly associated with feelings of envy or with the erotic meanings it will acquire" later on, and it is an integral part of a girl's "complex experience" of her own femininity and genitals.[8] A little girl's perceptions of differences need to be recognized and then brought into the open by her mother, since they have deep implications for the ways in which a woman understands her sexuality and the role of rage in her life.

Rage at Exclusion, Envy, Abandonment

In a great many of our interviews over the past few years, we encountered the common theme of women's fear of abandonment. It is understandable that a child would harbor fears of being left helpless and alone, but why, we asked, was it that so many women exhibit this fear in adulthood? Was fear of abandonment a defining characteristic for the female?

Experts in the field of psychology tell us there are two milestones in a girl's early life that play into her fear of being abandoned. The first, her perceptions of anatomical and gender differences, becomes the foundation for the second, her feelings of insecurity when she realizes, at four or five, that she is being excluded from the sexual life of her mother and father.

According to Louise Kaplan, the rage of the young girl concerning her parents' sexual life is "the critical trauma of her childhood."[9] Most likely, she has glimpsed her parents' bodies in various states of undress, has observed displays of affection between them, and has become aware of closed-off activity in their bedroom. Even infants hear and take into their subconscious the "struggle" of their parents in the bedroom, according to experts, who for this reason advise against keeping babies and children in the same room where intercourse occurs. One woman we interviewed remembered going to her parents' room as a small child because she "heard something going on." When she asked her parents what they were doing, they told her they were "wrestling" and that she should go back to bed. While she is filtering these impressions, the little girl is also striving to emulate her mother, who leaves her behind, outside the bedroom door.

Excluded, a girl becomes enraged: at her mother, who prefers to sleep with Daddy and seems to have it all—breasts, pubic hair, and the ability to make babies—and at her father, who prefers to sleep with Mommy. Always the child bridesmaid to her mother, never her father's bride, she feels like an outsider, living on the margins of erotic activity, never let in. Boys don't feel this exclusion in the same way, since they have the equipment, identify with the father and his power, and subconsciously intuit a future when they will take the father's place. If a woman's early rage at these two milestones is not resolved, she can feel envy, jealousy, and what we call exclusion rage in the wider social world every time she's left out of conversation or a negotiation or spends a Friday or Saturday night without a date.

Society reinforces exclusion rage as a woman grows into adulthood. When she is ignored at a board meeting or talked down to at the auto-repair shop, she can feel invisible. The groundswell of renewed female solidarity that followed the Anita Hill–Clarence Thomas hearings was powered by exclusion rage. Television cameras in that hearing room gave women visible proof of their lack of power in the political sphere. There was not one woman on the Senate committee.

Dana, one woman we talked to, experienced exclusion rage at the bank as she and her fiancé, Carl, were applying for a mortgage to buy a new house. Though they were going to use Dana's savings as a down payment and her credit record as references, the female bank official did not acknowledge her during the negotiations. Even after

Carl pointed out twice that the money for the loan came from Dana, the bank officer insisted on addressing Carl exclusively. Red with fury and trying not to take her feelings out on Carl, Dana left the bank deflated.

Exclusions may be real, as in Dana's case, but they may also be imagined. A woman who is prey to exclusion rage may feel fury at her boyfriend or lover if he focuses his attention on another woman at a dinner party or lingers too long in conversation with his boss. Slights like these can fan small brushfires of rage.

Laura, one of our interviewees, almost lost her second husband, Bill, because of her inability to control her rageful feelings. Laura's situation was particularly difficult, since Bill was a psychiatrist and most of his clients were women who told him the most intimate details of their lives and who sometimes thought they had fallen in love with him during the course of their therapy. Although she understood that this dynamic of transference was part of the therapeutic process, Laura was still plagued by the fear that he would become involved in an intimate relationship with a female client. She reasoned, If he was privy to their secrets, wouldn't this create a powerful bond? Sometimes, unable to curb her impulse, she called and interrupted his office sessions or chastised him at home for his imagined infidelity. Although he was patient and assured her there was no one else, she tortured herself, until she finally entered therapy and confronted these feelings.

Women like Laura, whose jealousy and rage interfere with their normal functioning, have not completely dealt with and resolved their separation from their mothers. For a girl, separation from a mother may be hampered by the parent herself. Many mothers, unable to disconnect themselves, project their own fears of separation onto their daughters.

For a female child, unlike a boy, separation from the mother most often begins when she gives up her same-sex erotic allegiance and superimposes her infantile sexual desires on the opposite sex. The mother is now forbidden territory—not a love object, but a rival— and one whose body is a bigger and better twin of her own.

The girl still longs for her mother's love, closeness, and protection, even as she switches her sexual attention to her father. Through the convoluted operations of the psyche, by engaging with a father who turns to her mother for love and intimacy, the girl regains her mother as protector and experiences the mother's erotic presence vicariously. The father becomes the fulcrum in this triangular balancing act that often repeats and reverberates in the psychic life of adult females.

When the little girl, through the support and understanding of both parents, negotiates her way through these psychic shoals, she sets the stage for her later development as a person with a strong ego and sense of boundaries. However, according to Dorothy Dinnerstein, author of *The Mermaid and the Minotaur,* the sexual contortions in the early years of a woman's development can lead to an adult heterosexual jealousy and a complex rage shaped and colored by an unsatisfied infantile desire for the mother. A woman's jealousy "is apt to be more deeply complicated than a man's by homoerotic excitement, her rage more blurred, her impulses to get rid of the intruder less pure."[10] This is why the rage of a woman scorned is so relentless, complex, and intense. The other woman is a reminder of a powerful mother who reactivates the rage and shame of early childhood.

In his startling fictional study of male-female relations, *The Unbearable Lightness of Being,* Czech novelist Milan Kundera dramatizes the real-life inheritance of rage passed on from mothers to daughters—daughters who in their own rage and resentment often repeat the sins of the mothers. The novel revolves around a love triangle in which a young woman, Tereza, plays out her pain and sexual ambivalence toward her lover, Tomas, and his mistress, Sabina. Tereza grew up trying to please her narcissistic mother and was "willing to do anything to gain her mother's love." Although beautiful and a capable photographer, she has little confidence, particularly about her body and her untested sexuality. Tomas, a doctor in Prague with a stable of mistresses, is touched by Tereza's innocence and vulnerability and asks her to move in and marry him. He believes he loves her because, unlike the others, whom he leaves after sex, she passes his ultimate test: He can sleep all night next to her, holding her hand.

But he is unwilling to give up the mysterious and outrageous artist Sabina, who feeds his fantasies in their lovemaking. One day, Tereza finds a letter from Sabina to Tomas inviting him for a tryst: "I want to make love to you in my studio. It will be like a stage surrounded by people. The audience won't be allowed up close, but they won't be able to take their eyes off us. . . ."[11] Tereza experiences vertigo when she first discovers the letter, but eventually "the image lost some of its original cruelty and began to excite Tereza. She would whisper the details to him while they made love."

Tereza's solution to her rage at Tomas's infidelity and her fears of abandonment is to fantasize ménages à trois in which she accompanies her lover to Sabina's studio and the apartments of his other mistresses. We can see that in her fantasy, Tereza has re-created the primal scene of her childhood, but this time she has let herself into the parents' bedroom. With Tomas and Sabina, she can play out her blurred and complicated feelings toward her mother. Loving and desiring both her mother and Sabina, she hates them at the same time.

But she is also able to understand her mother now: "her mother loved her stepfather, just as Tereza loved Tomas, and her stepfather tortured her mother with his infidelities just as Tomas galled her with his." Tereza's suffering is an exact duplication of her mother's anguish, only now, as a grown woman, she understands why her mother created so much pain for her when she was growing up.

Although all women may experience fear of abandonment, sometimes the abandonment they have experienced is real. Sherrie, one of the women we interviewed, was abandoned by her mother when she was five. "I realize now, after exploring all my rage and fears, that my mother was in an impossible situation," she told us. "But when it happened, and for many years afterward, I didn't know the truth about what was going on, and I was simply devastated." The pain of the young girl marks the woman's face as she recalls how frightened she felt. "She just left. I've tried to rationalize it and tell myself that she was being physically beaten by an enraged alcoholic, and of course she had to do something. But how could she leave me and my brothers there if it wasn't safe for her to stay?"

A high-functioning young professional involved in community affairs, Sherrie entered therapy when she was in her twenties to try to come to terms with her tangled emotions. As outgoing, energetic, and cheerful as she is, her mother's disappearance is a wound that is still fresh. "After six months, my father tracked her down in another city and persuaded her to come back to make things work. I remember the day. I was five or six years old and I pleaded with her: 'You're not going to leave again, right?' And I remember that night going from window to window to make sure they were all locked, because I thought that then she couldn't escape. I totally forgot that she could open the door and walk out, which is what she did the next morning. No good-bye, no nothing, just gone again."

The consequences of Sherrie's childhood were multiple and far-reaching: an adolescence spoiled by thoughts of suicide and the need to be the sexy center of every party, an emotional life defined by fear and depression. She has spent years learning to comprehend her mother's leaving—in therapy, at retreats, and in long group sessions. "I've been through week-long retreats where you bash the pillows, scream, and reenact the whole family scene. These sessions are extremely helpful. It's a slow process, but I hope someday I'll be completely free of my rage."

Boundaries and Buildup: Getting Stuck in Rage

> *What is our innocence,*
> *What is our guilt? All are*
> *naked, none is safe.*
> —Marianne Moore

Children who feel rage toward their mothers also feel an attendant guilt. At the same time they may wish to strike back at her, they are aware of how dependent they are on her. Caught in a bind of pushing their mothers away and wanting them near, little girls grow up con-flicted about their boundaries and feelings.

As the child separates more fully from the mother, she establishes emotional space between them. By the time she becomes a woman, if she has truly negotiated this separation, she has a sense of her own integrity. She has a clear sense of self, of where she ends and others begin. Her boundaries are intact and her behavior emerges from a central core of feelings, attitudes, and beliefs. She doesn't find it nec-essary to seek approval from others continually for her preferences, dislikes, choices, or desires. She thinks of herself as an autonomous being who has a right to her own place in the sun, who doesn't have to apologize for her existence or depend on others to make her feel worthwhile.

Women without boundaries (some psychologists use the term *po-rous personalities*) lack this sense of separateness, this clear vision of the distinction between themselves and others. Psychologist Susan Britain says that these women are often "daughters of mothers who have no boundaries of their own." Such mothers remain enmeshed in their daughters' emotional lives well after the girls need to separate. They send their daughters off ill-equipped to deal with the world and at the mercy of anyone who would exploit, manipulate, or ridicule them. These daughters have not learned how to protect themselves and they become the psychological "victim" types; they fail to evolve into autonomous adults and remain pathologically dependent. In their thirties and forties, they may turn to therapy to find out who they are. "Without boundaries," asserts Britain, "you don't get con-structed."

Samantha is twenty-eight, lives in Los Angeles, and works as a pro-duction assistant for a major television network. A graduate of one of the Seven Sister colleges who considers herself "an independent liberated woman," she looks, with her winsome, intelligent good looks, as if she could have stepped out of an Edith Wharton novel. Sam and her mother are very close and have been since her father died when she was two. Plagued by her father's seeming abandonment and fearful about her mother leaving, Sam remembers literally tying a string from her finger to her mother's waist "so I wouldn't lose her, too. I constantly quested for love and approval," she said. "I guess I still do."

In those very early days, Sam's mother was the center of her universe. Whatever her mother said, she accepted as true and right. If her mother was depressed, she felt depressed, too. As she grew older, she sought her mother's approval for all her decisions. If she slept over at another girl's house, she felt compelled to call home before going to sleep. But as she reached adolescence, their closeness became a problem. When she began going out with boys, her mother felt threatened and afraid she would lose her. She began eavesdropping on Sam's telephone calls and scrutinizing her letters. Though her love had given Sam a strong foundation, her clinging behavior made Sam feel guilty and perpetuated her childhood dependency. The walls between them remain semipermeable to this day.

Sam's first serious relationship with a man mirrored her relationship with her mother. Although she was financially independent and established in a career, she idolized David. Wanting to please him at every turn, Sam suppressed her own desires and followed his lead. In choices of restaurants, films, and friends, she deferred to him. Soon she felt so completely fused with him that she was unsure of her own identity. When she found out he had been seeing his old girlfriend behind her back, she was enraged but still clung to him. When David broke up with her two years later, Sam felt empty and ashamed for having trusted him.

Many times a woman without boundaries will pull herself together by using her feelings of rage, that primitive cement that helped her survive as a child. Rage becomes her survival tool, an all-encompassing security blanket that reconnects her to herself in some fundamental way. Many women we've interviewed describe their rage—which they connect with fears of separation, abandonment, fragmentation, or annihilation—as their way to recenter and ground themselves, to get back in touch.

Some women actually enjoy their rage and the power and attention it gives them and they become rageaholics. This kind of rage addiction gives birth to the clichéd image of women as enraged, Medusa-like creatures. Rageaholics deliberately set up scenarios that allow them to sustain both rage and control.

Other women, even at an early age, learn how to use rage to help them assert themselves. Describing herself as one of the "lucky ones"—a woman who comes from an intact, traditional, supportive family—Helen has always been aware of her rage and used it effectively and assertively since the time she was a young girl. "My parents always remind me about the time I crushed a watermelon, a baby watermelon, over my cousin's head when I was about nine or ten," she says.

In fifth or six grade in a girl's Catholic school, Helen was incensed when the nuns insisted that her diminutive younger sister clean everything on her plate at each lunch hour; her rage flared particularly when the nuns reminded her little sister about all the starving orphans in the world who would love to eat her meal. Finally fed up with the forced feedings, Helen stepped up to the nun, told her that her sister was not going to clean her plate anymore, and demanded that both girls be allowed to bring packed lunches from home. It worked.

"I learned to be assertive and take care of rageful feelings on the spot," she says. "At sixteen years old I wasn't afraid to speak up to a doctor whom I thought was being negligent and wasn't prescribing the proper doses of medication for my diabetic grandmother. I was furious with his incompetence and told him so, even though he was a pillar in our Midwest community and my parents were being extremely careful not to offend him. They were relieved when I spoke up on behalf of my grandmother. But I don't push the enraged button too often," Helen says. "I don't want to become one of those dragonladies people avoid."

Helen tends to be very cautious and thoughtful, both in her career as a talent agent in a large metropolitan city and in her comfortable marriage. She says she tries to look at all angles of each and every question and then tries to make decisions based on careful and prolonged deliberations. Still, when fired up with rage, usually over some kind of injustice, "My vision becomes myopic," she says. "I am able to focus and channel my thoughts into immediate action. It's as if I can leap from one tall building to another without one thought of what would happen if I glanced at the ground. I feel I can do anything."

Helen's rage is stirred up when she feels intensely that some injustice is occurring or when she knows that someone is being unfair. "I am constantly dealing with clients, artists and writers, whose livelihoods are dependent on the fairness of others," she says, "and I become furious when their incomes are in jeopardy. I know when this happens," she says, "because I register feelings of rage in my body. My nostrils start to flare—it's not a pretty sight—and I become cutting and sarcastic. I don't resort to foul language, but I may call someone 'dishonest' or 'incompetent.' It's usually a situation where my client is not getting paid, or the payment is being delayed; sometimes they are not given a chance at a job. Then I get up from my chair and have a tendency to pace. When I am pacing back and forth like a tiger, I know I am enraged."

In her job, Helen feels outrage on behalf of her clients, but she is also capable of feeling rage and dealing with it effectively on behalf of herself and her family. Helen's rage surfaced at home one Sunday evening as she and her husband were returning from the country to their brownstone on a quiet city street. After parking their car and mounting the steps to the apartment, Helen and her husband found a foul-smelling heap of overflowing bags of garbage, not theirs, in front of their door.

"It smelled up the entire hallway, and I could imagine what all our neighbors were thinking. My landlord is quite a character," Helen explains. "He told me that night one piece of our mail was on top of a heap of garbage outside the brownstone, so he assumed all the garbage was ours and put it on our doorstep. I saw red. I called him immediately—it was after midnight—and told him to remove the bags at once. He had been acting on one piece of circumstantial evidence and had made a false assumption. He appeared in less than five minutes.

"In business, I'm the same way. When I'm enraged, I immediately confront the individual. I am very direct and never go on hearsay; I can usually tell from someone's voice whether she is bluffing."

Fathers and the Rage of Rejection

> *I know I am but summer to your heart,*
> *And not the full four seasons of the year.*
> —Edna St. Vincent Millay

Medusa was the daughter of Phorcys, one of the lesser gods, who was said to be the son of earth and sea and was linked in this way to the sea god Poseidon, Medusa's defiler. In the myth, both men come to represent the principle of the father. Many women's sexuality, their perceptions about their bodies, and their views of men in general are determined by the posture and attitudes of their fathers.

According to the authors of *Mother-Daughter Revolution,* "fathering, like mothering, is political."[12] Often fathers, even when they accept the values of equality between the sexes, reward cute and impish behavior rather than competence or developing maturity in their little girls. Such daughters are programmed to evolve into "feminine" women and remain trapped in stereotypical female behavior.

Good fathering may be a political act, but it is also a sexual one. A father who turns his daughter into a "princess" sets her up for the rage of perfect little girls who later in life know only imperfection and discontent. By casting his child in this stereotyped role, a father robs her of her individuality and injects sexual intrigue into their relationship. "When father-daughter relationships focus too intently on a girl as a romantic heroine-in-training, down playing the fullness of her being, the relationship takes on subtle but discomforting sexual overtones."[13]

Judith Levine in *My Enemy, My Love: Man-Hating and Ambivalence in Women's Lives,* says: "More than mothers, fathers reinforce gender stereotypes in their daughters; they encourage even the littlest of girls to be flirty, pretty, well-dressed, warm, and pliant—in short 'sexy.' . . ."[14] Without consciously realizing what he is doing, even a well-intentioned father may emotionally seduce his daughter, filling her with false expectations, leaving the bedroom door slightly ajar.

In addition, researchers confirm a continuing widespread male and female preference for sons. Suffragette Elizabeth Cady Stanton wrote of a critical moment in her life, when her father, weeping over the death of his only son, "heaved a deep sigh and said, 'Oh, my daughter, I wish you were a boy.' "[15] Feeling her father's pain, eager to please and console him, she replied, "I will try to be all my brother was." She studied Latin, Greek, and math, working so diligently that she was awarded a prize in classics. "One thought filled my mind," she wrote. "Now my father will be satisfied with me." Her father was pleased with her achievement; he kissed her on the forehead and then he sighed and said again, "Ah, you should have been a boy!"

Women hearing words like Elizabeth Cady Stanton's father's may overcompensate to make up for their gender, at the same time feeling they will never attain their father's approval. Many turn their rage inward and denigrate themselves and who they are; some begin a life of man-hating or turn to other women exclusively. Stanton finally found affirmation from her father through her efforts on behalf of women's rights. She was able to negotiate this unaffirming passage and assert to the world the validity of female life. By turning her rage into action, she empowered other women as well as herself. Her father, in the end, was proud of her.

Fathers may fall into other traps. Those who believe themselves blind to gender often hold up the male model as an ideal, encouraging their daughters to play baseball, fish, and learn the intricacies of automechanics. While all these experiences may be potentially enjoyable and useful for the girl, when engaged in to the exclusion of any female activities, "they tacitly promote male models of how to be and act in the world. Appearing to treat girls equally by treating them as if they were boys affirms male superiority."[16] Fallout from this model of fathering is twofold: A daughter learns that she is of less value than a male, and if she chooses to compete in the world, she uses the masculine paradigm of relating.

Many of the women we interviewed described fathers who were critical or emotionally distant, or who preferred another sibling. Such women may suffer from self-loathing and low self-esteem, often develop a distorted self-image, and may become overweight, underweight, hypersexual, or sexually dysfunctional. Under hypnosis for a weight problem, one woman we interviewed discovered that the source of her lifelong obesity could be traced to the birth of her baby sister when she was four. As her father doted on her little sister and grew increasingly critical of her, there was a repressed "ugly" part of her that became enraged. Unable to challenge his criticism or to win his approval, she turned her rage inward and subconsciously gave him something very real to criticize.

In this complex emotional and psychological labyrinth, a father's response to his daughter during childhood and adolescence plays a large part in determining her relationship with her body and perception of herself as a desirable female. This first encounter with a male will shape her interactions with all the other men in her life.

Linda Leonard's study of the father-daughter relationship, *The Wounded Woman*, explores the ways in which a young girl's growth can be enhanced by a father who is sensitive to his daughter's need for autonomy and his crucial part in her development. "The father's role," she says, "is to lead the daughter from the protected realm of the mother and the home into the outside world, helping her to cope with the world and its conflicts."[17]

The Rage of Incest

"What would happen if one woman told the truth about her life?"

The world would split apart.

          —Muriel Rukeyser, "Kathie Kollowitz"

Some storytellers say that when Poseidon entered the temple of Athena to seduce the beautiful Medusa, he came in the form of a stallion; that is, he was ruled by his basic animal instincts rather than by his heart and human qualities. When a father is ruled by his sexual instincts, he may enter the sacred ground of his daughter's privacy, not only intruding on her emotional integrity but violating the sanctity of her body.

Sigmund Freud listened to his female patients' accounts of childhood molestation and incest and ultimately suppressed them or called them fantasies. A century later, our newspapers, magazines, and talk shows are full of accounts of childhood sexual abuse.

Undoubtedly there are some women and men, unable to grow up or unwilling to let go of their rage, who invent fictional scenarios of incest and abuse as adult excuses for their behavior. Others, who are suggestible, jump on the "victim" bandwagon, looking for an easy explanation for neurotic behavior. But there are those for whom the trauma of incest, molestation, and chronic abuse is corroborated and all too real. Like Medusa's rape, such a violation can transform a woman and infuse her with deep and enduring rage.

Rape and child molestation are among our culture's last taboos. Anytime these charges are leveled, as in the case of Michael Jackson, public outrage is a given. A woman, counseled by her attorney to hurl "child molester" at her estranged lover or spouse in a custody or divorce suit, may decide in her rage to use this ultimate weapon. More than financial misdealings, infidelity, or domestic violence, the violation of a child is still the worst offense. Mia Farrow, shocked and outraged by Woody Allen's affair with her adopted daughter Soon-Yi, sought to paint him not only as a "cradle-snatcher" but also as interested in little girls' "snatches."

Andrea, now in her late thirties, told us she was molested by her beloved father when she was four. She was lying on a kitchen counter to have her hair washed, her little legs splayed; when her father touched her, she was overcome by a rage she could not understand. "It seems to me since then," she said, "I've always thought of my body as open prey for anyone. I've never known how to protect myself or my privacy." A recent incident underscored her dilemma.

After a meeting with an older man her father's age whom she thought of as an adviser and trusted friend, he took her to his car and tried to embrace her. She pushed him away, got out of the car, and slammed the door. Although she acted on her own behalf, she felt guilty because of her past; she thought that somehow she must have encouraged him to make his advances. Andrea's childhood memory has influenced her sexual life, but by bringing her past to consciousness and understanding its connection with the present, she is able to transcend it.

Incest, buried rage, and the repression of memory are powerful themes for Jane Smiley in her Pulitzer Prize–winning novel, *A Thousand Acres*.[18] In this contemporary recasting of *King Lear,* set in the midwestern United States, three sisters and their alcoholic father confront their memories, play out their primitive jealousies, and recover their family secrets. Ginny, the eldest, is married to a good, if unexciting, man; her sex life is bleak; and while she thinks she's "standing on solid ground," she discovers that "there's something moving underneath it, shifting from place to place. There's always some mystery."

After her sister Rose reveals that their father sexually abused her from the time she was thirteen, Ginny returns to the bed of her childhood and her own memories of incest come flooding back.

> Lying here, I knew that he had been in there to me, that my father had lain with me on that bed, that I had looked at the top of his head, at his balding spot in the brown grizzled hair, while feeling him suck my breasts.

With this knowledge of "mysterious bulging items in a dark sack," Ginny's innocence is breached and her life is transformed.

Incest is the most extreme of violations and abandonments; yet a father can also abandon his daughter when he is physically violent, when he dismisses her, treating her as a person whose feelings don't matter, or when he stops investing his time and affections in the family. As Robert Bly put it in *Iron John,* "There is not enough father" in our culture and in our families.[19] Sons, Bly says, suffer from "father-hunger," but daughters also long for a father who is present and emotionally available. "A father's remoteness may severely damage the daughter's ability to participate good-heartedly in later relationships with men. Much of the rage that some women direct to the patriarchy stems from a vast disappointment over this lack of teaching from their own fathers."[20]

A good father is dependable and available. He lets his daughter know he loves her without sending seductive messages. He sets reasonable limits when she begins dating and understands her need for social and sexual exploration. He lets her know he trusts her. These attitudes build up her confidence as she navigates the waters of her development as a female. Happily there are more and more enlightened fathers who have this kind of understanding about their girl children. In an ideal world, parents would join together in support of a young woman's passage from innocence to experience. But all too frequently the passage is painful.

A woman's fall from innocence and her subsequent feelings of shame are a very old story: Pandora opens the box and all hell breaks loose. When she leaves the garden of paradise having tasted knowledge, Eve is held responsible for death, pain in childbirth, and human beings' permanent exile from Eden.

Most women are taught, by their families and their culture, that innocence, like virginity, is something to be preserved. But the lessons of life are fortunate falls and the forbidden apple of truth always transforms us. No woman is doomed to repeat her rage endlessly if she is willing to move beyond infancy and childhood into the pleasures of living as a fully conscious adult.

Athena, goddess of wisdom and war, was a virgin;
she watched the violation of her temple
hiding her divine disgust behind her shield.
Then fury swept her godly reason away,
she transformed the ravaged girl into a dragon;
Medusa's soft shoulders sprouted hideous wings,
the delicate hands became bronze claws,
fangs hung where her teeth had gleamed,
and a long tongue lapped her chin.
In place of Medusa's soft bright hair,
asps and vipers writhed from the roots
encircling her once lovely features. Finally
the goddess put a stare in Medusa's eyes—
a stare that turned men to stone.

Before and After Photos

> *. . . A woman's anger is as terrifying to a man as the wrath of an angry god.*
>
> —Frank Pittman, *Man Enough*

The way women look at themselves and the ways women are perceived in the culture make them prey to rage. A woman's looks, as we all know, are central to her identity. Her conditioning and her culture make her superconscious of her image, while her secret vice—frequent glances in mirrors, car windows, even dinner spoons—is not indulged in out of vanity or narcissism, but to allay her anxiety: to check herself out, to see whether she reflects an acceptable do-and-don't standard of beauty to the outside world. Whether she's Gloria Steinem, who calls herself "the pretty feminist," or Hillary Clinton, whose bad-hair days are fodder for the press, or someone's grandmother, she knows that her appearance is always at issue.

Medusa, the beautiful maiden transformed into a monster, represents the polar extremes of beauty and the grotesque, and her transformation bears a cautionary message. When a woman is too pretty, she risks rape; if she is raped, then enraged, she becomes ugly, at least in her own eyes. There is nothing neutral about any woman's appearance. If she behaves, she's a beauty; if she becomes too assertive or enraged, she's a beast. Naomi Wolf in *The Beauty Myth* writes that the beauty quotient of its leaders rather than the issues they were addressing became the focus of both media critics and social commentators, like Norman Mailer, commenting on the women's movement: "In drawing attention to the physical characteristics of women leaders, *they can be dismissed as either too pretty or too ugly.* The net effect is to prevent women's identification with the issues. If the public woman is stigmatized as too 'pretty,' she's a threat, a rival—or simply not serious; if derided as too 'ugly,' one risks tarring oneself with the same brush by identifying oneself with her agenda."[1]

What we have come to call the "Medusa quotient" played itself out during Bill Clinton's search for a female attorney general. His first choices, Zoe Baird and Kimba Wood, were both superachievers—rich, smart, and perhaps too attractive and too powerful for their own good. When Baird's comparatively minor infraction about her nanny's salary was revealed, her six-figure salary, good looks, and gender were more than most people could bear. The White House switchboards lighted up. A modern woman of intelligence and accomplishment was turned into a monster and the real issue of women and child care was overshadowed.

Janet Reno, who became an acceptable attorney general, described herself at the time of the confirmation hearings as "an old maid who never dates," neutralizing her appearance with this description, removing herself from sexual contention and the political ring of controversy where beauty and rage meet. Neither an angry feminist nor a glamour girl, Reno was like the porridge in the fairy tale: "Not too hot, not too cold, but just right."

For many women, Medusa's punishment, her permanent mask of rage, would be a fate much worse than having to stitch a scarlet letter on her breast or even spend time in jail. An appearance marred by rage is socially unacceptable for many women, almost taboo. We never saw an enraged Hillary Clinton at the time of the Gennifer Flowers episode during the 1992 presidential election or a truly irate Ivana Trump during the disclosure of husband Donald's liaison with Marla Maples. Instead, modern cosmetology gave us a made-over Hillary. Ivana was surgically metamorphosed; her sweet new face and svelte new body bore no marks of rage, and she turned her humiliation into profit in a television ad for hair color in which she declared that "being blond is the best revenge."

In history, art, mythology, and popular culture enraged men from Achilles and Hercules to Rocky and the Terminator are characteristically seen as heroes. Enraged women, on the other hand, are witches, shrews, and demons. Women fear looking *like* Medusa; men fear actually looking *at* her and becoming the next victim of her deadly gaze. According to Harriet Lerner in *Women in Therapy,* both sexes harbor "deep intra-psychic fears about female anger."[2] In a man, Medusa brings out feelings of vulnerability to female censure or attack; in a woman, she arouses fantasies of terrible mothers and primitive fears about her own deadly or magical powers. The faces and features of female rage in Western myth, literature, and art mirror these fears and reflect their intensity.

Greek and Roman mythology are replete with images of female rage. When Medusa was transformed into a snake-haired Gorgon, she became one of three such female monsters, and the only mortal one. The word *gorgon* now refers to any repulsively ugly or terrifying woman. The Furies, representing the most primitive form of female rage—unfocused, diffused, and relentless—are described by Aeschylus in the *Oresteia:*

> Black, and so repulsive,
> Their heavy rasping breathing makes me cringe,
> And their eyes ooze a discharge, sickening. . . .[3]

With the Harpies, like the Furies, female rage is connected with filth. The mythological equivalent of modern film's body snatchers, Harpies were part vulture, part predatory female. They flew above their victims, spreading pollution and contamination in their path. The Bacchae, fawn-skinned followers of the great god Dionysus, were celebrants of uncontrolled passion; fury endowed them with supernatural powers. Enraged, they would rip animals limb from limb with their bare hands, uproot large pine trees, and tear men's flesh to shreds.[4]

Native American author Jamake Highwater in *Myth and Sexuality* claims that the Western tradition has institutionalized the "ferociousness" of women: "This vision of the ferociousness of women as embodiments of dark powers, of irrationality, of the chaotic and savage forces of nature (as Nature itself) is constantly repeated as a fact of life in the literature of the Greeks. Subsequently, it became so fundamental an element in our own Western consciousness that we usually read the works of Homer, Hesiod, Aeschuylus, Sophocles,

A Bacchante *by Annibale Carraci*
Annibale Carraci's A Bacchante *captures the blend of rage, decadence, and ecstasy of Dionysus's female followers, the Bacchae, who would uproot pine trees and tear off animals' limbs.*

and Euripides without noticing that they brilliantly recount history as a vast slander against women."[5]

Women have been thought of as witches throughout the centuries; the rebellious, rageful women were the ones who tended to be demonized. In John Updike's comic novel *The Witches of Eastwick*, male fears and feelings of awe about female rage are expressed toward alienated, angry divorced women. Updike's coven of three middle-aged witches, "gorgeous and doing evil," can turn milk to cream, fly through the air, and rustle up thunderstorms. Their bodies are both mythic and curative: "for any man a garden stocked with antidotes and palliatives."[6] Their husbands have been transformed by their incredible powers. Alexandra's husband "rested on a high kitchen shelf in a jar, reduced to multi-colored dust, the cap screwed on tight." Jane's ex, Sam, "hung in the cellar of her ranch house among the dried herbs and simples"; while the third witch, Sukie,

Circe by Alice Pike Barney (ca. 1895) This pastel evokes Homer's seductive witch who turns men into beasts. Her arm encircles the head of a tusked boar, while her look blends a vampire gaze with the sultry come-on of the femme fatale.

had her husband "permanized" in plastic and used him for a place mat. Updike's relationship with his fictional women is always a love-hate affair. In his ambivalence toward women, he is able to capture precisely both male fears and women's anxieties about their own seemingly magical powers and the potency of their rage.

Thoroughly Modern Medusas

You did not know her all those years she thought she was homely, or see her poring over her baby pictures, making me tell her over and over how beautiful she had been. . . .
—Tillie Olsen, *I Stand Here Ironing*

Medusa's fall terrifies women because she mirrors their own worst fears about what they look or seem like when they are enraged. On her island of desolation, Medusa is surrounded by stony male corpses whom she has killed with her gaze. The only other creatures for miles around are the hideous Gorgon sisters, Stheno and Euryale. Scylla, too, is an image of isolation; in her final form, rooted to a rock, her only companion is another threatening female monster, Charybdis, a cavernous whirlpool that drinks in waves and spews them forth again.

Women tend to view the expression of rage as a threat to their relationships, their looks, their sense of security, and the ties that bind them. A woman's natural inclination is to "seek affiliation with others, to provide nurturance and support," writes Teresa Bernardez-Bonesatti, M.D., a pioneer in the field of women and anger.[7] "In anger, a person establishes automatic aloneness," expresses her autonomy, and breaks through the barriers of dependency. For many women, even the contemplation of aloneness is intolerable and inhibits them from expressing real feelings of rage.

We were surprised, in this enlightened feminist age of empowerment, to hear from one woman, a top law school student, that in response to sarcastic remarks made by her male colleagues about competitive women, she deliberately kept her grades down for fear of social rejection, isolation, and hostility. Even more sobering was the report of another woman that she participates in her husband's menages à trois with his graduate students rather than risk losing him. To unmask her rage and show her furious face would mean testing the security, such as it is, of her intolerable situation. It also might mean taking action and living on her own.

But women who repress their rage and don't speak of it or act on it often find it showing up on their faces or bodies in spite of their attempts to hide it: the furrowed brow, the worry crease between the eyebrows, the tight jaw, the down-turned mouth, the too-bright smile that looks like a grimace, or the permanent pout. Mary Jo Buttafuoco, who continued to support her husband, Joey, even after he was jailed for having sex with a minor, had her face disfigured for life by Amy Fisher, her husband's teenage mistress. Amy fixed on Mary Jo's face the features of rage that she knew should be there.

A Medusa transformation can occur when a woman's appearance is distorted through anguish or through undereating or overeating. Allison, one of the women we interviewed, experienced such a metamorphosis.

Five years ago, photographs reveal Allison as a stunning twenty-six-year-old with a broad, confident smile that expressed her warm, outgoing personality. She seemed to be half a perfect Yuppie couple. She and her husband, Andy, both worked on Wall Street as junior investment bankers and enjoyed generous salaries. They spent weekends exploring Connecticut and Massachusetts—searching out antiques for their dream New England farmhouse. Andy imagined it covered with snow—a welcoming fire blazing in the fireplace, kids and dogs running in and out. A year after their marriage, their dream seemed within the realm of possibility. With the blessings of their parents and financial help as well, Allison agreed to leave her job and Andy applied for law school. Fall found them ensconced in their New England farmhouse with Allison pregnant. But the reality was very different from the one they had imagined.

There had been stresses on Wall Street, yet Andy found the pressures of law school even more intense, while the prospect of a baby and added responsibilities terrified him. He responded by spending large amounts of money on designer suits, expensive cooking equipment, and weekly poker games. While Andy was overspending and staying out late, Allison began overeating. She was bored without a job, lonely during long evenings of waiting for Andy to come home, and angry at the onslaught of bills and their increasing debts, which Andy refused to address. Constantly on the phone with bill collectors, she knew she would have to suffer the humiliation of asking her parents for more money. Andy's first-year grades came and revealed that he was on the verge of flunking. Allison was furious and was unable to stop gorging herself, although her obstetrician warned her that she was in danger of becoming toxemic.

By the time their baby was delivered, Allison had gained fifty pounds, Andy had "maxed out" all the charge cards, and they were in debt to both sets of parents. When their baby girl turned six months old and Andy walked out and moved in with a female classmate, Allison describes herself as "Laura Ashley meets Medusa." "My rage was all over the map, I could feel it building up all the time—it had no boundaries, it was endless, it was a scary octopus with a thousand arms. This guy was such a bastard!" Her rage was so out there and uncontrollable, she suffered a mild heart attack.

Today, five years later, Allison is still confronting and contending with her rage, trying to understand what part her behavior played in the fiasco. She has just finished paying off the last of Andy's debts and, ironically, has started a bridal consulting business. Her rage comes freely now—when Andy comes to pick up their daughter for visits and she spots his girlfriend in the car or when she gets up alone to tend to her child in the middle of the night. She doesn't translate her anger into physical symptoms any longer, and she has started a support group for other women dealing with divorce and very young children. Overeating is still a problem, although her goal is to be able to fit into some of the Laura Ashley dresses she was able to wear when they were first married.

• • •

The rage of African-American women is particularly connected with insecurities about their appearance. Many women of color buy into the white culture's beauty myths and are both infuriated with themselves for being different and enraged at the world whose standards of beauty they don't fit. *The Color Purple*, Steven Spielberg's adaptation of the Alice Walker novel, contains two stunning portraits of female rage. One is Oprah Winfrey's interpretation of the majestic Sofia, whose pride and rage are punished by jail and disfigurement. The other is Whoopi Goldberg's Celie. Prune-faced and mousy, beaten and harshly abused by a duo of sadistic husbands, Celie's is the rage and shame of a woman battered not only for her gender but for her looks.

It has taken many years for Gail, a twenty-two-year-old African-American woman, to begin to feel beautiful. She's self-possessed and proud in her bearing; her voice is dignified and quiet, but with an undertow of anger. "I never fit in and I don't now," she told us when we interviewed her. "I describe myself as black, female, and queer. How outside can you get? I grew up in Bedford Stuyvesant, one of the toughest neighborhoods in Brooklyn. I had no relations with white people. My realities were my black church and all-black schools. I was always angry." Gail used to dream of living in "a white middle-class *House & Garden* kind of world." She can remember herself in her teens walking by store windows and seeing in their mirror a face that was hideous to her—the opposite of the Grace Kelly image she craved, and with an enraged expression to boot.

Gail's fragmented feeling about her African looks carried over into her sexual life. "Even though I had relationships with black men," she says, "I was getting crushes on white girls. I was so furious with myself—I was totally split. There were no romance novels written or how-to books handy about being in love with or having relationships with someone of the same gender. Even later, as I turned to feminism, that world had no place for me. Feminism is a largely white middle-class kind of operation. I didn't quite fit in to the queer movement, either, because, as I've explored my sexuality, I'm not one or the other, but both—bisexual."

In her first year of college, Gail was asked to write an autobiographical essay, and as she thought about her history, she began to see her struggles as positive forces in her development. This was Gail's first step in reclaiming her personal and racial identity; as she went through this ongoing process, her appearance changed. She discovered the African fabrics that suited her complexion and she stopped processing her hair and wearing makeup that lightened the tone of her skin. Today, she wears her hair in a crown of cornrowed braids and looks like a beautiful Medusa. As a teaching assistant in a department of Women's Studies, she makes a point of reaching out to younger black women to help them express their identities through writing. She also cultivates in them the attitude that black is beautiful.

The Medusa Triangle

When portraying rage in women, cultural images focus on two areas of the female body: her face and her genitals. To understand what we have come to call "Medusa dread," we turned first to Freud. In an essay aptly called "Medusa's Head," Freud explained that "the terror of Medusa" can be traced back to a boy's fear of castration and the terror he feels when he catches sight of the female genitals surrounded by pubic hair but missing a penis.

For Freud, Medusa's head, with its snaky corona, twisted features, and gash for a mouth, evokes "the terrifying genitals of the mother." As for the effect of her deadly gaze: "The sight of Medusa's head makes the spectator stiff with terror, turns him to stone." Medusa is an ancient hex sign for Freud, as he recalls Rabelais's image of "the Devil who took to flight when the woman showed him her vulva."[8] Philip Slater, a contemporary psychoanalyst and expert on Greek culture, agrees with Freud that the Medusa head is an image of maternal genitalia. But Slater equates the Medusa head and her snakes with male horror of the vagina itself, rather than with a fear of castration.

To illustrate his argument, Slater cites the case of Kenneth Elton, famous in the annals of psychoanalysis. Elton, who was convicted of sexually assaulting little girls, had been seduced at six by a woman in his neighborhood and was unable, as an adult, to consummate a sexual union with a woman unless it was in the dark. Later, in the course of his successful analysis, Elton dreamed that he was driving a motorboat that became clogged in sea grass. At times, the grass was so thick that it forced him to stop and clean off the propeller. Then as he looked over the side of the boat at the propeller, he could see that it was covered with "this long, black hair . . . that absolutely made me feel 'creepy'; in fact it looked to me like so many thousands of snakes straining to get at me."[9]

The "Kenneth Elton phobia," the fear of adult female sexuality, is

Le Viol *by René Magritte (1934) Magritte's* The Rape *suggests that a woman violated by rape is perceived only in terms of her sexual organs. She loses all her identity—even her face.*

both an ancient and contemporary male condition. In anthropology, of course, it is expressed in the image of the "vagina dentata," or toothed vagina, which, as Camille Paglia points out, "literalizes" male sexual anxiety.

According to Dr. Harriet Goldhor Lerner, a man may feel anxious and uncomfortable in the presence of the fully developed woman and her pubic hair, a Medusa triangle, either because she reminds him of his mother and activates infantile sexual memories or because he perceives the vulva as a wound and the clitoris as a "sucked-in penis." These anxieties translate into slang expressions that refer to a woman's external genital regions as a "gash" or "snatch."

Male fear of and fixation on the female genitalia adds to a woman's discomfort about her own body and sense of well-being. Cassie, one of the women we talked with, remembers a defining incident that colored her feelings about intimacy and her body for many years. She is now twenty-six, good-looking, stately at five foot eleven, and successful as a comic improviser. But for a year in junior high school, she says, "I was teased unmercifully by both guys and girls, and I got real angry. I was the group whipping post."

The crucial incident came at a ninth-grade party that turned into a petting session, when one of the boys discovered she was still undeveloped. "He went and told all the guys who gave me the nickname, 'H.P.,' for 'hairless pussy.' I was mortified when I went to class the next day. For months, I felt everyone was laughing at me. And it got worse. They teased me about my height and my large behind—even my big eyes, which I always thought were one of my good features. My rage at this cruelty was frustrated by the fact that I couldn't share my shame and humiliation with my mom. I was just too embarrassed. Ever since then, I've felt self-conscious about the way I look. I have trouble undressing in front of a man. I'm afraid he's going to laugh at me. I wish I could be comfortable with men, but instead I feel resentful and uneasy."

In mythology, Scylla's metamorphosis into a monster suggests several truths about this link between sexuality and rage. Ovid describes

Scylla's transformation in his *Metamorphoses*. Beautiful Scylla, whose only crime was to be loved by Glaucus, a sea god Circe desired for herself, is bathing in her favorite spring-fed pool when Circe intervenes to punish her:

> to her horror she found her legs were gone,
> And where her thighs should be she saw a girdle
> Of barking dogs' heads round her naked belly.[10]

As mythologist Edith Hamilton describes Scylla's predicament: "The beastly forms were part of her; she could not fly from them or push them away. She stood there rooted to a rock, in her unutterable misery hating and destroying everything that came within her reach. . . ."[11] The barking dogs, symbolizing rage, encircle her genitals, and no man can approach her.

Once integrated into her body, rage becomes part of a woman's personality and identity, colors her environment, and defines her image. To herself, she is miserable and unappealing, and she projects her pain and suffering into the world.

Female rage is usually intertwined with female anxieties about sexual appeal and desirability. Male fear of female rage usually contains displaced fears about female sexuality. This fusion and confusion of rage with sexuality accounts for the magnetic force of Medusa's gaze, which is deadly and seductive at the same time: Hers is a face mask of terror superimposed on a template of pleasure.

French feminist critic Hélène Cixous, revising Freud's penis-centered interpretation, tells us that Medusa is in the eye of the beholder. It is only men who associate female sexuality with death; when a woman looks at Medusa, she can see her pleasure and joy. "You only have to look at the Medusa straight on to see her," she says. "And she's not deadly. She's beautiful and she's laughing."[12] Judith Levine in *My Enemy, My Love* cites Suzanne Moore's essay "Here's Looking at You, Kid," which suggests that "the fear experienced by men of women's Medusa-like stare" is "in reality a fear that the female gaze will soften everything in its path."[13] Fear of women's rage, in other words, may be seen as fear of impotence.

Glamorous yet frightening images in art and fiction and on film—femmes fatales, "black widows," bisexual he-women—tell us what female rage feels and looks like to men. In the late-nineteenth century, in response to the new, liberated woman, male artists conceived of the "gynander": a woman striving for male privileges who threatened the status quo of the male-dominated home. As Bram Dijkstra in *Idols of Perversity* points out: "The Medusa with her bouffant of snakes, paralyzing eyes, and bestial proclivities, was the very personification of all that was evil in the gynander."[14] In a lithograph of 1888, the artist Fernand Khnopff superimposed a horrific giant Medusa head, pulsating with phallic tentacles and raging in sexual frustration, over the pubic area of a voluptuous chained-up woman.

Bram Stoker's 1897 novel, *Dracula,* is the culmination of male backlash against the new vote-seeking woman whom Stoker endows with vast sexual appetites.[15] In this nineteenth-century masterpiece of vampirism, the heroine is Lucy Westenra, an untransformed young maiden who calls herself a "horrid flirt" and is pursued by three suitors. Stoker implies she would like to marry, even sleep with, all three. Lucy is on holiday with her friend Mina Harker when Dracula climbs into her window at night and sucks the blood from her veins. Once bitten and, as Stoker implies, sexually initiated, Lucy's bloodthirstiness and lust can never be sated. Languid and tired after each encounter with Dracula, she is given blood transfusions from her admirers. Stoker hints that Lucy's injections are sexual and represent the symbolic semen of all the men she wants to marry. But the injections are futile: Lucy dies.

To the horror of her three suitors and physician, she returns as a vampire. They know they must stop her evil forays. They see that her enraged sexual self has taken over: "The sweetness was turned to adamantine, heartless cruelty, and the purity of voluptuous wantonness." She growls, snarls, and hurls threats; when confronted with the doctor's crucifix, she grows more enraged:

Lucy's beautiful color became livid, the eyes seemed to throw out the sparks of hell-fire, the brows were wrinkled as though the folds of flesh were the coils of Medusa's snakes.

Lucy has become a Medusa, a "foul thing," sexually wanton and transformed by female rage. The suitor whom she had promised to marry drives a stake through her heart.

A century later, Medusan vampires still haunt the male imagination. In Paul Verhoeven's controversial film *Basic Instinct*, the Medusa is Catherine Tramell, played by Sharon Stone. Cold and calculating, hyper- and bisexual, she is a femme fatale, a psychofemme and a best-selling author of murder mysteries. The film opens with a crime: A nightclub owner makes passionate love to a blond-haired woman and, at the moment of climax, she ties him up with a long silk scarf, then plunges an ice pick repeatedly into his neck. The scene has all

The Vampire *by Edvard Munch (1895/1902)*
Edvard Munch's woodcut and lithograph depicts a woman, with long hair and encircling arms, silently sucking blood from the neck of a male victim. For Munch, Stoker, and other late Victorians, her act is a metaphor for seduction.

the ingredients of a male fantasy of female rage: sex, fury, and death, with a pinch of domination thrown in.

Medusa's face makes a cameo rather than a starring appearance in the movie. We glimpse her briefly through the director's lens as he pans over Sharon Stone's crotch in the scene that made the movie famous. One glimpse by the male policemen and they are not turned to stone, but "turned on" by Stone.

In *Basic Instinct,* female rage does not wear its familiar face of ugly fury; instead, it is expressed as high drama sex, glamorized sibling rivalry, lesbian rage, and slasher behavior. Sharon Stone is both the sexual vortex that threatens to suck men in and the cause of their anxiety about performance. She is portrayed as the quintessential female demon, exemplifying the fusion of rage and sexuality.

The writer Anne Roiphe suggests that "maybe this whole rotten system of patriarchal religion and boy's clubs and unequal pay for equal work is all based on fear of the vagina."[16] The bottom line about Medusa is that she is a complex and composite symbol that blends female sexuality and rage in a strange and uncanny way. She can be a stern and judgmental queen of vengeance and a reminder of the mother as giver of law and possible punishment. She petrifies men because she inspires in them feelings of lust as well as helplessness; she raises anxieties about impotence, sexual performance, and genital size. Men may also be enraged by what they perceive as Medusa's judgmental gaze.

A combination of desire and dread seems to have motivated those so-called football heroes of Glen Ridge, New Jersey, who were tried for raping a mentally retarded eighteen-year-old girl with a broomstick. The innocent young woman, thinking they wanted friendship, misunderstood the assault, even as they finished probing her with a fungo bat. Their punishment? They were sentenced to up to fifteen years and may be released in as little as twenty-two months. And they are free on bail until they exhaust their legal appeals, a process that could go on for years.

Male rage and female sexuality also became the issues at the inves-

tigation of the now-famous 1991 Tailhook Convention for navy and
marine officers at a Las Vegas hotel. Navy women enticed to a third-
floor hotel corridor were attacked by almost eight hundred men.
"The assaults varied from victims being grabbed on the buttocks to
being groped, pinched, and fondled on their breasts, buttocks, and
genitals," the report said. One man described the hallway as a "pin-
ball machine," with each guy getting in his shots as the women were
handed through the gauntlet.[17]

When those drunken officers groped and grabbed in the darkness
of that beer- and urine-soaked corridor, they not only exposed their
own fears about female sexuality and their own rage at women's
bodies but transformed their female colleagues into angry Medusas
whose outrage caused "the Navy's biggest scandal in decades" and
implicated at least 140 senior officers. The officers' punishments,
which amounted to a few letters of reprimand, immunity for the
worst offenders, and a slap on the wrist for the remaining flight officers, were the cause of additional female rage.

Incidents like these take on the aura of rituals; they become a collective way for men to cut women down to size and punish them for
being desirable. They will probably continue to occur in our culture
until women stop accepting the status quo and use their rage constructively to change things.

The face is the focus of male rage against female sexuality in Clint
Eastwood's Oscar-winning film, *Unforgiven*. The film opens with a
shot of the tombstone of the hero's wife, who died of smallpox. It
reads: "She was a comely woman once . . ."—an epitaph that could
be written for many women. In an early scene, Delilah, a beautiful
young prostitute, pays dearly for a giggle as a cowboy client pulls
down his pants. While his summoned sidekick holds down "the
bitch," the cowboy accuses her of stealing his money and threatens
to "cut out her tits." Instead, he slashes her face with a razor blade,
giving her a Medusa grimace and turning her into "damaged goods."
The owner of the brothel explains to the sheriff: "No one's gonna
wanna pay money for a cut-up whore." Delilah's sister prostitutes,
who witnessed the disfigurement in the Big Whiskey brothel, take up

her cause. Their outrage about the slashing and the sheriff's light sentence propels the plot forward when they offer a thousand-dollar reward "humping money" to any person who will kill Delilah's attackers. Eastwood's camera is never far from Delilah's face, which carries the permanent scars of a woman who dared to cast a judgmental gaze on a male body.

Shrews, Sickos, and Psychofemmes on Film

She'll not recover from her rage, till the lightning of her fury has struck somebody to the ground.

—Euripides, *Medea*

Culture's images of shrews, sickos, and psychofemmes have been with us since ancient times. Medea, Phaedra, Dido, and Clytemnestra are all classical images of female rage gone out of control. Clytemnestra's saga has been retold several times recently. Director Garland Wright pieced together ancient play fragments to create a new production at the Guthrie Theater in Minneapolis. Clytemnestra's contemporary "cry for vengeance," according to *The New York Times* reviewer "sounds suspiciously like a call to sisterhood."

Even as the women's movement progresses, so does backlash. The enraged woman has become a movie staple in recent years, and she has been portrayed both more positively and realistically and more demonically than ever before. Some film directors and television producers have taken the woman's part; most have seized on the most pathological extremes of female behavior for entertainment purposes.

The psychopathic Annie Wilkes of Stephen King's novel and Rob Reiner's film *Misery* is an enraged female monster who fits every misogynistic stereotype King can think of. Annie pries a man out of his wrecked car after a blinding snowstorm. By coincidence, he just happens to be best-selling romance novelist Paul Sheldon, whose "number-one fan" is none other than Annie. Sheldon becomes

Annie's victim, forced to recuperate from his accident under her sadistic regime.

Annie Wilkes, abandoned by her husband, is as ugly and pathetic
as she is deadly. By the time Sheldon meets her, she's already killed
her father and several newborns and nurses. She not only embodies
male fears about women and rage but reflects women's anxieties
about their appearance, their intelligence, and their emotional explo-
siveness. Her personality is split: Sometimes she behaves like a devoted nurse, sometimes she's the total woman, and sometimes she
issues sadistic threats; though she is an adoring fan club member, she
burns Sheldon's precious manuscript in a Weber cooker.

King seems to be saying that not only does rage make women ugly
but under the skin of every "ugly" woman is an even uglier tangle of
serpents waiting to spring. Beneath her bulk and falsely compliant
hero worship, the repulsive Annie rages against men, yes, but also
against the gods who have made her. She is Medusa after the transformation, a blind date from hell, the Elvis fan, the borderline psy-
chopath, and one of the first female serial killers all rolled into one.
King's satirical fantasy allows us to laugh at our fears, but we come
away with one image: the female with her knife raised, ready to
strike.

The film that shattered all the stereotypes about women's rage
and ugliness was *Fatal Attraction,* with its beautiful and seductive
image of a modern-day Medusa; now even beautiful women can't be
trusted to control their rage on-screen. Today, when we think of an
enraged female, Glenn Close as the blond hypersexual Alex Forrest
immediately flashes into consciousness. Alex is a successful and
seemingly self-possessed career woman, complete with high-style
moussed-up curls that turn Medusa-snaky once her true nature becomes exposed.

Attraction is fatal for Alex because she suffers from what psychoanalyst Ethel Pearson calls "the psychology of extreme unrequited
love."[18] We discover early in the film that her father died when she
was very young, a cinematic hint that her obsession with Dan, the
family man who makes love with her one weekend when his wife is

away, may be replaying an Oedipal attachment. When she finds out Dan has no intention of carrying on the affair once his beautiful wife, Beth, comes home, she slashes her wrists. Later, in her rage, she boils Dan's daughter's rabbit and attempts to murder his wife. She is the bitch who always comes back, a pathetic monster of her own making.

Alex Forrest's revenge on Dan elicited universal cries of "Kill the bitch!" from theatergoers, both male and female. While many women could understand and identify with Alex's sense of exploitation and humiliation and the rage evoked by Dan's empty phrase, "I'll call you in the morning," few could sanction her horrendous acting out. The powerful Alex embodies our deepest, most primitive fears about the danger of female sexuality and the potential for female rage. Alex's rage is towering, monumental. Her behavior arouses men's psychic fears and fantasies about their mothers at the same time that her glamorous appearance excites their lust. Women can disown their own fury by siding with the good woman, Beth. In doing so, they also disown sexual appetite.

At last, in the early summer of 1991, when Callie Khouri's script of *Thelma and Louise* was brought to the screen by director Ridley Scott, women found a vision of female rage they could applaud. *Commonweal* magazine called the film "a cultural milestone," while Jon Tevlin in *Glamour* called *Thelma and Louise* the first sign that female rage had entered the cultural mainstream.[19] From the moment Louise picked up a gun and shot her buddy Thelma's taunting ("Suck my dick") assailant in cold blood, women of all ages bonded in the darkness to indulge in a collective revenge fantasy—against womanizers, controlling husbands, men in general. The makers of the film unwittingly "sank a drill," as *Time* magazine called it, into "familiar American soil and somehow found they had tapped into a wild-rushing subterranean stream of inchoate outrage and deranged violence."

Thelma and Louise were beautiful Medusas with shining red hair and eyes that sparkled. Careening down the southwestern highways or parked out under the stars, their metallic green T-Bird was a vehicle that caused many women to dream of change. Women can identify with the untransformed Thelma, an infantilized housewife walking on eggs with her beer-guzzling, sports-crazed male chauvinist pig husband. They can empathize with the waitress Louise patiently waiting like Odysseus's Penelope for her commitment-phobe musician boyfriend to come home. Thelma and Louise's fabled road trip begins as an all-girl weekend getaway and ends with apocalypse in the desert. Thelma changes from a pathologically dependent wife into a fiery, sexually awakened bandit; Louise, a take-charge control freak, lets her hair flow free and stops worrying about tomorrows.

What was striking about the Khouri-Scott vision was that for Thelma and Louise, rage meant freedom, a reconnection with nature, sexuality, and female bonding. This time, female rage looked glamorous and luscious: It was lipstick, shiny red curls, bikini bathing suits, and glorious smiles, not scary hair and tortured eyes. Although ultimately it pushed Thelma and Louise over the edge of the canyon, rage cemented their hands in kinship, not only with each other but with all other women in the theater. More women of all ages are openly acknowledging their rage and anger now. As Nancy Friday says in *Women on Top:* "the witch is out of the nursery, and the fury of women, feared by men and women alike, is loose in the land."[20]

3 | The Inner World of Rage

Medusa was helpless, bewildered, ashamed
of what she did not commit, repulsed
by her own grotesquery, terrified
of petrifying her loved ones with a look.
She flew to exile on her loathesome wings
and marooned her horrific self on a dismal island,
hideously, piteously, wailing to the winds
mourning her torn innocence, her beauty, her
    sanctity.
Debauched by a god, deformed by a goddess,
she turned the sailors to stone who sailed by
to stare upon her hideous form, and they sank
into the sea, their own tombstones.
Then, looking into the inky water she saw the ugly
reflection of her pain. She seemed at times
to frighten even herself.

Emotional Survival Kits

*Twenty years ago there wasn't even a whisper of women's
rage, which shows how well the defenses were working.*
—Nancy Friday, *Women on Top*

Just as Medusa retreats from the world into her isolation, a woman's
rage may also go underground and become buried under a mental or
physical subterfuge. Women employ extreme measures to conceal
their rage. Some disguise their fury with tightened neck knots and
autoimmune-system diseases that develop silently in the body; some
gain or lose weight; others transform their dangerous feelings into
phobias and self-mutilations or even multiply personalities. "Rage
comes disguised in many other forms; depression covers up rage,
anxiety cloaks rage in panic, while panic attacks and anger attacks
are both characterized by rapid heart beats, sweating, and flush-
ing."[1] Peeling off a woman's disguises and looking behind the veils of
her mind-body deceptions and her skillful masquerades reveals the
rage underneath.

After her rape and transformation, Medusa is exiled with two other Gorgons on a deserted island; there she is unable to conceal her snaky head, and her gaze turns men and beasts to stone. Medusa's rage is her defining characteristic.

But most women marked by rage go to great lengths to disguise it. In order to make the surface attractive, they keep the raging monster inside them hidden. Thus they become adept at what psychiatrists call splitting, a defense mechanism by which painful emotions like rage are split off, denied, or isolated from consciousness. Most women, conditioned from early on to survive in a "female is inferior" environment become so deft at compartmentalizing their feelings that they are unaware of the ways in which they numb themselves. Faced with loss, abandonment, or any other psychic trauma, they isolate mind from body, separate their thoughts from feelings, and flee.

In the early days of psychoanalysis, women who exhibited splitting behaviors were called hysterics, phobics, and hypochondriacs; they were put in trances, given shocks and hydrotherapy, and sometimes institutionalized. Many practitioners, products of their own cultural and gender biases and faced with the very real discomfort of dealing with enraged females, unwittingly perpetuated these symptoms by labeling splitting behaviors not only neurotic but psychotic and sick. Enlightened therapists acknowledge the splitting process and help women to integrate their painful emotions into their psyches.

Women are whizzes at planning operations and finding ways to avoid going crazy in a world where all too often their needs are not considered and they feel they cannot risk expressing anger. In conducting our interviews, we have marveled not only at the variety of female survival skills but at the ability of so many women to partition pathological behavior from daily functioning. One woman we talked with is a bulimic who throws up after every meal yet gives devoted care to her disturbed child. One is a professor who suffers from crippling panic attacks at the mall and still gives superb lectures in class. One is an alcoholic who puts perfectly prepared dinners on the table for her family each evening.

When rage is disguised by weight gain, depression, illness, or even silent compliance, it may distract a woman from the reality of an intolerable situation. At the same time, being sick or feeling helpless can provide her with a cover for inaction, protecting her from the apprehension of a reality she can't tolerate or doesn't want to face. When a woman censors her anger and suppresses rage over a long period of time, she not only distorts the reality of her outer life, but also creates an inauthentic inner world of blurred visions, illusions of dependency, and fantasies of powerlessness. She loses her sense of herself and becomes unfamiliar with the sound of her own voice.

Certain personality styles evolve when a woman's real self goes into hiding. She may become a *control freak,* the woman who is unable to show warm and tender emotions; her perfectionism and need to control the way others do things drives everyone around her mad. As she focuses on details and making everything perfect, she usually misses the big picture about herself. With her constricted emotions, her patterns of rigid thinking, and lack of spontaneity, the control freak must have everything her way and preplanned. When she cannot control others, she becomes enraged. Usually she expresses her anger in petty and indirect ways. She gets back at a waiter by obsessing about the tip, leaving a skimpy one instead of making a constructive comment; she punishes her husband by blowing up at a friend or talking about him behind his back.

Another enraged personality type is the *attention seeker.* These lively and dramatic women are always drawing attention to themselves. Prone to exaggeration and craving novelty and new excitements, women who need constant attention assume various roles in every situation—the victim, the princess, the martyr—unaware they're playacting. Friends are made quickly, yet once ensconced in a relationship, the attention seeker can be a demanding, bottomless pit. Because of her feelings of powerlessness and dependency, she needs constant reassurance and the spotlight. When she is not the life of the party or the conversation turns to someone else, the attention seeker may retrieve the spotlight by throwing fits and tantrums.

Passive-aggressors express rage covertly by never living up to their commitments and by performing inadequately at work or in their social lives. They find ways to sabotage a promotion or a relation-ship, yet hurt themselves in order to get back at others. Their rage and anger parade as procrastination, dawdling, stubbornness, inten-tional inefficiency, and "forgetfulness." A woman who arrives half an hour late for lunch may be unconsciously telling her friend she's furious with her or that this friend is really not that important; a woman who always gets sick for an important meeting is sticking it to herself as well as to her boss.

The *geisha* is a woman who's constantly pleasing others and put-ting herself in second place. Unable to separate her thoughts and feelings from other people's, she lacks self-confidence and bounda-ries and she tolerates all kinds of exploitation and abuse. Her aim is to maintain the status quo at any cost, and in her state of hostile dependency, she relinquishes her rights of independence and free-dom of speech while resenting those she empowers. A doormat who doesn't feel she deserves to express anger or rage, this woman uncon-sciously captures it in her body before it escapes. The result may be chronic fatigue, TMJ syndrome of the jaw, panic disorder, or agora-phobia. Her rage is like a powder keg; once ignited, she can literally blow a fuse and suffer a stroke.

Female Rage Zones

To prevent rage from seeping into conscious awareness, women will literally split off rage from entering their heads by unconsciously re-taining it in jaws, plugging it up in the sinus passages, constricting it in the throat, or capturing it in their ears or teeth. Karen, a nurse and medical psychotherapist, told us, "Women have compulsive jaw hunger. We love potato chips, crackers, and salt. Sometimes our jaw is the only organ talking about our rage. We chomp on our anger. You should see the tiny women who come to see me whose jaws are bulging or whose neck muscles are overdeveloped. They have learned from infancy how to repress rage and cut it off from the head."

Karen and other therapists, including those who work with the experiential effects of rage, conclude that most women feel rage in a band that extends across the upper third of their bodies. The lower edge of the band runs in a line about two inches below the throat, while its upper limits form a line right above the eyebrows. Women carry the weight of the world on their shoulders, literally.

Callie's rage is so embedded in her neck and shoulder muscles, she hires a shiatsu massage therapist to stand on her shoulders and press her elbows as hard as she can into the bulges of knotted rage that have formed in an area between them. Kate spends hours in the dark, nauseated and wearing a Lone Ranger–type mask to shut out the bright yellow lights that accompany her migraine headaches. Other women we've talked with tell of asthma attacks, infected jaws, neck pain, massive tooth problems, and gum disease—all physical conditions exacerbated by rage that is unexpressed. As Aristophanes put it in *Lysistrata,* "we're women and our rage is in our teeth."

Some of the origins of splitting are cultural and have to do with the way women think they are supposed to speak, look, behave. To behave in a ladylike manner, women who grew up before the mid-sixties buried their feelings in depression or used alcohol or tranquilizers to help them control their rage. Today, women have more latitude when it comes to behavior, and younger women are trapped in another bind: In an effort to conform to the culture's standards of the way women should look, they develop eating disorders, which alter physical appearance.

Depression

> . . . *poor Ophelia.*
> *Divided from herself and her fair judgment . . .*
> —*Hamlet,* act IV, scene 5

Depression is masked rage; it conceals a woman's unacceptable feelings. On the surface, a depressed woman may seem compliant, cheerful, and eager to please, catering to her partner's or children's every

Ophelia *by Sir John Everett Millais (1851)*
In Hamlet, *Shakespeare's fair Ophelia turns rage into literal madness when faced with the death of her beloved father, Polonius, and the withdrawal of Hamlet's love. She drowns herself in a grassy stream on a bed of her favorite flowers.*

whim. She faces the world as a caring and compassionate woman, while her real self hides and silently burns. "The outwardly conforming self," explains Dana Crowley Jack, an expert on depression, in *Silencing the Self: Women and Depression,* "accepts the social norms for female goodness or for worldly success and tries to comply with them."[2] Underneath that inauthentic mask of goodness lies a secret but real self that grows more and more blurred as rage grows, and needs and desires go unrecognized.

This division or polarizing of the self is, according to Jack, "the core dynamic of female depression." A depressed woman manages her rage by isolating and hiding it. As "the woman begins to experience two opposing selves," she disconnects from her core of genuine feelings and the lack of connection impairs her normal functioning and performance.

> These women put the authentic self into solitary confinement, forbidding it to think, feel or communicate with others. . . . If the part

of the self that is banished to solitary confinement sees no possibility of escape without disaster and becomes resigned to its fate, the whispers of the authentic self become less and less audible. They may eventually seek communication through physical symptoms. . . . The link between self-silencing and anger is clear.

Linda told us she never realized how depressed she had become until she began taking antidepressants and her world came back into focus. As a columnist and features' reporter for a midsize city paper, Linda was the image of competence and self-assurance. She drew praise for her weekly column from her editors and the public; women's groups frequently asked her to speak, while the news media called on her for commentary. On her job, she was a high-functioning career woman and community leader, but at home she felt defeated, unempowered, and alone.

When we spoke with Linda, she had gained perspective on her depression and now understood that her own family history and her husband's psychological problems were contributing factors in the double life she had led. "To the outside world," she told us, "I was a successful journalist, mother, and hostess. In my own bedroom, I was an object of derision and scorn. I felt my husband's entire purpose in life was to rain on my parade. I was leading this bizarre double life and I didn't know who I was—by day, a superwoman; by night, a real wimp who was simmering inside."

Linda's husband, Don, was a hard-driving and successful real estate developer who liked the cachet of his wife's success but needed to control every aspect of her life—including her career. He told her what clothes to buy, what movies to see, which people to invite for dinner. Her own suggestions always met with disapproval. After eight years of his ruthless criticism, she was experiencing intense anxiety and depression, which landed her in a local hospital emergency room. "Although I knew somewhere deep inside me that something was rotten, I had disguised my anxiety and rage under the cloaks of depression and bodily symptoms. I told myself I must be okay—after all, I was a big success on the job. Meanwhile, I was trying to be the most loving and supportive wife in the universe. Black lacy nightgowns and perfectly cooked Silver Palette dinners by candlelight, freshly squeezed orange juice, and handmade sweaters did nothing to improve our relationship. The béarnaise sauce always had too much lemon. And the surprise of the sexy nightgown became the occasion for more demeaning comments. It got to the point where I could only ask questions of my husband; I couldn't produce a declarative sentence when I was around him." Linda was assigned to the head of outpatient psychotherapy, who sent her home with a prescription for a major tranquilizer and began working with her to uncover her rage. Remarried now and happy in both work and love, it is difficult for her to comprehend that earlier part of her life.

Dr. Roy Schafer of Columbia University has treated a series of successful career women like Linda who are caught in what he calls "a maze of power and rage."[3] They shared a tendency to enter into painful relationships with "narcissistic and sadistic men" and presented problems of depression. On the job, these female patients showed high levels of "cognitive, administrative, and social skills." In their relationships, however, "all power seemed to pass from their hands." They became "helpless, blindly repetitive, self-accusatory . . . very often unaware of the rage they felt at the way they were being treated." Like Linda, they had lost their ability to articulate thoughts and feelings, "went on clinging to their tormentors," and characterized themselves as deficient or unlovable rather than as exploited and enraged.

Why did these bright, accomplished women tolerate and actually cling to men who "were determined to undermine [their] self-confidence and reality testing" and to destroy what Schafer calls their "moral and ethical core"? Schafer found that women who exhibited symptoms like Linda's were all "good girl" superachievers whose fathers lived on the sidelines of the family when they were growing up and whose lives, consequently, tended to be enmeshed with their mothers'. These women had never developed sufficient ego structures or boundaries. Striving to overcompensate for being female and highly dependent on others for approval, "their way of being in love could be viewed as helping them to keep in check overt expressions of their rage and envy, and at the same time obscure their relatively retarded individuation. . . ."[4] Being in love with narcissistic men and feeling depressed were unconscious ways, first learned in childhood, of concealing their rage at and envy of powerful male figures.

When a woman is depressed, the dynamic between the man and woman is disturbed. She's not communicating her authentic feelings and is leaving him out in the cold. In a way, a depressed woman turns the loved ones around her to stone with her subdued affect and her inability to communicate her full warmth and love. Her condition often alienates the very people whose support and tenderness she most desires and needs.

But much has been learned about the treatment of depression in the last few decades and no woman needs to remain in that gray twilight world.

Alcohol and Rage

A drink would put things right. Drink was not to help forget, but to help remember, to clarify and arrange untidy and unpleasant facts into a perfect pattern of reasonableness and beauty.
—Brian Moore, *The Lonely Passion of Judith Hearne*

When enraged females in classic literature and opera decided to destroy themselves, pyres and poisons were their methods of choice. Dido, the queen of Carthage, hoists herself on a pyre of wooden sticks and immolates herself, as Aeneas, her Trojan lover, sails away to found Rome. Emma Bovary, consumed by debt and narcissistic rage, consults the local pharmacist and does herself in with deadly poison. In modern times, however, these dramatic solutions have gone out of vogue, replaced by subtler strategies—alcohol and drug addiction.

Alcohol is both a sedative and an uninhibitor, anesthetizing a woman's anger even as it fills her with illusions of glamour and an enhanced personality. A few cocktails allow a woman to express her aggression without the attendant guilt. In *The Wounded Woman,* Linda Schierse Leonard contends that, "Rage can be veiled in many ways. One way is via addictions. With alcohol, the rage can come out when one is drunk, but without the conscious and responsible acceptance of it."[5]

Alcohol is another way a woman can leave herself, her conflicts, her memories, and her rage behind. Many times, a woman becomes an alcoholic in order to hide in isolation like Medusa, away from a family that has hurt her. Women alcoholics keep their rage literally bottled up in the liquor closet; many are closet drinkers whose addiction may go undetected for years. For this reason, women alcoholics are more difficult to identify than male alcoholics; psychologists estimate that many of them are secretly dealing with rage from painful memories of childhood sexual abuse.

Eleanor is seventy-five years old, a college graduate, and a voracious reader. She started drinking fifty years ago, with a few cocktails before dinner. She found that drinking cheered her up when she felt depressed. She found it especially important to drink at parties, where she felt herself a nonentity next to her husband, a publisher, who was often the center of attention. Later, after she was divorced, she drank to forget that she was alone and sad. She would start drinking at five every afternoon and continue until her dark self-critical thoughts lost their edge and she could crawl under her electric blanket and go to sleep. Finally, when she found she couldn't get out of bed in the morning without a drink, her children insisted she enter a hospital detoxification unit. With their support, Eleanor was able to dry out and has been sober for three years.

"I was brought up in the twenties and thirties," she told us, "in a small city outside New York. Although it was the Depression, my family was wealthy. I was the youngest of five, and the only girl. My mother was almost fifty when I was born. Father died when I was twelve. I was really the poor little rich girl, neglected emotionally yet overly indulged by my parents and nannies."

Eleanor's childhood was claustrophobic: A heart murmur kept her from attending school until sixth grade. "We had a large house, lots of attic rooms with dormers, where we used to play. My brothers were my companions, but I was particularly close to Steven. We would read together, play records—he was four years older, very handsome, and a terrific athlete. I looked up to him, and he adored me. Then when I was fourteen, he adored me too much. He loved me as a woman." For years, Eleanor was haunted by this memory of the months when they were lovers. She began having recurrent nightmares where she was attacked by wild lions and bears. Though she was in therapy during her early sixties and talked about Steven, she skirted the main issue. Her rage only emerged when she stopped drinking some years later.

Eleanor, like most alcoholics, drank so she would not have to confront her painful feelings and take responsibility for her own life. Now that she has been in intensive therapy and has stopped drinking, she is able to experience a broad range of emotions for the first time in her life. Eleanor now can feel rage throughout her body. Sometimes she staggers and trembles. Inevitably, when she allows the feelings to surface, she feels energized and empowered. Suppressed so long and buried under layers of memories, her emotions are newfound energies that reconnect her to her family, nature, and her past.

Many women, particularly of Eleanor's generation, turned their anger inward, depriving themselves of natural emotions and authenticity. Protecting, even idealizing people who hurt them, they dwelled in that prefeminist twilight of silence and compliance, unaware of their own possibilities, their emotions, and their real selves.

Fantasy Island

> *She lay there 'neath her covers*
> *Dreaming of a thousand lovers*
> —"The Ballad of Lucy Jordan"

Women have always led rich fantasy lives. Fantasy can compensate for a life without passion and add spice to extended relationships or long-term love. Although it is a mild form of splitting, a woman's fantasizing is harmless if kept within bounds, and it can teach her about her secret wishes. Yet many women are late-twentieth-century Emma Bovarys who long to escape from their ordinary existence and live in a dreamworld of fateful encounters and elegant balls. In their real lives, they maintain what Dalma Heyn calls their "erotic silence"; they talk about domestic logistics with their husbands over dinner and go for months without initiating any intimacies. Having fed themselves on inner visions of romance, they are doubly disappointed when reality hits.

The danger inherent in fantasizing becomes clear in the extreme example offered by Dr. H. P. Laughlin in the following case history. Dr. Laughlin calls this more dangerous type of splitting "an unhealthful fantasy-pattern" designed to disguise the underlying emotion and drive all the anger inside.[6] Dr. Laughlin describes his patient as a twenty-nine-year-old mother who "presented a picture of emotional fatigue, weakness, and was nearly narcoleptic." She slept approximately fourteen hours a day and had absolutely no energy; even crossing a room was tiring.

In therapy, the doctor learned that the young mother was suffering from "an overwhelming, diffuse, unconscious rage. This emotion was evoked by nearly everyone in her environment. Essentially it [the rage] was in response to terrific frustration, as her strong underlying needs to be cared for were not being met."[7] The young woman experienced herself as perhaps "irritable" on a conscious level, while the true extent of her rage was expressed covertly in an obsessive fantasy about the death of her husband and her child. In fantasy, "she would go to the door and be met by a delegation from her husband's office telling her that her husband had been killed in an accident. The fantasy would then proceed in organized detail up to and after the funeral." These fantasies took up hours upon hours of the young woman's day and were visualized so much that they took on the quality of hallucinations. She remained in a state of chronic fatigue, unable to stand on her own two feet. The young woman's fantasizing allowed her to cover up her rage and postpone action, while she expressed her infantile needs and dependencies in the form of illness.

Other women, using a similar strategy, bury the enormous energy of their rage under the obsessions of hypochondria or phobic reactions. Yet in spite of these subterfuges, rage oozes out as fantasy, as in this young mother's case or in the hypochondriac's symptoms. The fantasies of obese females are particularly graphic and intense. In a study conducted by Jungian analyst Marion Woodman, eighteen of the twenty women tested preferred fantasy to reality; fifteen of the twenty women dreamed of a paradise they inhabited with their fathers.

Obesity and Dieting

When I am furious with Dick, I tear open the fridge door,
and grab anything I can find and wolf it down.
　　—Marion Woodman, *The Owl Was a Baker's Daughter*

Obesity is a cultural and media fixation in the United States tabloids, and such magazines as *People* obsessively monitor the fluctuating hiplines and bulges of superstars like Liz Taylor and Delta Burke, all the while correlating weight gain with marital infidelity and abandonment and weight loss with happiness and success. In the age of images, we've become more and more concerned with surface. As Naomi Wolf says in *The Beauty Myth:*

More women have more money and power and scope and legal recognition than we have ever had before; but in terms of how we feel about ourselves *physically,* we may actually be worse off than our unliberated grandmothers. Recent research consistently shows that inside the majority of the West's controlled, attractive, successful working women, there is a secret "underlife" poisoning our freedom; infused with notions of beauty, it is a dark vein of self-hatred, physical obsessions, terror of aging, and dread of lost control.[8]

It's no wonder that today's little girls are aware of body image at age two and three, that by fourth grade 80 percent of them are on self-imposed diets, and at twelve most girls are into serious dieting.[9] As college professors, we know that one out of eight of our female students is using laxatives or vomiting to control her weight.

Carolyn Blackman Miroff, a psychiatric social worker, sees herself as basically a "healer." Her practice includes women of all ages who suffer from the three major eating disorders: compulsive eating, anorexia, and bulimia. "Sometimes I see myself as sitting at the edge of an abyss and catching the lemmings before they leap over the edge," she says, describing her therapeutic interventions. Her desire is to save the young ones before it's too late. "The young girls I see are crippled by the rage of their grandmothers, the rage of their mothers, the rage of their fathers; they hate their brothers' fat jokes, and many resent their passive, overweight mothers. These girls will do anything not to be ridiculed and criticized and tormented like Mom." Desperate to obtain male approval, taking note of their fathers' and brothers' oohing and aahing over the models in the *Sports Illustrated* swimsuit issue, teenage and college girls are bent on becoming everything their mother is not. By eating only unsalted popcorn and cans of diet soda, they mock what they regard as her high-carb diet; by applying makeup meticulously for hours on end, they distance themselves from what they see as her carelessness about her appearance. They strive for straight A's to underscore her lack of achievement and they aim for pencil thinness to accentuate her womanly hips.

While they intensely desire to be different from their mothers, what these young women fail to understand is that their behavior, just like their mothers', is a way of seeking approval. "Every bulimic or anorectic remembers an incident just before she dropped to the infamous one-hundred-pound mark on the scale, when she heard a mother, a brother, a girlfriend point a finger at a fat woman or make a disparaging remark," Miroff says.

Therapist Ellyn Kaschak explains the preadolescent female's concern with her weight as a "general need to be pleasing to Father." Daddy, on his part, may send her telepathic and subtle messages about staying thin to preserve her desirability.[10]

Nina, one of the women we interviewed, developed early. At nine, she was wearing bras and menstruating; at twelve, she was beginning to lose her trim athletic figure and was putting on weight on her hips and thighs. Her father, an extremely attractive man who was preoccupied with his own looks, became obsessed with his daughter's weight gain even though she was only ten to fifteen pounds overweight. She still remembers the hurt she felt when he suggested she go to fat-girl camp. During her first year of junior high, he arranged for her to be excused from school twice a month and drove her to a Park Avenue diet doctor. After six months on amphetamines at age twelve, she had lost fifteen pounds, but the pills caused an irregular heartbeat and depression and her weight yo-yoed back up when she stopped taking them. Nina's weight kept fluctuating until recently, when she began to understand that her weight gains had nothing to do with hunger. Although Nina's dad died fifteen years ago, she may still slip into those archaic food patterns—confusing brownies with fury and folding anger in her muffin mix.

Compulsive Eating

Infants become aware of hunger when their tummies aren't full enough. Later on, if actual physical hunger becomes merged with emotional deprivation, a child may seek emotional comfort from food. A girl who is trained early to deny her own needs and to meet the needs of others learns that her "hunger" doesn't count and it becomes unreal, unfamiliar, and strange to her. She replaces the physical sensation of hunger with what diet expert Geneen Roth calls "the hungry heart." Female hunger is not necessarily a growling in the belly or a perception that it's time for nourishment. Throughout many women's lives, hunger is a metaphor, symbolic of every need they have learned to deny themselves.

Any woman who suffers from an eating disorder has a distorted view of her physical appearance, not only in her mind's eye but even when she looks in the mirror. Incapable of seeing herself as she really is, having no identity she recognizes, she imagines she is either an ideal version of herself or the hideous person she is afraid she may really be. In the most common instance, a woman with no weight problem sees herself as vastly overweight. In extreme cases, the opposite can be true.

Nina is five foot six. She can weigh up to 172 pounds, she told us, and she sees herself as Jane Fonda, while at her ideal weight of 115, she looks in the mirror and sees herself as unattractive and ungainfully overweight. The reality of her appearance is beyond her grasp.

Heidi Waldrop is a freelance journalist, a recovering overeater, and the author of *Showing Up for Life: A Recovering Overeater's Triumph Over Compulsion.*[11] In 1985, Waldrop weighed close to three hundred pounds and needed both hands just to pull herself up to a sitting position. When she looked in the mirror, her eyes "locked on the distorted, bloated face . . . entranced by the bleary-eyed puzzled stare." A self-created Medusa, she encased "the bad person" she thought she was in a hermetically sealed prison of fat. For Waldrop and many other women excess weight is a camouflage for powerful emotions like rage toward others, and a visible means to punish the self. It may also provide the overeater with the illusion of control, or it may distract her from dealing with significant problems and issues.

Although she knew she must change her life, Waldrop's story is a life-and-death struggle not only with chocolate cakes, candy bars, and Doritos but with a self that had been buried under layers and layers of fat since she was twelve. During psychotherapy she realized that "I had been hiding who I truly was because I had always feared my parents wouldn't love me when I was angry or depressed."[12] It wasn't until she began to see herself as a food addict and committed herself to a twelve-step program that Waldrop slowly began to lose her excess weight. In the process of shedding more than 150 pounds, she learned that compulsive eating had been a way to prevent her feelings from coming up. Now she feels "comfortable in my own skin" and "unencumbered by anger."

Anorexia

Now I can be all things. I can be a mother and I can rip your head off too.

—Tori Amos

There are now so many teenage and college women with eating disorders that one singer-songwriter, Tori Amos, has made a reputation giving voice to these young women's laments. In her album *Little Earthquakes,* Amos weaves a narrative in shorthand of adolescent angst. One of her songs, "Me and My Gun," is an interior monologue set at a rape scene inspired, Amos says, by *Thelma and Louise.* In "Silent All These Years," she describes a teenager's feelings about her father: "I got the anti-Christ in the kitchen yellin' at me again." Exquisitely in touch with a young woman's inner world, Amos uses a sugary sound to make raw rage palatable, as she asks her tortured listeners, "Why do we crucify ourselves each day?" Eating disorders thrive on the disjunction between the rage inside and the feminine image these young women feel they must present to the world.

Allie passed her adolescence in the grip of anorexia. "Creative, beautiful, and brilliant," as one friend described her, she excelled in her high school classes; she was vice president of student government, a cheerleader, and a band member; she painted, sang, and wrote poetry. But her African-American father and Caucasian mother, whom she describes as "refugees from Woodstock," began in their middle age to attempt to control her life. She was not allowed to date, she had a nine o'clock curfew, and she faced daily searches of her room as her mother looked for incriminating clues into her personal affairs. Behind her parents' backs, Allie was in a state of rebellion. She lost her virginity with a boyfriend in junior high and in high school she smoked pot, took LSD, and slept around. By her sophomore year, her parents had become physical in their attempts to control her, and she engaged in frequent fistfights with her mom. She was enraged at her parents and also at her brother, who was a model child.

In the spring of 1990, when she was in the eleventh grade, Allie, five foot eight inches, medium-boned, and weighing a perfectly normal 130 pounds, decided to go on a diet. Over the summer, she lost ten pounds, eating only chocolate chip cookies and drinking diet soda. By January 1991, she was down to ninety pounds, and she still thought she was too fat. "I was only skin and bones," she told us. "I looked like a skeleton wearing big baggy clothes with size-one pants falling off me." Like many anorectics, Allie's face bloated and ballooned out with water, while her eyes sank into their sockets, and coarse dark hair started growing on her breasts and then all over her emaciated back.

"I used to hang out at the airport and watch all the planes taking off. They were symbols to me of flight, and all I wanted was to fly away," she said, remembering that dark period. "I was trying to express myself, but my parents were so wrapped up in themselves, they never wanted to see how really thin I was getting. It scares me now. I looked like I was going to die." Allie's strategy of not eating not only disguised her rage at her parents but also drew attention to herself by making them "see" her as she was slowly disappearing. Their failure to recognize her symptoms confirmed for her their level of uncaring and neglect. Even if she literally starved to death, as she almost did, her mother would still be too paralyzed to act, while her father, so wrapped up in his own rage as an African-American man, would continue to tyrannize his family. Until she moved two thousand miles across the country and entered college, Allie didn't have the perspective to see what she was doing to herself. There at the counseling center, she entered intense individual therapy and began to separate her identity from her mother's. As she learned to express her rage directly, she returned to normal weight and began enjoying every aspect of college life.

Disorders like anorexia and compulsive eating both derive from early experiences and are related to problems of self-esteem. During childhood and adolescence, the psychology of anorectic and obese women is similar. "In both pathologies," writes Jungian therapist Marion Woodman, "the girls are repressed, too compliant, too desirous to fulfill their parents' expectations, even to fulfill their parents' unlived lives."[13] According to Carolyn Miroff, "What happens in a typical case is that the young anorectic girl sacrifices her own childhood to help her mother. She presents herself as falsely mature and self-sacrificing: 'Don't worry about me, Mom,' is her message—'I don't have any needs.' "

The sacrifice of the self is so profound and so effective in the middle years of this young woman's development that by the time she reaches the verge of adulthood, she hasn't grown up herself. She has been made to behave but not properly parented; fights over food become her way of expressing rage at neglect or attempting to control her parents. Eating is the one thing Mom can't make her do. Miroff describes the anorexic woman as seemingly uncommunicative: She gets her parents to notice her by not eating and growing skinnier. If the developing girl doesn't get enough attention from her parents or if the attention they give her seems dismissive or mocking, her narcissistic wounds may become so great that she feels she doesn't deserve to live or breathe, much less eat. As she perceives herself to be more and more trivial in their eyes, she starves her body down to nothing—which is her expression of what she thinks they think she's worth.

A woman's body expresses the way she feels about herself in double messages. If she's too fat, she's saying, "I can't control my appetites, and it doesn't matter what I look like, anyway. But you can't ignore me." If she's too thin, she's saying, "This is your ideal woman—I'm barely there at all."

Bulimia

The 1989 black comedy *Heathers* has become a college film classic. Set in a suburban Ohio high school, this saga of teen suicide, adolescent anger toward authority, and, as all the girls put it, "megabitchery" is populated with diet Coke–heads, bulimics, fat boys, and geek squads. The film takes its title from a female power clique of three girls named Heather that tyrannizes almost everyone in the school. As the film exposes the inner world of teenage girls' rage, we see their death wishes for prom queens and chauvinist pigs come true; we come to know their viciousness, their contempt and hostility for boring, "out of it" parents, and their unending sarcasm; we are privy to the sounds of purging in the high school lav.

Many young women with eating disorders particularly admire this dark comedy because it expels all the feelings they are trying to suppress. Expelling is the specialty of bulimics, who binge and purge, or gorge and compulsively exercise. Judith Brisman, director of the Bulimia Treatment Associates of New York City, explains that bulimia has many intrapsychic functions but that one factor can be "a release of anger."[14] Unlike the anorectic we interviewed who ate one piece of lettuce during an hour-and-a-half lunch, the bulimic tries to have her cake and not eat it, too. All the world saw the photos of Princess Diana eating layers of ice cream on the honeymoon yacht, and some people read about the Prince of Wales's heartless comment: "Is that going to reappear later? What a waste."[15]

Author and weight-workshop leader Geneen Roth explains that any compulsive behavior like the bingeing of bulimia is "marked by an awful absence of the self." She describes her own compulsive eating as "the feeling of being possessed. When I binged, it was as if a demonic spirit entered my body and took control. My movements were wooden, my will dissolved. I felt hypnotized, in a trance."[16] Pat Boone's daughter, recovered bulimic Cherry Boone O'Neill, says that in the height of her seven-year bout with the eating disorder, she would eat compulsively until she could "barely stand up."[17] A binge consisted of a box of doughnuts, a bag of cookies, a pint of macaroni salad, and a half gallon of ice cream. Sometimes she binged four times a day. There were also tedious rituals involved: The cookies had to be combined with milk; ice cream was favored because "dry foods don't come up very well."

Purging is a protection against the self and its rage, for there is actually a physiological and tranquilizing component in every post-meal trip to the bathroom. As therapist Pam Killen explains, "Vomiting releases endorphins that soothe the rage and act as palliatives for murderous feelings. Some women, maybe even Princess Diana, throw up their rage so they won't take it out on or hurt their children."

Actor Tracey Gold's food obsession came from what she calls her own struggle with "inner issues." Tracey's eating disorder, a combination of anorexia-bulimia, called bulmarexia, was triggered on the set of the sitcom "Growing Pains," when the producers of the show insisted that the actress lose her adolescent padding. In an interview with Diane Sawyer of "Prime Time Live," the painfully thin twenty-two-year-old admitted that the sitcom's writers' running gag about her weight gain in the script had gotten under her skin and enraged her. She had told them it was hurting her, Tracey said in a tone of undisguised anger, but the jokes in the show's dialogue continued.

When the producers told Tracey she had to lose the weight or leave the show, her parents found her a diet doctor who taught her the techniques of a bulimic. She trimmed off twenty pounds in about two months by chain-drinking tea and diet Coke to inhibit appetite. Her weight kept inching down until she weighed only eighty-three pounds. When she ate, she would purge herself immediately afterward. Her "meals" consisted of pasta and chicken microwaved to a minuscule mass. As her weight decreased, so did her sexual desire and appeal.

Today, Tracey is back up to a skinny ninety-three pounds, back to work, and on Prozac. Although she says butter still terrifies her, she is beginning to recognize and examine the issues underlying her eating disorder and learning how to cope with uncomfortable emotions. She has even made a promise to her fiancé that they will be married in the near future.

Self-Cutting and Mutilations

DEAR ANN LANDERS: I was stunned when I picked up the *Bakersfield Californian* and read the letter from the 17-year-old girl who mutilates herself with razor blades. I thought I was the only one in the world who did that.

FROM BROOKLYN: This is for the girl who cuts herself because the physical pain blocks the emotional pain that she finds unbearable. . . . I quit carving on myself nearly three years ago. . . .

DEAR FRIENDS: . . . I had no idea there were so many of you (self-mutilators) out there. My mail has been staggering. Information is available through the Hartgrove Hospital Treatment Program for the Treatment of Self-Injury in Chicago. The number is 1-800-DONT CUT.[18]

From chewing tacks to scratching the skin with a bristled hairbrush, from sticking needles into palms to creating geometric patterns on the wrist with a razor blade, self-mutilators try to tattoo their rage and other painful emotions indelibly on their skin. Even Princess Di reportedly cut herself: Once, she used a serrated lemon slicer on her wrist; once, when Prince Charles was in the room, she "picked up a penknife lying on his dressing table and cut her chest and her thighs."

Like the anorectic or compulsive eater who learns early on to suppress rage and her own desires, the self-cutter "is unable to communicate her anxiety and rage and longing in words," according to psychoanalyst Louise Kaplan.[19] Carolyn Miroff calls self-cutting "a profoundly abused woman's creative way of containing her rage at herself and her suicidal thoughts"; while Pam Killen describes the act of cutting itself as "a strategy of binding her rage, keeping it under control." Women of all ages, but particularly girls in adolescence, use acts of what has come to be called "delicate self-cutting" to keep their minds from confronting volatile emotions connected with early trauma, the onset of puberty, or love deprivation. Cutting distracts from murderous impulses and is a more diluted means than suicide or homicide of expressing murderous rage and vengeance.

"The usual site of the cutting is the ventral surface of the wrist, but sometimes the arms, the legs, torso, or face will be chosen," says Kaplan. "Sometimes the cuts are carefully wrought, sometimes simple parallel lines but also intricate patterns; rectangles, circles, initials, even flower shapes."[20] Just as compulsive eaters enter a trancelike, hypnotic state during bingeing, "the delicate self-cutter suspends conscious awareness of her self and the world around her. Splitting that part of her mind that feels and thinks about intolerable emotions and situations, she enters an inner, depersonalized world where she is only in the moment and cutting." At the sight of her own blood, calm is restored and, like the bulimic relieved by the endorphic flood from vomiting, she feels centered once more: She has "succeeded in repressing the fantasies, thoughts, and emotions that have set the stage for her self-mutilation."[21]

Marcia, who attends a prestigious East Coast university, was abandoned by her own Southeast Asian mother when she was only two and brought up as an adopted daughter in a loving American family. Hers is a rage that comes from childhood trauma and abandonment, and although she tries to let it out in other ways, she succeeds best when she's sticking little needles in the crook of her arm. "If women were allowed to be angry," Marcia contends, "we wouldn't have so much rage."

Marcia is a painter, but she admits that her rageful canvases evoke such comments as, "That couldn't be the work of a woman." For Marcia, self-inflicted pain is often experienced as pleasure. Art can be a substitute for sticking needles in her arms; sometimes she ends up a painting session with her palette knife gouging into and slashing her canvas. "Half of the time when I paint," she says, "I feel like I'm slashing myself and at the same time hurting this other living thing. I split, but at least I feel passion. Passion is a very foreign thing for most people in this culture."

"Nice-girl" mutilators who carve their aggression into the skin are punishing themselves instead of others. "One of the reasons a delicate cutter is unable to communicate her anxiety and rage," says Kaplan, "is that she has learned never to bother her parents with unpleasant thoughts or feelings."[22] Some girls, who don't actually cut themselves, express rage at their rite of passage into adulthood by compulsively plucking their eyebrows, scalp sites, lashes, and pubic area. This strategy is an oblique way of expressing rage that is also a visible cry for attention.

Pseudosymptoms and *Agnes of God*

> *I am accused. I dream of massacres.*
> *I am a garden of black and red agonies.*
> —Sylvia Plath, *Winter Trees*

At Physicians Hospital in Elmhurst, Queens, New York, a group of eighteen women of mixed but predominately Hispanic origin participated in a study of the relationship between rage and pseudo-epileptic seizures. One of the research assistants on Dr. Jason Lawson's project described the attacks as identical in appearance to four-minute epileptic seizures. "What we discovered was that the seizures had their origins in women's rage," the assistant told us. "The women would become unconscious, their limbs would shake, and they would bite their tongues. But if you rubbed a cotton swab around the rims of their eyes, they would blink—a reflex action and a true sign they were awake.

"When we began talking to them, we discovered in all the women, ages seventeen to forty-nine, underlying volcanoes of long-buried rage. We heard how they hated their children, their husbands, their families of origin. Never before had they talked about their own rage and frustrations." The researchers also knew that the seizures always occurred in front of other people and that none of the EEGs showed signs of epilepsy. They concluded that the seizures were self-induced, allowing the women to discharge rage with their bodies by thrashing around under the guise of illness, while at the same time drawing attention to themselves.

Many of the participants spoke of rage connected with the coming of middle age and the onset of menopause. Some talked of loneliness, though they lived in families of eighteen or more members, saying some of their bleakest moments occurred in rooms full of family. All women in the study were in a state of denial; more than one of them told the psychiatrists that her abusive husband was "the best man on the whole earth." Some also practiced self-mutilations or self-induced respiratory failures, holding their breath and turning red, then blue with rage.

During one group session, the women expressed awe and even admiration for a wife in the neighborhood who had finally become so enraged that she physically maimed her husband. In the later stages of the study, the women learned to look in their mirrors and scream or to punch a pillow, tear it apart, and curse. "We also told these women it was fine to cry—that crying would release their pain and rage, that crying would ground them in their bodies once again, a place they were always trying to escape."

Symptoms such as alcoholism, eating disorders, and pseudoseizures are not only forms of splitting; they also allow a woman to enter an altered state of consciousness. Professional therapists call the process of entering these altered states "dissociation." To dissociate is to disrupt, unconsciously, "the normal integrated functions of consciousness or identity."[23] On one end of the dissociative spectrum are minor phobias and compulsive eating, its mildest forms; at the other end are multiple personalities; and in between are amnesiac events.

One memorable film, Norman Jewison's *Agnes of God*, uses the case of a French-Canadian novice to pursue this range of dissociations. The film's opening scenes of calm and silence—whispered prayers, snowy white doves, the inner recesses of a womblike convent—are interspersed with bloodcurdling screams and images of blood-drenched hands. A dead baby has been found strangled by its own umbilical cord, wrapped in bloody sheets and stashed in Sister Agnes's wastebasket. The authorities assign the mysterious case to Dr. Martha Louise Livingston, a psychiatrist and chain-smoking lapsed Catholic.

Dr. Livingston investigates Sister Agnes, who suffers from a split personality, spontaneous stigmatic bleeding, anorexia, and hallucinations. Through persistent questions and then hypnosis, she discovers that at the age of two or three Agnes suffered monstrous abuse by her mother: She would be made to undress and her mother would ridicule her body, then burn her vulva with a lighted cigarette. During the course of the film, Agnes is able to unearth the traumatic incident, explore her feelings of shame, and transfer her rage at her mother to the psychiatrist. However, she is never able to reintegrate her polarized personalities: the first, a loving nun with beatific visions; the second, a two-year-old child convinced that she is "bad" and so enraged, she murders her innocent baby.

Rage and the Disintegration of the Self

Much madness is divinest sense . . .
—Emily Dickinson

Perhaps the most dramatic and sensational of a woman's survival strategies is multiple personality disorder (MPD), the subconscious creation of a rainbow of personalities or different ego states. Once considered rare but now acknowledged by psychotherapists as more common, MPD is seen as a subconscious defense against psychosis or suicide. By literally splitting off parts of her core self, a woman in a highly sexually or emotionally abusive environment makes an emotional escape, fragmenting into personality parts or ego states, each with its own history, its own emotional life, its own eyesight and physiology, and each, of course, with a different name.

Each ego state or personality is called an "alter," and some are older and more developed than others. One fragment of the self may be cerebral and help at school or on the job. Another alter might be seductive, while still another may carry all her family's rage.

In essence, the MPD multiplies her self into fragments to compartmentalize the horror of early experiences and to bury her rage, hurt, and shame. Usually, the initial traumatic events occur between the ages of two and five—the time when the personality of a child is pliable and she lives in a world of the imagination. The personalities stay frozen at the age of trauma, whenever it occurs. There are firm boundaries between each of the alters in the spectrum of personalities. When one alter comes to the surface and responds to the administration of a tranquilizer, for example, another submerged personality fragment will remain totally separate and anxious.

Nancy is forty years old and has had MPD since the age of three, perhaps younger. She gave us permission to speak with her therapist about her case, and he agreed to talk about her history with anonymity, in the hopes that other women might recognize themselves in Nancy and get help. In her case, MPD helped her to survive what she claims was a chronic and sexually abusive situation that went on well into her adult years. She is bright and creative and works as a supervising nurse when she is able to function on her own. She had never gotten any relief from her suffering before Dr. Reed (not his real name) diagnosed her case.

According to Nancy's account, she was two when her father first fondled her, telling her as he did so that he was expressing his love. Dr. Reed cannot verify her memories but knows that Nancy learned early on how to separate her emotional states from her ego. When her rage became unbearable, she would black out and enter another ego state. While her depressed mother stayed in bed and neglected the family, Nancy says she became the wife and mother. Not only did she supervise her two younger siblings; she was sexually molested by her father and uncle almost daily. "I came to believe and was taught that what they were doing to me was for my own good," she says. Inside the confines of the home, there were no secret places or boundaries; yet there was an enormous wall around the family and its secrets, separating it from the world outside.

Many people had been puzzled over the years by the way Nancy could change her state of mind and even her voice in an instant. All she knew was that she missed appointments, suffered with suicidal thoughts, and seemed unable to remember large chunks of her life. Easily victimized and exploited, she felt guilty about her family and didn't take care of her personal needs and appearance.

After three months in treatment with Dr. Reed, Nancy's separate alters began to emerge under hypnosis. When she mapped out and drew charts of her newfound inner family, Nancy discovered it was her cerebral personality, "Ann," who had gotten her through college and nurse's training. Her most frightening alter was "Freddy," modeled on the slasher Freddy Krueger of *A Nightmare on Elm Street* movie fame. An embodiment of Nancy's family's rage and fears, Freddy acted as the top cop of the alters; when anyone from the outside tried to get close to Nancy, Freddy would try to make Nancy kill herself, literally turning the family's rage against her.

Today Nancy is learning to expel negative emotions directly instead of burying them in her mind. She has also begun the process of reintegrating her separate selves and fragments and finding her central core. For the first time in her life, she is able to experience normal sensations, like registering whether she's too hot or cold. Her cure will be complete when all the various alters merge and her whole self feels strong enough to be exposed to vulnerability once more. Dr. Reed emphasizes that Nancy's response to her trauma was "an utterly logical and creative solution to her unbearable situation." He adds, "Yet all women in this culture learn to dissociate to some extent. It is a common way that women learn to survive."

In Dr. Ellyn Kaschak's opinion, the woman suffering from multiple personality disorder is saying, "I'm here but I'm not here" and "You can't hurt me because you can't find me."[24] Because the woman's personalities are walled off from one another, her inner world is a honeycomb of boundaries. When it comes to the outside world, she has no boundaries and is totally vulnerable.

The goal for every woman is to come out of hiding and give herself permission to act in the world as a flawed but healthy human being. When she can be honest with herself and disclose her thoughts and feelings to others, she no longer has a need to fragment herself and silence her rage.

Perseus was a brash and brave young man
whose mother was Danaë; Zeus his father
had come to her bed as a shower of gold.
Perseus was born of this sly union.
The son and mother, abandoned by the god,
wandered until they came to a land
ruled by the evil tyrant Polydectes,
who wanted Danaë for his wife.
He offered them uncharitable hospitality,
hating the boy for his kinship to the gods.
To appease Polydectes Perseus promised him
a prize: the famed Medusa's head as trophy.
The tyrant urged the boy on,
to die among the rocks that once were men
who dared glimpse Medusa's snaky head.
But the gods are a close family: Wise Athena
gave her father's child her mirrored shield
to deflect Medusa's deadly gaze.
Wily Hermes gave him an unbreakable sword
and told him how to find the Grey Ladies,
strange wrinkled crones who knew the whereabouts
of the monstrous Medusa.

The Slow Tango

It was tonight, when the wonderful didn't happen. That was when I realized you were not the man I thought you were.

—Henrik Ibsen, *A Doll's House*

While both men and women carry infantile memories into their adult relationships, women tote an additional burden, the dependency cycle, in their gear. The cycle revolves around their expectations about love, marriage, and romance; the dependency those expectations foster; and the resulting rage when dreams and realities clash. Although some women repeat this cycle over and over, other women, who learn to acknowledge their rage directly, as it comes up, are able to retain their autonomy, their separate identity, and a balance of power with their partners even when they are in love.

We live in an era of airtight prenuptial agreements, artificial insemination, computer dating services, and condom vending machines. On the other hand, the market is flooded with romance novels, "chick flicks," TV sitcoms that portray love as pure bliss as well as a laugh riot and marriage as the consummation every woman deserves. The exalted expectations an American woman brings to a heterosexual relationship are bound to fill her with rage and puzzlement when things don't work as they do in books or movies.

What women think they want is romance, the promise of the slow tango moving surely toward a consummation that Robert James Waller uses so well in the immensely popular *The Bridges of Madison County.* Waller's heroine is a fiery forty-five-year-old woman who has spent her life in a comfortable and companionable but passionless marriage. One day, when her husband and children are away, a dream lover appears in her driveway; he stirs up old passions, reawakens her sexually, and changes her life forever. Some women of all different ages respond to Waller's formula, including many who are liberated in their careers and in their ideology.

Even movies that are meant to take the woman's part often perpetuate the romantic notions that get women into so much trouble in the first place. Nora Ephron's film *Sleepless in Seattle,* in which the lovers played by Meg Ryan and Tom Hanks finally get together at the top of the Empire State Building at the very end, replaying the tearful reunion of Deborah Kerr and Cary Grant in the fifties film *An Affair to Remember,* is the very essence of romance and a comment on it. Ephron, acutely conscious of the female predilection for romantic love, says, "our dream was to make a movie about how movies screw up your brain about love, and then if we did a good job, we would become one of the movies that would screw up people's brains about love forever." Ephron, who is able to portray shattered romance so accurately because she's been there, and who has written *Heartburn,* a novel about it, says, "women have always made the mistake—of having unrealistic expectations."[1]

Dependent Women in Love

How many of my angers, my sudden, inappropriate rages, my jealousies, stem from my own self-imposed dependency, which up to now I have inappropriately called love?

—Nancy Friday, *Jealousy*

In the early stages of falling in love, many women tend to close their eyes not only to a man's bad habits and minor quirks but to possible character flaws, emotional and psychological problems. What Gloria Steinem calls "the circus of romance" distracts a woman with its enticing sideshows and keeps her from concentrating realistically on the main event. Rarely do women surrender to love and at the same time keep their heads and their perspective. Remember Stephen Sondheim's musical *Into the Woods*? Cinderella glows with happiness on her wedding day; the day after, she's back at the palace arguing with the Prince over the new shoes she's bought. Even when women are aware of potential problems in a relationship, too often they go ahead and get married, thinking that he will change. Women tend to think as Lady Diana says she did during her now-famous courtship. Aware of Prince Charles's liaison with Camilla Parker-Bowles, she was still convinced she could change him and make him prefer her youth and freshness to the more experienced competition.

Illusions about a partner are accompanied many times by naïveté about love itself. There are few high school and college courses that provide information on the various aspects and stages of love, its natural cycles, its idealizations and illusions, and the shoals on which it might flounder. What a woman does learn from dating is to curb her rage and disguise her anger—skills she will undoubtedly bring into a marriage or long-term partnership. Afraid of losing what she has, she becomes expert at preserving the status quo; she swallows her rage, pulls in the snakes, and seemingly lets him hold the sword. Her dependency on the relationship may prevent her from resolving conflicts with confrontations that would clear the air. She may repress her anger for emotional and financial reasons; it may be too difficult or frightening for her to follow her heart, take a risk, and make a change. In more violent scenarios, she may fear his physical strength.

Naomi Wolf, in *The Beauty Myth,* says that for many women "there is a certain attractiveness to dependency—something we're so used to that it's almost synonymous with being female. We need to overcome our psychology of insufficiency." Lack of independence shows up most prominently in a woman's love relationships where she may be a powerful woman on the job but turn into a jellyfish during the rush and early phases of a new romance.

Women often mistake dependency for love, which they tend to experience as "sweet surrender." Women escape all kinds of limitations—at least for the moment—by surrendering to love; Emma Bovary and Anna Karenina are merely the best known of an almost endless list of literary heroines who flee the restrictions and suffocations of marriage by embracing passion. Psychoanalyst Ethel Pearson and others believe a woman establishes and consolidates her identity by finding love and making a permanent connection: Her quest for an ideal love relationship has been the female counterpart to a man's search for autonomy and adventure. Because they don't have power in the world, many women derive what power they have from their relationships. For a woman, the stakes in a relationship may be higher than for a man, precisely because her identity is more dependent on its survival. Conversely, when she faces abandonment or rejection, her rage and hurt at these endings can be deeper and more intense.

Most researchers now believe passive and dependent behaviors are not genetically determined in females but have been ingrained by upbringing and culturally reinforced. As discussed, women's early declarations of independence from their mothers are much more tentative than a man's. Women find it harder to sever the cord, even from an abusive, invasive, or absent mother, and to seal off the boundaries between their mothers and themselves. In adolescent and adult relationships, many women open themselves up to love's vulnerability and when the romance is over have trouble reconnecting to their sense of wholeness. Women struggle all their lives with these questions of boundaries, fuse with partners more easily than men, and find it hard to tell where "she" begins and "he" begins and ends.

As Charles Whitfield, M.D., says:

In a healthy relationship there is an equality of pursuing and distancing by each partner. The other contacts me and initiates communications, get togethers, and activities about as often as I do. There is *mutuality*. In a less healthy relationship, I may do most of the pursuing and the other most of the distancing—or the reverse.[2]

Dependency, lack of clear boundaries, and passivity have been the hallmarks of traditional femininity. These qualities enable women to communicate feelings readily, open up, even express vulnerability. Yet the same qualities may make them more susceptible to pathological dependency. "Such women," writes Dr. Harriet Lerner in *Women and Therapy,*

> do not take action to solve their own problems, do not clearly state their opinions and preferences out of fear of conflict or disapproval, turn fearfully away from the challenges of the outside world, and avoid successful and autonomous functioning at all costs.[3]

Complicating a woman's dependency and boundary issues is the pattern created by her early dynamic with her father when she was striving against her mother to win his love. For many women, the quest for the father becomes in later life a do-or-die battle for a man. In place of her mother, all other women become her erotic rivals. Competing for available men, a scarce commodity in many American cities, is the female equivalent of Sunday-afternoon football and elicits rage toward other women.

Females, like Avis, try harder and are more competitive about love because they fear its loss so intensely. In the dynamic, as women see it, men give love in order to get sex; women give sex in order to get love. All people play out the drama of their earliest relationships with partners. When this dynamic is unconscious, a woman will have problems with her relationships. She will expect others to take care of her and approve of everything she does. She will look to others to make her feel complete.

Gloria Steinem's book *Revolution from Within* was generated by her love affair with newspaper magnate Mort Zuckerman, whose power and its trappings she says compensated for deficiencies she perceived in herself. Steinem explains her obsession with this man as "mourning for the power women need and rarely have."[4] It was the Dantesque hell of their breakup, she says, that really caused her to look inside of herself for the first time in the process of writing the book.

In the earliest stages of dating, a woman may act deliberately cool and independent in order to make a man fall in love. She disguises her most intimate desires and uses what Steinem calls her prefeminist "primordial skills." Playing hard to get and requiring pursuit are traditional female postures, say psychologists Barry Dym and Michael L. Glenn, "that are fine with the majority of men. They enjoy being involved with a woman seemingly so unlike the devouring creatures of their nightmares, a woman who *doesn't* want to control them."[5] During courtship men, too, try to please. They may bring roses, engage in hours of intimate conversations, and show tenderness and patience while making love. If both men and women continued to behave in marriage as they did in courtship, matrimony would be a thriving institution.

Male Distancing Strategies

Female dependency terrifies men—when men are afraid of being trapped, they distance themselves. Women are puzzled and often enraged by their distancing strategies. On the casual dating level, there's the "hit-and-run" evening: He seems to have a great time, kisses her at the door and promises to call, and that's the last time she hears from him. In a more intimate relationship, he engages in passionate lovemaking, tells her what a great bed partner she is, and then slips away in the middle of the night, leaving her to wake up alone in the morning. Or he seems deeply involved in the relationship but leaves her waiting by the phone while he spends Saturday night with the guys.

In longer-term relationships and marriages, these distancing techniques become even more intense and rage-producing. The women we interviewed described men who withhold sex and intimacy; partners who can't say "I love you" but find no problem flirting with and making advances to other women; husbands who work not only days but evenings and weekends; and the most enraging distancing behaviors of all, infidelity and chronic womanizing. In extreme cases of distancing, women have told us about men's sadistic or phobic behaviors, and violence.

Kristin is thirty-eight years old and lives in Boston, where she works for a software company. Though she has yet to marry, she has dated many men and is wiser than she'd like to be. "What men really want," Kristin says, "is a woman who is sophisticated and will share their interests but who isn't going to challenge them or cause any problems." A spirited, attractive woman with sunny Mediterranean good looks and a volatile personality, Kristin would like to meet a man who will think she's "worth hanging in there for. A guy who will think, I am so lucky to meet this woman. She has integrity, intelligence, and a passion for life."

In her experience, relationships end when emotions come up. Whenever a woman dares to express strong feelings openly, the response is, "Check please," and the guy disappears. "Men hate arguing and anger in women," she says. "They even start squirming when you tell them how much you love them. They feel when you express your feelings that their mother is about to appear, ready to order them around or drop some kind of bomb of verbal abuse."

Six months ago, Kristin had begun to wonder whether she ought to go into therapy to learn to control her temper and express her emotions without alienating men. Then she met Charlie, a resident at a large Boston hospital who lived around the corner. This time, she thought she had found *the one*. For three months, they enjoyed each other's company, going to hockey games, listening to jazz, or just quietly reading together. She accepted the fact that his medical career had first priority and that his time with her would be limited; she felt their values were compatible. She thought that with him she could show her feelings and bring problems out into the open. For their first three months together, their love life was exciting and deeply satisfying. Then one night, he pointed out a slight rash on his genitals and jokingly asked whether she had given him a sexually transmitted disease. Attributing this to the well-known medical student's penchant for developing every disease in the book, she laughed it off. Several days later, she was astonished when he brought the subject up again and suggested that she had been unfaithful. Cut to the quick, she lashed out in anger and slapped him. He apologized, but now she was the one who couldn't let the issue go; she harangued him about it over and over again and found that she was seeing him less and less frequently. Finally, he announced that he no longer wanted to continue the relationship. Although Kristin bemoaned Charlie's "inability to stick with her," she failed to see her own part in the demise of their affair. Kristin had put her trust in Charlie and didn't understand that her own intensity and need to control every situation led to the distancing she was experiencing with all men. Many women like Kristin don't understand that men who distance are dealing with fears of their own.

Some Realities About Men: Or Why *Fatal Attraction* Terrified Every Man in America

Hadn't he told her again and again that love had nothing to do with sexuality?
　　—Milan Kundera, *The Unbearable Lightness of Being*

According to Dr. Frank Pittman, author of *Man Enough,* "women will never be able to understand men until they realize that the most frightening thing in life for men is the anger of women."[6] What Pittman calls "this strange panic in the face of female anger" has its roots in a man's childhood and in "the engulfing power of Mama." A man rarely hears what a woman says when she's enraged: Her tone

of voice alone has called up the awful maternal sound of his childhood. "We strap ourselves in, turn off our receivers, and wait in
terror for the storm to pass," Pittman says.

The story of Medusa's slayer, the young warrior Perseus, cast out
to sea and sharing a tiny boat with his mother, Danaë, is a metaphor
for the intense feelings sons and their mothers have for one another.
The voyage of Danaë and Perseus is a prototype of the dreams men
have about their mothers, dreams that float through a man's subconscious, activating fears, fantasies, and desires.

Numerous women have told us about their husbands' fierce attachment to their mothers and the pain it causes when it seems to

Danaë *by Titian (c. 1554)*
*The lovely Danaë, mother of Perseus, was locked by her father in a
brass tower with only a slit for light to prevent the prophecy that the
son she would bear would kill him. Every night Zeus would enter her
cell as a shower of gold and vanish at dawn.*

take precedence over their loyalty to themselves. The rock group The Police recorded a song several years ago with the lyric "Every woman I go out with turns out to be my mother," which tells us volumes about male fears and desires. The songwriter seems to be complaining that every woman he dates becomes nagging, controlling, and overbearing just like his mother. His maternal alarm may be tripped not only by behavior but by an audio or visual reminder—a little thickening around the waist, a hint of a face wrinkle, a strident tone of voice. No matter how young and pretty she is, the song implies, as soon as he sees a hint of his mother, he dumps her for somebody new. On the other hand, the song may also mean quite the opposite: that a man cannot forget the sexual power and magnetism of his mother and is always seeking to find her again in the arms of another woman.

"There are essentially two very different images of women that run through all male fantasy," according to psychoanalyst Ethel Pearson. "In the first category, there are women who are split off from the image of the mother; they are enraged or highly seductive—vixens, witches, black widows, furies, and femmes fatales. At the other extreme in the second category are earth mothers and women who are nonsexual—Betty Crockers, vestal virgins, and the girl next door."

This male tendency to split women into either sexually neutralized "good" mothers or rageful "terrible" mothers derives, according to Pearson, Pittman, and other contemporary analysts of intimate relations, from the moment when a boy realizes that his mother's love is not his exclusively. At this crucial juncture for many men, love and sex split, as they separate the good mother, who feeds them, from the bad mother, who has power over them. These men connect sexuality with seduction, dominance, and the power of the female, while they reserve love and affection for an approving, unsexual "good" mother.

Because of these split-screen images of women, many men who may be ardent before marriage equate their wives with their mothers and have trouble experiencing them as real or desirable. One woman we talked with describes a moment early in her marriage when her husband, just returned from his mother's funeral, took her to the bedroom mirror and placed his mother's fur jacket on her shoulders. Since then, she has worn his mother's "mantle" in many different ways and is just now coming to terms with how to discard it.

The narcissistic blow that leaves a man ambivalent about his mother and causes his anxieties about sex and women is actually double-pronged: When he discovers that his mother has another love, he also finds out that his father—a bigger man with superior genital equipment—is his rival. This double perception—of his mother's preference for his father and his own genital inadequacy— enrages the child. Sometimes, according to Pearson, a boy's narcissistic striving for his mother "may become linked to aggression directed at women." For such a man, any woman is a reminder of his mother's power and her potential to deride his potency and size. Some of these males spend the rest of their lives proving their masculinity; others will need to dominate and control one woman; still others will seek simultaneous relations with two women or more.

Perseus's boast to his prospective stepfather and the assembled guests that he will vanquish Medusa is clearly an assertion of his manhood; the feat he proposes will prove his ultimate "swordsmanship." In psychoanalytic terms, Perseus's pledge that he will conquer Medusa and return with her head on a platter can be seen as an expression of murderous rage toward his mother for marrying the king, as well as a bid to outdo the rival father.

Camille Paglia in *Sexual Personae* calls love "a crowded theater," with family members and past loves occupying the seats. Sexologist John Money describes lovers as following "love maps" drawn from our earliest memories and experiences. These love maps determine what roads we take in relationships, what kinds of partners we choose, whether we need to create triangular relationships, and what situations trigger rage. Many of the behaviors that enrage us in relationships spring from hidden currents in our unconscious and are beyond our control. Woody Allen said it all in explaining his liaison with Soon-Yi: "The heart wants what it wants."

What Do Men Want?
The Low-Maintenance (LM) Woman

And what they felt as they became silent and sexless, as they
assumed the qualities of the perfect wife, was rage and sadness
and loss.
 —Dalma Heyn, *The Erotic Silence of the American Wife*

The perfect wife is a mistress.

 —John

Feeling dependent, women often attempt to make themselves into what they think men want. Women think men want a Martha Stewart in the kitchen, a sex bomb in the bedroom, a best friend, a secretary and social director, and an ego booster who seconds their opinions and carries out their plans. If they lack confidence in their authentic selves, women choose to try to meet these impossible demands, to be what Dalma Heyn in *The Erotic Silence of the American Wife* describes as "Beautiful, smiling, supportive, contented, giving, feminine—she is, in one word, good. . . ."[7] This doormat behavior produces additional rage and self-sacrifice, with its attendant stifling of real emotions and muting of personal desire.

Yet judging from the female behavior that turns men on during courtship and keeps healthy marriages intact, what men really want is an independent woman who is not afraid to express herself and doesn't have to be taken care of. She shows independence, coolness under pressure, generosity, empathy, and she likes to have sex. Low-maintenance women in film—Katharine Hepburn, Audrey Hepburn, Grace Kelly, Lauren Bacall, Ingrid Bergman—have screen images that shatter male stereotypes about women in love: They are not neurotic or hysterical, and they never whine. Sophisticated, elegant, and self-possessed, they don't cling or express anxiety and they definitely know how to manipulate rage. Their direct expressions of feeling turn men on and come from their true selves.

When Harry Meets Sally:
Biology, Expectations, Destiny

> *The birthday of my life*
> *Is come, my love is come to me.*
> —Christina Rossetti

The latest scientific studies of romantic relationships come to the conclusion that women and men equally crave and desire all aspects of love—the passion of romance, the warmth of intimacy, and the security of long-term friendship.[8] But while the need for trust, caring, and respect, as well as love and passion, may be shared by both sexes, men and women have clashing biological imperatives: He's born to breed and look for eligible mates; she's programmed to nurse and nurture. "Nature apparently meant passions to sputter out in something like four years," says Helen Fisher, author of *The Anatomy of Love*—time enough for a man to establish a relationship, produce offspring, and then take up with another partner. Ignorant of this biologically ingrained "four-year itch," and perhaps of other natural cycles, many couples may confuse genetic imprinting with rejection.

When faced with real life situations, we're lost.

Adding to the confusion, our images of love and romance and what to do in relationships are shaped by what Barry Dym and Michael L. Glenn, authors of *Couples: Exploring and Understanding the Cycle of Intimate Relationships,* call the prevailing "Cultural Narratives." The culture—represented in books, movies, TV sitcoms, and stories in magazines about the lives of celebrities—tells us the way love is supposed to be. These narratives always seem to reflect current trends, yet they coexist with and are undermined by earlier and still prevalent narratives.

In the fifties, the narrative was about monogamy, fidelity, female dependency, and "happily ever after." In the late sixties and seventies, women didn't wear bras and premarital sex was taken for granted; the movie *Bob and Carol and Ted and Alice* made couple swapping look middle-class; orgiastic love-ins seen in many movies were considered acceptable for counterculture youth. The romance in *Wall Street* between Darryl Hannah and Charlie Sheen epitomized the ideal eighties' live-in relationship—lots of sushi, lots of money, and fitness-inspired sex. Side by side with this Yuppie zeitgeist, New Agers emphasized the soul in relationships; at the same time, serious consciousness-raising focused attention on issues of child abuse and domestic violence.

In the nineties, gay and lesbian lifestyles have been recognized by the mainstream culture. For heterosexuals, there are lots of friend-ships, little formal dating, a supply of durable condoms, and the ex-pectation that somehow intimacy will develop. At the same time, the earlier narratives persist, causing confusion and muddying expecta-tions.

Cultural narratives with their clashing expectations are the sub-ject of the film *When Harry Met Sally*. How, why, and where Harry meets Sally is less relevant than the attitudes and expectations about love and marriage each brings to that meeting. Harry, for example, conforms to several male stereotypes: He believes that men and women can't be friends because sex always gets in the way and that the reason Sally is so uptight is that she "hasn't had great sex yet." Though he's afraid she wants to trap him into marriage, when faced with the loneliness of a life without her, he rushes headlong toward a romantic ending.

Like many women, Sally remembers every aspect of their relation-ship—where they first met, their first date, first kiss, and particularly the first night he used the *L* word. After they have sex for the first time, Sally wears a stuffed-animal grin on her face and all her mar-riage fantasies rev into high gear; Harry stares at the tube, wondering how long he has to hold her before he can get up and go home to his own bed. Harry believes that no woman has ever faked an orgasm with him; Sally expresses her rage at Harry for harboring his delu-sion by faking one convincingly in the middle of a crowded deli.

When Sally meets Harry, she disguises her anger and insecurities about abandonment under a blanket of sweetness and agreeability. Her high-maintenance qualities emerge nonetheless. She is an obsessive compulsive who alphabetizes her video cases; in a restaurant, her pickiness is way up there on the high-maintenance scale with her complicated orders: "apple pie, but only if it's heated, and whipped cream, but only if it's real, and a chef's salad with oil on the side." There is a fine line between expressing one's needs and becoming a royal pain, and Sally crosses that line. With her, everything is a major production. Like most high-maintenance women, she discharges her rage at men not in angry outbursts but in passive-aggressive and indirect ways, making it difficult for Harry to relax and enjoy himself, to detect her real feelings or to trust her.

In the world of celluloid, they walk happily into the sunset. However, when his and hers narratives don't match, in real life anger and resentment are usually added to all the other baggage men and women bring into relationships. Unreal expectations combined with harsh realities and a pinch of fear about the possibility of contracting AIDS create a stew of potential rage and confusion.

The Stages of Marriage

The ideal partner of today is a cross between a psychotherapist and a good parent.

—Dym and Glenn, *Couples*

According to that old fifties song "Book of Love," relationships, like novels, fall into natural chapters. Although some books, like some marriages, read longer than others, consensus among professional researchers and Ph.D.s who specialize in studying romantic relationships is that there are three broad stages in the development of a relationship. The first is the stage of passion, the initial period when love is new and seemingly endless. Like chocolate or a runner's high, a lover's euphoria is biochemical and can last for a day, several months, or even years. "Lovers often claim that they feel as if they are being swept away. They're not mistaken; they are literally flooded with chemicals. . . ."[9]

The love chemical, phenylethylamine, can retain its potency for two or three years, keeping lovers addicted to love and on a perpetual and passionate high. Authors Dym and Glenn call the beginning of a relationship its "expansive stage"—a time of mystery, discovery, and biochemical bonding. In this period, boundaries loosen, partners listen, and the other person is seen in an ideal light. Both partners feel sexy, brilliant, and transformed by the prospect of life's endless possibilities.

But like love, the love chemical fades, and from this stage of attraction and excitement a couple either moves into a quick ending or, when bonds of affection and trust have formed, into love's more modulated or muted phases. If a relationship survives the waning of passion's flames, a couple enters a time of bonding and attachment, when the idealization slips away and a partner is loved for who she or he really is. In this less exciting but more comfortable and realistic kind of love, endorphins flood the brain, bringing another chemical brain fix: "a sense of security, peace, and calm."[10]

In spite of all the early chemistry, a great many marriages end in rage and sadness. The circumstances of marriage set it up as a potential powder keg—the enforced intimacies, the shared disappointments, the failure of cherished dreams, the exhaustion of raising children, and the pressures of building successful careers. In addition, there may be spousal competition, the clash of different values, sexual dysfunction, possessiveness, and jealousy. The area of couple communication is another breeding ground for resentment. As Deborah Tannen points out in *You Just Don't Understand,* when there is lack of directness about expressing needs, or a deliberate repression of honest feelings and desires in a partnership, rage and volatility are the normal residue.

Moonlight Kisses Fading in the Warmth of the Sun

*In the hours leading up to his marriage to Lady Diana Spencer,
Prince Charles lay in bed with Mrs. Camilla Parker-Bowles.*
        —James Whitaker, *Royal Blood Feud*

In the pain and pulling back, or second stage of a relationship or
marriage, hope for its survival may seem dim. Yet this is a normal
part of every long-term relationship and by getting through it a couple emerges stronger. In this phase, as idealizations about a partner
slip away and disappointment sets in, "the relationship that opened
and transformed us now closes us down."[11] The woman who hears
too many complaints or criticisms may begin to lose her confidence;
instead of feeling sexy, she may desire food or drink. Both sexes at
this time may long desperately for intimacy with a partner who lis-
tens, who is generous and helpful, who is sexually inventive and
doesn't always ask after lovemaking, "Did you come?" A woman
who feels disillusioned or rejected by her partner may begin to fantasize or develop obsessive crushes on other men. Some seek out affairs
at this point in the marriage; the less adventurous may spend hours
reading Danielle Steel or Barbara Cartland novels; others may sink
into depression.

Many women allow the secret Medusa inside themselves to come
out of hiding with their partners at this time. During this period, all
a woman's infantile fears and phobias may blossom; her hypochondria and fears of flying or crossing bridges or leaving her own house
can add to marital misery. Women can also become passive and silent or turn shrewish and abusive. One man we talked to told us how
after three years of marriage his wife started making scenes in public
restaurants, yelling at him for tipping too little and taunting him in a
loud voice about his preference for catsup on eggs. In response, a
man may turn to other women, withdraw into silence, leave the
house for the bar, or become more aggressive and controlling. One
woman told us her husband alphabetized the foodstuffs in their cup-

board; another said her husband gambled away the household funds.

If passion alone was the basis of the relationship, if there is no trust and friendship between the lovers, they are likely to split up at this stage. In all relationships, dwindling desire becomes a source of anguish for both partners. A woman who doesn't know how to take her sexual pleasure and feels dependent on a man to give it to her is likely to be enraged, both by her husband's diminished sexual interest and by her own powerlessness to do anything about it.

Female sexuality is still a territory that needs exploration and is for both sexes what Freud called "the dark continent." A woman's genital organs are a scene of contradictions and oppositions: concealed and yet not sealed off, a place of birth and the "jaws of death." Her pleasure is equally complex. Many men have viewed female sexuality in the same way many women look at the insides of a car engine: too complicated, too messy, and almost unnecessary for them to understand. Sexual rage ran high in our interviews with women who don't take responsibility for their own pleasure. There are some women of all ages who feel rage at themselves because they have become expert at faking orgasms and don't know how to ask for or achieve a real one. While more women and men are becoming increasingly enlightened, many, like John Wayne Bobbitt, still view a woman's pleasure and concomitant orgasm as irrelevant, or secondary to their own. Such attitudes toward women's sexual pleasure keep men and women emotionally distant from one another.

In finding ways to deal with rage, says New York City psychotherapist Sandra Cross Strawbridge, women must first come to terms with both their bodies and their sexuality. "A major source of women's rage," she says, "is in the bedroom. What's going on in that little world gives us a pretty good idea of how we're doing outside it." She suggests that women ask themselves several defining questions: How do I feel about myself in there? Is the giving going only one way? Do I feel desirable? Am I achieving orgasm? Am I satisfying him? The answers to these questions will not only tell a woman how she's doing in the bedroom but will provide a gauge of her health, assertiveness, sensitivity to others, and well-being in the rest of her life.

"About forty percent of women have never had an orgasm," according to Strawbridge. "But the good news is that as women are finding out about their bodies and sexual responses, the percentage is going down. Women think that their power is all tied up in their sexuality, and that their sexuality is bestowed as a gift by men. But once women give up the myth that their sexual power comes from men, they also can give up the notion that men or society are supposed to care for them. We don't have the right to think that men can provide for us, whether it be financially, socially, or sexually. Our power comes from pulling together both our minds and our bodies, not just the sexual part."

From the time of Aristophanes's *Lysistrata,* it has been a tradition for women to display their anger by withholding sex from men, disguising complex and unconscious resentments about pleasure with clichés about a headache or menstrual cramps. "The reason a woman chooses sex to demonstrate her rage," wrote Dr. Sonya Friedman in 1977, "is because it is the only weapon she has."[12] In the nineties, therapists, including Dr. Friedman herself, advise against using sex as a strategy in sexual warfare. Instead, they teach women the techniques of real assertiveness and the assumption of personal responsibility for their own sexual pleasure.

Stuck in Marriage Rage

Some marriages that survive the second stage of growing pains, disillusionment and waning passion, get stuck in a cycle of perpetuating rage. The couple resorts to using cruel and vicious gender stereotypes during arguments, dehumanizing each other. As the rage between them escalates, each feels trapped, despondent, and betrayed—blaming each other becomes not only a sport but "a bitter routine."[13]

Rage scenarios are a way for a couple to communicate with each other by not communicating. Unable to deal with the roots of their pain, they rage instead of talking it over. The classic example is the rage of George and Martha, a college professor and his wife, in Edward Albee's play *Who's Afraid of Virginia Woolf?* The couple tear each other apart in front of a new colleague and his wife during the play's memorable drunken evening. They seem to be fighting over the balance of power in their relationship, but they do so in order not to speak of the real cause of their anguish, the death of their son.

Power and its apportionment is the underlying issue in *The War of the Roses,* the marriage-rage film of the eighties. Oliver and Barbara meet at an auction where Barbara (Kathleen Turner) outbids Oliver (Michael Douglas) for a piece of antique porcelain. In the beginning they are both turned on by the competition; then, after they marry, Barbara reverts to the traditional wifely role and remains secretly competitive. She wears a bun, stumbles over French while boring Oliver's law partners at a dinner party, stuffs her kids with sweets, and doesn't believe in discipline. The more submissive she is, the more he dominates her, the more enraged she becomes. Above all, her rage is an expression of her envy of Oliver's power—over her, over their lifestyle, out in the world. As she desperately tries to revalidate herself by redecorating their mansion and starting her own catering business, Oliver's indifference to her career, as well as her own feelings of subservience, drive her mad. Her attempts at retaliation infuriate him. Soon they are at war; they communicate by committing hostile-aggressive acts. *The War of the Roses* is a cautionary tale. Barbara and Oliver are both so bent on winning that they lose track of what's happening between them. They end up killing each other.

Infidelity: The Crux of Female Rage

HARRY'S FRIEND: *Marriages just don't break up over infidelity; it's just a symptom.*

HARRY: *Yeah, but that symptom is fucking my wife.*

—When Harry Met Sally

Some marriages end because they can't support the rage and tension any longer; other marriages collapse under the weight of infidelity. More women we interviewed were enraged about infidelity than about any other subject; one woman called infidelity "the crux" of female rage. For a wife, the disclosure of her husband's infidelity is all her nightmares coming true. Infidelity is a profound blow to her ego that brings back all the fear, rage, and feelings of rejection she had in early childhood. In her view, the abandonment she avoided has become a reality; instead of seeing infidelity as a symptom that something's wrong with a relationship, most women naturally personalize a partner's affair, blame themselves, and demonize him.

History, literature, and opera have provided all of us with myths and archetypes of treacherous women and male lotharios. Each sex attaches different meanings to adultery; each individual because of her or his upbringing, prior relationships, and level of confidence reacts to infidelity in varying ways. Some women see themselves as "wronged" and infidelity as a heinous act of betrayal, while to their husbands it's often just a fling. In Europe, where there is less emphasis on romance and more on material arrangements, both women and men view affairs as natural responses to the vicissitudes of passion. In the United States, a love affair that may be entered into for some missing romantic excitement is likely to break up a marriage.

Men assume they should lie to their wives about their infidelities. But a woman whose husband is having an affair may feel intense rage because of the cognitive dissonance produced by deception: She has the feeling that something's up but doesn't know if what she senses is real, particularly if a partner denies her suspicions. One woman we interviewed told us she had suspected for months that her husband was fooling around and was actually relieved when friends told her they had seen him enter another woman's house. When she finds her sister's earring on the bedroom carpet, Anne, the betrayed wife in the film *sex, lies, and videotape,* announces to her straying husband, "Tell me the truth, John. I will be more upset if you're lying to me."

Infidelity occurs when a relationship becomes weak and lacking in vitality; in this climate, either the man or the woman may become vulnerable to the charms of the opposite sex outside marriage. For some couples who have not addressed the issues between them, infidelity comes as a catastrophe; for others, emotionally healthier, it can be a constructive wake-up call.

Jean and Raymond married in the fifties, when she was twenty-one and he was twenty-five. She stayed at home and provided him with a warm and relaxing atmosphere, comforting food, and company when he came home from tension-filled days in his busy law office. Their marriage produced a son and two daughters, and when the children were old enough, Jean became a community volunteer. They collected antiques and took early-morning swims in their pool together. They were a team in marriage and child rearing. At their thirty-fifth wedding-anniversary party, they were feted by family and friends as a loving couple. The day after the anniversary, Ray suffered a heart attack.

Jean nursed him back to health and he returned to the office and resumed his normal duties. Six months later, he was swimming laps and making business trips. Not only was he back to his old self; he seemed more youthful than before. But Jean became concerned about his health because he was working so hard. Often his hours extended into evenings, and some Saturdays his business took him out of town. She had no idea that he was having an affair with a lawyer in her thirties assigned as counsel on the opposite side of a case.

One day, going through their credit-card bills, Jean noticed some charges at Saks that she couldn't remember having made. When she questioned him, Ray broke down and cried, then told her about Claire. Jean's reaction was fury: She burst into tears; she began smashing their antiques—the teacups, the Staffordshire dogs, the crystal Deco lamps. Finally, Ray, who had stood watching in disbelief, grabbed her and held her. She burst into tears again. He told her he felt so old after the heart attack and that this young woman's attention restored his confidence. "If I could make love to her and not die," he said, "I felt strong." Not only that, Claire did not continually criticize him; she didn't get mad if he was a few minutes late for an appointment or left towels on the floor of the bathroom. They talked to each other openly for the first time in many years, and Jean realized how sterile their relationship had become because of her need to control everything. Ray agreed to break off the affair.

Three years later, Jean and Ray are still together. A part of the thirty-five-year trust they had built is gone, and Jean still experiences intense feelings of rage when she allows herself to think about Ray's affair. But Jean is committed to spending the rest of her life with Ray and to working together with him to preserve openness and clarity of feelings in their marriage.

Creating triangles in relationships is an unconscious strategy that serves multiple purposes and may be used by both women and men. "Either lover may be tempted to introduce a third party to escape the intensity of love," says psychoanalyst Ethel Pearson. A third-party relationship may also be deployed to punish a spouse, to compensate for a defeat such as job loss or major illness, to prove one's masculinity or femininity, or to punish oneself for too much pleasure or intimacy. Infidelity is a symptom of other breakdowns in the system of a relationship: communication, trust, respect. Women and men who understand these dynamics are well armed if an infidelity occurs. Yet some women, whose egos are fragile, get stuck in recurring rage after the discovery of a partner's affair.

Barbara is sixty-five, attractive, slim, and intensely energetic. She has four grown children and a total of seven grandchildren. Recently divorced, she now calculates she had been lied to for thirty of the thirty-seven years she was married. The marriage always had problems, particularly in the sexual area, and in her drive to sublimate desire, Barbara became compulsive about her house and obsessed with extracurricular activities. Her many interests include yoga, alternative medicine, and healing, all of which her husband ridiculed; she is an accomplished artist as well as a writer of children's literature. Together, she and her husband had built a thriving travel business in New Jersey. He was the salesman; she handled the books.

She had just returned from a four-day weekend retreat on a Sunday night in May of 1990 when at dinner her husband said he had something he wanted to tell her. "Very calmly, he said, 'I've been seeing someone else for two years now. I can't go on with this double life. I've moved my clothes out of the house. I've seen a lawyer and I think you should see one, too.' And then he walked out the door with a parting shot: 'She doesn't believe in past lives.' My mouth got completely dry and my tongue started to burn. I had no breath—I felt like a pack of wild horses had trampled over me," recalled Barbara in graphic detail. "I felt so much rage. I felt as if I had been stabbed and I was living in a nightmare."

Barbara's rage is still vivid; she can pinpoint every detail in her narrative of the marriage's breakup, each date and conversation, and her every reaction. The centerpiece of her narration is her memory of the two years during which she had been sexually rejected. She had believed him when he said he was impotent and could no longer make love. She was unaware that with her compulsions for neatness, her need to control things, and her passive-aggressive expression of anger, she had begun to remind Glenn of his own mother, who had squelched his spontaneity when he was a young boy. When he left the house and she realized that he wasn't coming home anymore, that he was living with another woman, her alternating rage and grief became overwhelming.

"To my utter horror," she told us, "I found out he had had affairs with all my housekeepers and several of my close friends. He had made passes at the children's friends. I wanted a huge train to run over his legs and paralyze him from the waist down; I walk around with a pain in my heart all the time." Barbara's rage fantasy, in which her former husband is immobilized below the waist, projects her feelings about her own sexual desirability and serves to dispel some of her pain. Rage is now her constant mantra.

After the pain of infidelity, there is naturally a period of mourning during which fantasies that punish and destroy the wounding spouse are appropriate, even healthy. However, many women, like Barbara, remain stuck for years in the rage and bitterness of infidelity. They obsess about their personal injury, demonize their former husbands in every social conversation, and subconsciously stay tied to their spouses in protracted legal battles and custody fights. These women find it difficult, if not impossible, to move on. Not having learned how to take responsibility for their own happiness, they rehearse their rage over and over again.

Joanne, another woman we interviewed, was able to dispel and move beyond the rage of infidelity. Joanne had always prided herself on her detached attitude toward jealousy. Her husband, Bradley, a college professor, "always made a big deal out of jealousy and couldn't understand why I was never jealous. It was my belief that jealousy was an infantile and unproductive feeling that never got you what you wanted," Joanne told us in the logical and thorough way she has of recounting the events in her life history. "But when I discovered that the nice graduate student who came to the house with her little girl was really my husband's girlfriend, I burst into his study and screamed at him. In my fury, I had an exquisite sense of my own hideousness, my contorted features and the grimace on my face. As I felt my face burning and my tongue thickening, I literally hissed. I felt like Medusa."

Joanne is the director of a large association of hospitals in the Midwest and a responsible and highly effective person. She had never experienced real rage in her twenty-year marriage to Brad, but she admits she had been frequently angry about his chauvinist attitudes and the derogatory remarks he sometimes made about her, particularly in front of their two children. She describes him as charismatic; almost hypnotic in his ability to charm a dinner party audience; "physically and emotionally overwhelming." Until a friend told her about Brad's girlfriend, Joanne imagined they would grow old together. "It was the first time I had ever felt something I could call rage," she told us. "It was such a feeling of powerlessness. I felt all my bodily fluids rising up and trying to burst through my skin. Rage was trying to come through the top of my head." Although

Brad declared his undying love to Joanne, in the end he was unable to separate from his girlfriend.

At first, Joanne's rage took the form of obsessions and low-level revenge. She scanned the family telephone bills for her husband's long-distance calls to his mistress, rifled through his study, ripping up letters, books, and postcards from her. She visited a series of minor destructive acts on the girlfriend: For two weeks, she called her at four in the morning; one evening, she sent twelve pizzas to her house; once she corrected the grammar in a love letter and returned it to the sender marked up with a red pen. While these acts felt good at the time, Joanne knew she had to find a permanent and more constructive way to deal with the overpowering rage she felt toward her husband.

After he returned from a vacation to a place where she had always wanted to go, her rage was even more intense. Always a letter writer, she sat down and wrote to him, articulating her strong feelings about their relationship and what it meant to her, the nature of his trespasses and his act of betrayal. "The letter was long, clear, direct, and written in the most powerful language I have ever used. I ended it by saying, 'Please do not respond. You have already had the last word.'" That letter allowed Joanne to put it all behind her. It stopped the recriminations and de-escalated the battles over money and child custody. "I could let go of my feelings as I wrote them to him," Joanne says. "His behavior was the last word. But I regained my power by communicating my rage."

Her letter not only allowed Joanne to redirect her rage outward toward her husband; it became her method of reconstructing her self. As she articulated the reasons why she was so enraged, she defined once again her personal values. By asserting that she, too, could have a last word, she refound her voice. Once she wrote her letter, she no longer suffered the feelings of powerlessness and weakness that come with chronic rage. When she had told her version of the truth, she could move on with the rest of her life.

The Remains of the Day

When a couple enters the dark night of the soul in a marriage, it takes tremendous strength, determination, and commitment to get through the rage and disappointments and to piece back together the shattered remains. If they do make it out of the dark wood and want to continue the marriage, a couple enters a clearing where compromise and resolution can replace turmoil and the rituals of rage. In this third, or partnership stage, what Dym and Glenn call "resolution," wisdom, acceptance, and temperance predominate. For these lovers, says Ethel Pearson, their marriage becomes "a context rich with meaning: they maintain a joint memory bank, share long-standing jokes, constantly re-edit the family mythology. . . ."[14] Some even maintain a "mutual fascination" and "passionate engagement" with each other. Conflicts are settled through negotiation rather than regression, while differences blend into a more mature acceptance of ambiguity as the given and forgiven conditions of human life.

There is still a balance of power, but power is on a seesaw—tipping back and forth to each partner at different times. In unhealthier relationships, where one person has too much power, the powerless partner experiences rage at her dependency. Healthy independence matched by mutual interdependence means there is appropriate intimacy and sharing as well as distance and privacy. Rather than fused and enmeshed, partners know they can live without the other, but they choose mutual love.

Justine's marriage has just hit the thirty-two-year mark. She and Sandy are still together and going strong; their relationship, which began in the early sixties, survived emotional trauma, a three-year separation, and now his retirement. "I got married when I was twenty years old," Justine says, "and the first thing I was enraged about was, How did I get here? Lots of women in my generation had this experience. We had gotten married and done what we were supposed to. We couldn't understand why we were so miserable."

One source of Justine's misery was her mother-in-law, who moved in with the couple after they were married. Another problem was that her husband had been the only man in her life, and she was totally overwhelmed sexually. "I had a lot of questions about sex—it didn't feel the way I thought it was supposed to—and I couldn't ask my husband or my mother-in-law. In my confusion, I felt totally isolated and alone. I also felt so trapped and thought I couldn't cope socially. When my first child was born, I thought my life was over for good." After a second child, she had what she calls a minibreakdown. "I was twenty-three years old, everything in my life revolved around my husband's job, and I had no say in anything we did.

"My rage took the form of paranoia. I remember once we were at the movies and some people were talking in the row behind us. At the end of the film, I went up to them and asked them why they were talking about me. They thought I was crazy, and I guess they were right. My mother-in-law indulged and adored my husband. My rage at her was actually displaced rage at him. Like many women, I had also brought rage into my marriage from childhood."

Justine was lucky; in the midst of her torment, she realized that no one could save her but herself, and she started putting her existence together piece by piece. The first step was taking out a library card in her own name. "The first book I read was *Lady Chatterley's Lover*, where I learned about female sexual pleasure and marital boredom." From there, she moved into counseling and with her therapist's encouragement she discovered her need to be effective in the world at large and she went back to college, ultimately entering law school. Ironically, as she began to unearth it, her rage at her husband and his mother increased. "My rage at Sandy became clear and focused. I began to see that our upbringing and expectations were extremely different. He still wanted me to be the perfect mother and wife. He had never seen the inside of a kitchen, and I needed his help with the housework and the kids once I was back in school. His mother only made things worse."

When Justine went to work full-time as a lawyer, her entire family was upset, but financial independence from Sandy and a balance of power between them became her compelling goal. Her success brought them financial security, but he translated her desire for economic autonomy as withdrawal from him and the marriage. She resented his lack of trust in her and hated his attempts at control. "Our marriage has been very difficult," Justine says. "My mother-in-law was in and out of institutions, we went through a three-year separation, and we have found that we are very different people. Without counseling and an acceptance of an entirely new dynamic in the relationship, we would not be together."

Today, with the major problems in their marriage resolved, it brings them many pleasures. They are as different from each other as they ever were: She wants excitement, material comforts, and vacations; he would be happy living on a diet of yogurt, with a few books for friends. They have managed to negotiate their preferences into a his-and-hers blend of the opulent and the Spartan. He has retired, and he reads and attends classes at the local university during the week while she works and enjoys the glamour of a big-city law firm. In her middle age, Justine has found her formula for a happy and productive life and learned to think of her rage as "an old friend."

Freud's question from the beginning of the century—"What do women want?"—is the crucial one every woman must answer for herself before entering into a long-term relationship or marriage. Boundaries in place, she needs to determine not only what she wants but what her values, expectations, and long-term goals are and she needs to forgo what she may perceive as the rewards of emotional dependency, for in a dependent state she can never feel her power. Chaucer wrote centuries ago in "The Wife of Bath's Tale" from *Canterbury Tales* about a young knight sent out on a quest who discovered that what women desire is "sovereynetee." In the 1990s, the answer to what do women want is the same: They want the sovereignty to make choices and to have power over their lives. Sovereignty is there—women can claim it when they are able to be themselves.

5 The Rage of Age

Perseus came to the dismal cave of the Grey Ladies
and asked them how to slay Medusa.
The ancient hags said no one could slay Medusa
without the helmet that could make him invisible
and the winged sandals that could make him fly,
and the magic pouch that could hold Medusa's head.
When Perseus asked for the magic objects,
The three hags refused to tell where he could find
   them.
The Grey Ladies had among them only one tooth
and a single eye to share among them.
So they were passing them one to the other.
Perseus snatched the eye and tooth
and in so doing, forced the Grey Ladies
to reveal their secret.

Seers, Prophetesses, and Wise Women

Although the mature yet beautiful faces of media stars like Lauren Hutton, Jane Fonda, and Gloria Steinem clearly suggest that a woman's prime time may be her fifties, many women spend thousands of dollars on plastic surgery, trying to erase their bags and wrinkles. Our culture's view of aging females dooms a woman to years of loss—of looks, bone mass, and male attention. Some movie directors, modeling agencies, and magazine editors have begun to present images that urge us to rethink the relationship between beauty and age; nevertheless, reality tells us that a woman's primary value remains invested in her face and figure and not in her life experiences.

The Grey Ladies whom Perseus meets on his quest to arm himself in his encounter with Medusa live in a land that is shrouded in twilight. As symbolic figures at the edge of darkness, they represent the diminished capabilities of the aging female. They hold only one secret, and when they reveal it, they betray Medusa and cause her death. The myth presents them as virtually toothless and blind. With no "bite" left, no power in their voices, they also have no resistance.

Destiny *by Goya*
These three Grey Ladies were encountered by Perseus on his quest for
Medusa's head. After Perseus snatches the one eye and the one tooth
that the three share, they disclose the secrets of the Gorgon.

Unlike their sisters on the moor in Shakespeare's *Macbeth,* the
three Grey Ladies in the Medusa myth appear without a cauldron.
The cauldron of myth is "the source of life, wisdom, inspiration,
understanding, and magic, the Mother vessel tended and cared for by
women."[1] Containing a stew of life-giving and sustaining knowledge, it is the symbolic womb of feminine wisdom. Any Grey Lady
without a cauldron is woefully incomplete: what is left to her but
pain and self-pity?

The modern counterparts of the Grey Ladies are those older
women who are unaware of themselves as potential sources of wisdom and power and who consequently have suppressed their hopes,
aspirations, and desires. Many betray themselves, never having demanded more than "one eye and one tooth." But graying women are
beginning to break the stereotypes about aging and articulate their
desires. Some, like Betty Friedan, Germaine Greer, and Gail Sheehy,
are pioneers in the field of female aging; their eloquence in illuminat-
ing their lifetimes of experience is part of an ancient feminine tradition.[2]

The ancient world venerated older women as receptacles of holi-
ness and wisdom: They were oracles, sibyls, seers, and prophetesses

with access to the invisible world of spirits and mysteries. Originally *hag* meant "holy one," while *witch* comes from "wit" and *crone* meant "wise woman." In today's culture, these are terms of disparagement associated with bag ladies and aging comedians. Yet there are contemporary cultures that revere the wise woman—cultures in which time is more fluid and cyclical and the cause of less anxiety and fear. Old age in this paradigm becomes a time to draw together the threads of one's life, to seek wisdom, and to care for and counsel the less experienced. Native Americans of the Southwest, for example, have traditionally called on Grandmother Spider for help and guidance. As a spider spins a strong and beautiful web out of herself, bridging the gaps between space, women pass female ways to their daughters through the experiences of daily life, ceremony, and tradition. Aged women are receptacles of wisdom, judgment, and expertise; the elderly are nourished and honored, their role considered crucial for the development of succeeding generations.

At the root of women's anguish over aging is the Western attitude toward age that denies older women respect and acknowledgment and the opportunity to share their wisdom in their later years. Western culture views time as linear and finite, an hourglass that runs out. Our goal is to stay young—a focus that keeps many people from leading authentic lives. In Betty Friedan's latest book, *The Fountain of Age,* she investigates what authenticity means. "There is," she writes, "a great need to knit together the pieces of our life. . . . And then you become a truth-teller."[3]

The Grey Sisters' individual uniqueness vanished, their identities merge. They live apart, separated from all social intercourse. Like the monstrous women whose secret they guard, they know the pain and rage of being undesirable. Today, the Golden Girls can be seen as the Grey Ladies' TV sitcom counterparts: The Grey Ladies share a tooth; the Golden Girls, more enlightened, share a home, men, and what fortune they have.

A woman's sexuality peaks in her forties and fifties and remains a vital part of her sense of self for the rest of her life. But many women feel they can't express their vibrancy, libido, and passion as they grow older—largely because of the lack of available men. By the time they're in their thirties and forties, some women are left in the lurch—abandoned for someone who is a more manageable, less experienced version of themselves. These women need to understand that they are sexual beings whether or not they have partners and that their sexuality can be expressed in many ways.

In his quest for freshness, in search of his own waning youth, a man sometimes turns suddenly and angrily on his long-term partner. If a wife or a girlfriend reminds him too much of his mother or his own human weaknesses, he may reject her and push her abruptly aside. To assuage his feelings of guilt, Madeline Bennett, author of *Sudden Endings,* told us, he projects on his mate a terrible fury she calls "bad object rage." Either spouse may exhibit this baffling turn-about in behavior, but commonly a man will use his spouse's age as a way to blame her for his lack of adventure, fun, sexual excitement, and personal fulfillment.

A woman who experiences this intense and unexpected rage from her partner feels erased, emotionally abused, sexually inadequate, and totally confused. Bennett explains that the man's behavior is usually triggered by some kind of trauma: "the loss of a job, the collapse of a business, or serious illness."[4] The traumatized spouse who is doing the rejecting "unconsciously diagnoses his partner as the bad part of him or herself." He projects all his own shame, guilt, self-hatred, and rage on a partner, and then, by rejecting the partner, he exorcises himself. Bad object rage may be accompanied by other symptoms, such as lack of empathy, sadistic behavior, and the inevitable attachment to a new partner.

A woman swiftly and cruelly abandoned for someone younger can explode with the full force of female rage. The story of Betty Broderick, a California housewife who murdered her husband and his new bride, has become a modern parable.

Betty's troubles began in 1983, on the day her husband, Dan, a wealthy lawyer, came home and announced he was unhappy with everything in his life. He didn't like their elegant house, he hated their upper-middle-class California lifestyle, he didn't like their friends, and he particularly didn't like her. "I was old, fat, boring, ugly, and stupid," she remembers him telling her. "He immediately went out and bought a red Corvette, you know, the car of his teen-aged dreams, and he got a young girlfriend, who, coincidentally, looked just the way I used to look."

At the time, Betty was an attractive thirty-four-year-old college graduate whose life had revolved around her husband since she was seventeen. She had worked as a teacher to pay Dan's bills for Harvard Law School and had handed over her paychecks to him from the first. She had stayed home and raised their four children while he spent long hours working as a malpractice attorney, building up a fortune. Their marriage was rocky at times but seemingly stable. Friends described her before the breakup as a "supermom" and "normal, the most together woman I ever met."

Betty found out about her husband's affair sometime later, when she went to his office on his thirty-ninth birthday to surprise him with a bottle of champagne. There, she found the remnants of an intimate birthday lunch he had shared with his twenty-two-year-old personal assistant and mistress; she was told they had "left for the day." She went home, doused his custom-made suits with gasoline, and set them on fire. After he moved out, to get his attention and to dispel her sense of annihilation, Betty Broderick put on Medusa's mask and smashed her way back into Dan's life. She took scissors and cut him out of family pictures, went to his house with cream pies and smeared them all over his clothes, broke his windows with champagne bottles, and left obscene messages on his answering machine.

According to friends, what really tormented Betty was that she had been replaced by the other woman—at charity benefits, at her children's ball games, and in her husband's bed. After giving the best years of her life and her money to this man, Betty had been discarded for a newer, younger model of the woman she had once been. Her rage ignited into a bonfire when Dan and his new wife, Linda, began to mock her sadistically as an unattractive older woman. In legal documents and harassing mail, they characterized her as "grossly overweight" and "crazy." She told the court they sent her ads for wrinkle creams and weight-loss programs and a picture of the two of them cut out of a magazine, along with a note that read: "It must kill you to see these two so happy together. Eat your heart out, bitch!" Unable to control her overwhelming rage, Betty eventually eliminated its source—by shooting Dan and Linda in their bed.

Speaking to the public via a TV hookup from her prison cell to the Oprah Winfrey show, Betty Broderick said that her mistake was to sacrifice her own needs completely in order to support her husband's career and raise their children. She had never imagined a time when she might want to function independently or create an autonomous life for herself within the marriage. She thought she was indispensable, but she was stuck in her happy young married role, and was supplanted by a young woman who in her husband's eyes could play it better.

A Change of Lives

As with most passages in life, entering midlife can be either a positive or devastating experience. Some women find themselves caught between a past in which their lives were full of purpose and a future that yawns ahead, looking empty and bleak. Other women at this stage are able to take another route, using their rage at biological change for spiritual and erotic self-deliverance. Fortunately for women, menopause, with its mysteries, anxieties, and confusions, has finally begun to be explored with much insight and wonder.

In *Used People,* Shirley MacLaine portrays a newly widowed woman who must finally confront her own longings and desires. In a climactic scene, she tells her youngest daughter what might happen if she really began to examine her unlived life and the sacrifices she has made for her husband and children. "If I looked deep inside at what happened to my life," she hisses, "there'd come out of me such a rage it would blow this building apart; it would blow you apart, and it would blow Queens off the goddamn map!" But after facing her rage, internalized and built up for so many years, she allows herself to feel desirable again and enjoys the attentions of a romantic widower played by Marcello Mastroianni.

Germaine Greer, in her provocative book about menopause, *The Change,* speaks of the rage released toward the end of a woman's biologically productive life:

> Some of our negative feelings about menopause are the result of our intolerance for the expression of female anger. . . . We are not really surprised when menopausal women spit out bitter home truths to their children, but we pretend that it is hormonal imbalance that is speaking, turning anger into illness so that we can evade the implication of it.[5]

Husbands and children often dismiss an older woman's rage as hysteria rather than confronting her pain. One woman we interviewed said her son had labeled her "borderline psychotic" during her menopause, unaware that she had endured an arranged and loveless marriage for thirty years, having given up the man she truly loved. This "spitting out" of rage that Greer writes about is really a menopausal woman's clearing of her throat, an attempt to say out loud what she has repressed for decades.

She may be a wife and mother who loved and served her family well but received little gratitude or love in return. Raging silently like Joanne Woodward in the film *Mr. and Mrs. Bridge,* she may turn to her husband in late middle age and ask, "Did you ever love me?" Panicky at the poverty of her emotional life, Mrs. Bridge is desperate for anything to fill the void and warm the chilly marriage bed. In the end, such a woman feels trapped. Like Mrs. Bridge, caught in a snowstorm when her car dies halfway out of the garage, in real life many women feel wedged between the constricting walls of conventionality and fear. The lucky ones will realize rescue must come from within, that they must find their own source of fulfillment.

Menopause is a period when women may feel doubly betrayed: by a body they don't fully understand or seem to have control over and a society that tells them that their value is waning. In Gail Sheehy's *The Silent Passage,* a successful movie executive reacts to her change of life, saying she was flushed with rage because aging meant "I might be perceived as having no power."[6] Many women at work feel they are combating not only sexism but ageism.

As a woman wrestles with who she has been and who she is becoming, menopause can be a time for her to look back over her life and see which friends, ideas, values, and behavioral patterns should be discarded and which should be retained. She has entered autumn, a time when gardens are dug up and turned over, not because they are no longer productive, but in preparation for a new season of growth. The earth is still warm from the summer's sun and the fall foliage presents a blazing palette of brilliant colors. There are days of grace in November as well as in June. If women are to restore the cauldron and place of honor to the Grey Ladies, they must see hot flashes as "power surges" and reintegrate menopause as part of the natural cycle.

The Rage of Caretaking

The Pietà is an image of woman beloved throughout the world. Michelangelo's great masterpiece of the Virgin Mother lovingly holding her fallen son dramatizes women's experience of caring for men who die in their arms, as does the new Washington memorial to women who served in Vietnam. The average woman's life span is ten years longer than a man's. An older woman will frequently find herself left alone without male companionship and love. Some may feel a kind of dark cosmic joke at work: They are given additional years but spend them sacrificing rather than enjoying themselves.

Especially with protracted illnesses and caregiving, older women oscillate between compassionate love and hate. Sometimes family ties are not only the tie that binds but the bind that ties. One woman we interviewed, an eighty-two-year-old widow, was active and curious, ready to enjoy all the things she couldn't while raising a large family and caring for a husband. But when her sister-in-law died and her ninety-year-old brother moved in with her, she found herself again a caretaker and pulled apart by conflicting loyalties. One woman was enraged during the final months of her ninety-two-year-old partner's life because his children were more interested in his will than his basic needs for love and attention. Her rage grew more intense after his death when they refused her the painting he had promised her.

Many older women feel incomplete without a man and after a husband's or companion's death venture out in search of another mate. Because the pool of eligible older men is ever-shrinking, a woman needs to find other prospects besides men that broaden her knowledge and deepen her experience. Life can open into other possibilities for a woman alone; free now from the responsibilities of those who depended on her, she can travel, teach, start a business, write, paint, fulfill her creative dreams.

Reclaiming Our Daughters

Your mother did it to you. And her mother did it to her, and back and back and back, way back to Eve, and at some point you stop it and you say "Fuck it." I start with me.
—Postcards from the Edge

The Grey Ladies in Medusa's story represent female treachery. After only momentary hesitation, they yield up their secret to Perseus, betraying Medusa to get back their eye. In *Iron John,* Robert Bly says that in order to liberate the "wild man" in himself, the boy must steal the key from under his mother's pillow. It "is a troublesome task. . . . Attacking the mother, confronting her, shouting at her . . . probably does not accomplish much. . . . The key has to be stolen."[7] And so Perseus seizes the moment when the sisters are passing their shared eye to one another. He reaches in and snatches the eye, just as the patriarchal culture usurped the ancient vision and power of the matriarchies.

The old women's mistake is an ancient one that is also common today. Conditioned to sacrifice for husbands, family, and loved ones, to act without thinking when anyone asks for help, women may not envision the consequences of their actions. When they no longer have power of their own, they become ineffective guardians of other women's lives, as well. For older women to reclaim the cauldron, they must see all younger women as potential daughters and themselves as role models.

The most anguishing betrayal between women is a mother's betrayal of her daughters. The work of Nancy Friday, Harriet Goldhor Lerner, and Debold, Wilson, and Maleve has revealed just how precarious the "dance of intimacy" between mothers and daughters is. Much as she desires to shield and protect her daughters, even the best-intentioned mother can find herself treading the thin line between female bonding and suffocation. During the significant passages in the lives of the mother and daughter—adolescence, marriage, childbirth, menopause—the friction between them is at its height. A classic example is the premenopausal mother of a prepubescent girl; she brings her own memories and anxieties to her daughter's rite of passage and in addition is reminded by her daughter of the ending of her own ability to bear children.

Mothers and daughters both suffer in this clashing biological climate, but when the two find a way to recognize these issues, they can move toward deeper connections and love. In Amy Tan's *The Joy Luck Club*, we see how four mothers' secrets and hopes for their children are often at odds with their daughters' expectations for themselves. Each of the young women longs for autonomy and also desires her mother's love and approval. But until they know their mothers' personal histories, they cannot put their own lives into perspective and choose their own best paths. Each young woman in turn gives up her rage at her mother and achieves deep union when the silence is broken and the wounds of the past are exposed. When June's mother tells her at last, "I see you," she heals her daughter's feelings of insubstantiality and ties her once again to the maternal source. Another daughter receives her mother's support when she confides her pain over a marriage that has soured. "What does it matter if you lose him?" her mother asks. "It is you who will be found."

The "club" of women serves as a model for an authentic mother-daughter reunion and a vehicle to dissipate ancient rage. Older women who can tell the truth to themselves can heal their own lives and impart their wisdom when they pass it on to their daughters. If women begin to think of themselves collectively as mothers, or women who guide and care for many daughters, they can change the patterns of matriarchal betrayal.

Jean Harris is a real-life model for this kind of mothering. Sentenced to fifteen years in prison for the murder of Dr. Herman Tarnower, the Scarsdale diet doctor, Harris wrote a book about the years of rage and pain that led up to that life-altering moment. "I had been screaming for help for years but somehow whatever came out never rang true, or never sounded important enough to take seriously," she writes.[8] Although she was a highly respected headmistress of a prestigious Washington girls school and the mother of two sons, she didn't value her own feelings. Like many women who repress their rage, she discounted its messages, and while it smoldered, she tolerated her lover's verbal and emotional abuse and his affairs with other women. "In the end, I had become a nonperson to Hy," she says.

Like many women who should know better, Jean Harris placed herself at the disposal of the man she loved. Although she knew that other women sought out the highly prized bachelor Tarnower, she never believed that he would actually bring other women into the bedroom where they slept. "Imagine such hubris and naivete in a grown woman," she writes. Believing in the fiction of his exclusive passion and surrendering herself to romance and the glamour of his life, she was vulnerable for rejection and open to betrayal. Jean Harris had no idea of the depths of her rage.

The night of the murder, she had begged Tarnower to see her once more. She arrived at his Scarsdale mansion intending to end her own life, and she might have done so if she hadn't seen the visible proof of his betrayal—another woman's negligee draped on a hook in her lover's bathroom.

It might be expected that Jean Harris's imprisonment would have embittered her. In fact, she serves as a model of how rage can be channeled and used constructively. Accustomed to competing with other women, at the Bedford Hills Correctional Facility she came to view them with compassion. On her first night in prison, when she walked into the recreation room and saw all the other women engaging in everyday activities—visiting quietly, fixing their hair, ironing—she was touched by the familiarity of it all. "They're so remarkably ordinary. This is the dark side of the moon, but the women look so ordinary. They're people. They're women. And they're mothers. It was a sobering moment of discovery," she says.

Harris became a teacher's aide in the high school–equivalency program. She then moved into the Children's Center. Converting her depression at personal rejection and imprisonment into advocacy fueled by rage, she worked to give incarcerated mothers more time with their children. She saw women giving birth handcuffed to delivery tables; she taught a parenting class, during which she learned that the most deprived and humiliated women can become models of nurturance, compassion, and independence.

Jean Harris found in the work at Bedford a way to exorcise her past rage and become absorbed in issues that put her personal problems into perspective. Today, out of prison, she continues to work on behalf of mothers in prison.

Older women like Harris reclaim the cauldron of the wise women: By teaching younger women, by sharing their experiences, and by channeling personal rage into compassionate action, they break the cycle of generations of betrayal. Audrey Hepburn, who traveled the world for UNICEF on behalf of starving children, and Mother Teresa, who embraces the outcasts of our time, gave us just a taste of what matriarchy in all its power can accomplish.

It's a cultural imperative for older women to initiate younger women. Mothers need to teach their daughters about female mysteries like menstruation and childbirth and make them wise in the ways of the world. But sometimes when a mother's rage remains unresolved, she becomes a partner in the most dangerous relationship in the young girl's life. Poet Anne Sexton had such a mother, according to her biographer, Diane Wood Middlebrook. As Sexton reportedly put it: "Mother didn't want to be motherly."[9] Both of Sexton's parents were heavy drinkers. Her mother, Mary Gray, was vivacious and self-absorbed. "She was also emotionally unpredictable; Anne never knew when she was going to be horrible or nice." Not only did Mary Gray compete with and attempt to "squelch her daughter"; she made her submit to periodic "genital inspections," disguising abuse under the pretext of checking for cleanliness.

Anne Sexton's experience may sound bizarre, but it was echoed in several of the interviews we conducted. We can merely speculate that some mothers, when confronted with the spectacle of their daughters' vulnerability, wish to violate it.

In Sexton's case, she was also violated by her father. For comfort and compassion, she turned to her great aunt, Nana, who sexually "cuddled" with her in bed for many years. Later, when the old woman went mad, screaming that Anne was not the young girl whom she once knew, Sexton felt guilty and responsible for Nana's condition.

When she became a mother herself, Sexton was thoroughly enraged and unable to deal with the burdens of motherhood. Having suffered invasion by the three significant adults in her life, Middlebrook says, she had no clear sense of who she was. She felt exposed, injured, and vulnerable.

Anne Sexton tried to obliterate her anguish with sleeping pills and to exorcise her torment in her poems, but neither strategy could save her. Like her mother, she became fascinated with her own daughter's prepubescent body; she entered her child's bed for comfort and "cuddling" as Nana used to enter hers. Middlebrook re-creates a night Anne's daughter Linda remembers: "it was dark, but she realized that her mother was lying astride her, rubbing against her, and kissing her on the mouth. 'I felt suffocated. I remember pulling out of bed and throwing up. Mother followed me into the bathroom and soothed my head.' "

Though Sexton had perpetuated the family legacy, her daughter Linda Gray Sexton gave the rage a more public, less lethal form by allowing Middlebrook to tell her mother's story in a controversial book. Not only did Linda provide graphic details of mother-daughter incest; she also allowed the release of confidential tapes, recorded while her mother was under hypnosis during therapy. As executor of Anne Sexton's estate, Linda was able to perform a turnabout and revise, to her own satisfaction, an interpretation of her mother's life. By exposing these family secrets to the world, she not only came to terms with personal demons but allowed other women an intimate view of female incest in an upper-middle-class American family.

In other cultures, there are other ways in which older women initiate young ones into womanhood by betraying them. Although we have known the facts about female genital mutilation and clitorectomies from anthropological works and feminist books such as Marilyn French's *The War on Women,* it is only with the publication of Alice Walker's novel *Possessing the Secret of Joy* and her documentary and book *Warrior Marks* that the subject has become part of the public discourse in the United States.

In Walker's novel, Tashi, a young Olinka woman whose mother refused to have her operated on as a child because her sister had died following the surgery, submits as an adult. She wants "to be accepted as a real woman . . . to stop the jeering."[10] It is only after her external sexual organs are excised and her vaginal opening sewn nearly shut that she begins to understand the great price she has paid for a partner's pleasure.[11]

After her initiation, Tashi's rage surfaces and she finds out that her sister, a known hemophiliac, died during the operation, while their mother assisted the *tsunga,* or cutter. "Your mother helped me hold your sister down," M'Lissa, the *tsunga,* says. Years later, when she hears that M'Lissa has been honored by the patriarchy, Tashi becomes enraged once more. "I feel the furies, the shrieking voices, wrap their coils around my neck." Tashi has put on an African version of Medusa's mask. "I recognized the connection between mutilation and enslavement that is at the root of the domination of women in the world. . . . It's all in the movies that terrorize women. . . . We are the perfect audience, mesmerized by our unconscious knowledge of what men, with the collaboration of our mothers, do to us."

Tashi's story is a parable for all women who feel betrayed by an older generation's ideas of what a woman and her body should be. There are hundreds of thousands of women in Africa, the Middle East, and the United States for whom genital mutilation is a reality. When women understand that they all need to become one another's mothers, they can channel their energies into missions that will rescue the Tashis of the world. The National Organization for Women has placed genital mutilation on its human rights agenda, bringing this previously hidden secret of the female realm to light.

One of the most powerful and positive contemporary stories of the way female wisdom can be passed down from one generation to the next is related in Fannie Flagg's novel *Fried Green Tomatoes at the Whistle Stop Cafe* and the film that was made from it. The action unfolds in a series of conversations between Ninny Threadgoode, an elderly resident of a nursing home, and Evelyn Couch, played by Kathy Bates, a frilly, frumpy woman addicted to sweets who's on the verge of menopause and also on the edge of divorce and a nervous breakdown.

Mrs. Threadgoode, whose very name evokes the ancient role of females as weavers of tales, tells Evelyn the stories of her own girl-hood and coming of age. Evelyn has been trying to put the spark back into her lifeless marriage by experimenting with every quick-fix self-help solution she can find. But dressing in Saran Wrap, preparing nouvelle cuisine, and attending a class on female sexual response do nothing to change the way she feels about herself or reduce her rage at her husband, who ignores her attempts at seduction. She discovers a better way by listening to Ninny's stories about Idgie and

Ruth. These two friends took stands in the course of their lives: against a battering husband, the Ku Klux Klan, a Southern court.

Ninny tells Evelyn about "Tawanda," Idgie's nickname for the Medusa in herself. Evelyn is accustomed to stuffing her Tawanda with powdered doughnuts, and when she breaks this self-destructive habit, her rage comes to the surface. Seizing upon Tawanda's energy, Evelyn initiates crucial changes in her life: She renovates the inside of her house, buys new clothes, finds a job, and brings Ninny home as a permanent guest.

Jessica Tandy's Ninny Threadgoode is the Grey Lady who is not complicit with the male and can act as a helpmate. Ninny and her stories allow Evelyn to hold a mirror up to her face and confront her fury, an image she was unwilling to gaze at before. Once she does so, her appearance is transformed. She smiles, her skin looks healthy even without the Mary Kay cosmetics she now sells, her face loses its puffiness, and her eyes become clearer as she turns into the woman that she should be. Her relationship with Ninny empowers her to claim responsibility for her own happiness, to redraw her boundaries, and to enjoy her body and sexuality.

Far from being a time of diminished expectations, aging gives a woman the chance to take on new roles. The more an older woman regards herself as the keeper of the cauldron, the less competitive she will be with her daughters and other younger sisters. As she assumes her place as a surrogate mother or an older, more experienced friend, she enhances her own identity and makes it clear to herself and those around her that maturing does not have to limit a woman's autonomy; instead, it can be the gateway to power.

The Grey Ladies told Perseus of the Stygian Nymphs
who were the keepers of the winged shoes,
the magic pouch, and the cap of invisibility.
Perseus sailed to the home of these nymphs,
glad place of joy and revelry,
and told them of his tyrannized mother
and his need of the treasures in their keeping.
His sorrowful voice enchanted the nymphs;
they put into his hands the magical things.
He promised to return. They're waiting still.

The Gifts of the Nymphs

In the myth of Medusa, the Nymphs of the North betray their Gorgon sister by providing Perseus with the equipment he needs to slay her. The Nymphs give Perseus the attributes of male power to which every young man feels entitled: a magic wallet, a helmet of invisibility, and a pair of winged sandals. These attributes are as powerful today as they were in ancient times, and women everywhere recognize how formidable they are in a man's possession.

The magic wallet symbolizes the financial clout that powerful men take for granted and women are just beginning to pursue. Money and financial foresight confer autonomy and a sense of self-possession, and for too long women have relinquished the power of acquiring money to men.

Hades's cap confers invisibility on the wearer and represents the lack of accountability women bestow upon men. Women's silence makes it possible for men to disappear without a trace and avoid paying child support, to abuse their daughters, and to batter their wives.

The winged sandals of flight, the third gift of the Nymphs, symbolize a man's mobility and freedom of movement. Mobility is another indicator of an individual's autonomy and power. Many women harbor the illusion that they are dependent on their circumstances and have no options. They fear leaving a toxic marriage or dead-end job. Women fear the winged sandals of flight; they fear they will fall, they fear the struggle, and they fear the risk. If they are successful, they fear the heights.

Their sense of their own powerlessness engenders in women rage toward powerful men. Fearing retribution and loss of attractiveness, they are loath to direct their anger at the opposite sex. Instead, they may turn on their equally weak sisters. Other women are not only seen as less formidable; in their own powerlessness, they are both genuinely enraging and safer to bash.

A Man's Woman and a Woman's Woman

In an attempt to validate themselves, many women become what is called "male-identified," subconsciously adopting male values,

The Three Graces, *a Roman fresco from Pompeii. Perseus visits the Nymphs of the North to discover the whereabouts of Medusa. They provide him with three gifts: winged sandals, a magical pouch, and the helmet of invisibility.*

viewpoints, and perceptions. A woman who is identified with male values will not necessarily think like a man or even act like one, but she will define others according to the dominant culture's generic vision of women and ally herself with the men. The actress Debra Winger, quoted in New Woman's "Thump on the Head to . . ." column, expressed pride in her affinity with the male outlook as she attempted to distance herself from her own gender. "I don't work well with other women—especially conceited, stuck-up women. I work better with men. I'm a man's woman, not a woman's woman, thank God."[1] What she meant was that she does not like to work with prima donnas, yet she adopted a stereotypical view of spoiled females and took a general swipe at all women in her angry comment.

To be "a man's woman" literally means being possessed by a man, to be "the woman of a man," but it also means putting the male first. A man's woman who has call-waiting on her telephone automatically stops talking with her female friend if a man calls. She breaks a long-standing dinner date with her girlfriend at the last minute if a man asks her out for the evening. For women friends on the receiving end of her partiality, her actions confirm their second-class status and engender feelings of betrayal and rage.

The Greek goddess Athena, who sprang symbolically from the head of her father, Zeus, is the ultimate male-identified woman. When, in Aeschylus's Oresteia, she is asked to pass judgment on the case of Orestes, who murdered his mother in cold blood, Athena casts her lot in favor of the young man, saying, "No mother gave me birth/I honor the male in all things except marriage." As Jean Shinoda Bolen points out in The Goddesses in Every Woman, Athena represents the "woman who quite naturally gravitates towards powerful men who have authority."[2] Strictly her father's daughter, she champions the patriarchy. She may erase incriminating evidence from a presidential tape, doctor computer files, or lie on the witness stand, putting herself on the line for a partner or a boss.

During the Anita Hill–Clarence Thomas hearings, many female viewers experienced feelings of betrayal when a panel of three women testified on behalf of their boss, Judge Thomas. Coldly and calmly, these women dished up Professor Hill to the all-male Judiciary Committee as probably in love, the woman scorned, and a careerist. Judge Thomas had not asked for their testimony, they said, but they couldn't sit by and watch his name be tarnished by a vengeful woman. Denying the reality of Anita Hill's suffering, they underscored their loyalty to the patriarchy by deploying its stereotypes and co-opting its terminology.

Virginia Lamp Thomas, Judge Thomas's wife, joined the chorus of Anita Hill's detractors. In *People,* she characterized Hill's testimony: "... what's scary about her allegations is that they remind me of the movie 'Fatal Attraction' or, in her case, what I call the fatal assistant. In my heart, I always believed she was probably someone in love with my husband and never got what she wanted."[3]

Virginia Thomas did more than come to the defense of her husband: She tried to demonize Anita Hill, casting her as a modern Medea, scorned and bent on revenge. In this, she was following the cultural tradition that encourages women to vent their rage on other women, who seem to be easier targets than the men who actually betrayed them. Virginia Lamp Thomas blamed the woman in the triangle; Mary Jo Buttafuoco, betrayed by her errant husband, Joey, directed her rage squarely at the other woman, whom she called "that slut Amy Fisher."

How would a woman who is not male-identified act in a similar situation? Hillary Clinton, when confronted with Gennifer Flowers's accusations, acknowledged that she and the then governor had had problems in their marriage and told television viewers that their private life was not for public consumption. Her strategy here of defining her own boundaries and squarely confronting the extramarital issue defused the controversy and undermined Flowers's credibility; she also stood by her man with great dignity. The power of Hillary Clinton's rage was concentrated on winning the White House rather than on defaming Flowers.

A woman who refuses to be a man's woman treats other females with compassion rather than suspicion. She exhibits empathy, not antipathy, for other women, knowing that if one woman makes it to the top, all women are elevated. The actor Jodie Foster is consciously her own woman rather than a man's woman. "I have to take roles that I understand, because if I don't get the character—if it's a woman, for example, and something bad happens to her and all she does is cry and scream and totally can't cope—I have to back away. . . . People have been telling us for centuries that women don't survive things, and that's just not true."[4] Foster, a woman's woman, will not perpetuate the distortions of female experience by playing to the stereotypes. But a woman's woman is not exclusively supportive of women, another unhealthy extreme. She also treats men with equanimity, since fairness is her operative principle, not gender.

Rage and the Other Woman

One of the deepest wounds a woman can inflict on another woman is to become the third party in an adulterous triangle. Athena in the Medusa story performs the functions of the other woman; it is Athena who provides the hero with a shield of polished bronze that deflects Medusa's intensity and enhances his glory. Whether she is the more manageable younger woman or the experienced seductive lover, the other woman is someone new for the man to conquer or impress. She may boost his sagging ego, make him feel newly attractive and desirable, and allow him to confront female sexuality and power in a diluted or refracted light. A younger woman, particularly, fulfills these needs and requirements: Her sexuality and power are not full-blown, her ideas and habits not yet ingrained, and her rage can be manipulated and diffused.

Many variations of the love triangle can be seen in our contemporary mythology. Amy Fisher and Soon-Yi Previn exemplify the man's desire for the inexperienced woman. The marriage of Charles and Diana was essentially destroyed by Prince Charles's continuing relationship with his experienced pal, Camilla Parker-Bowles.

In Woody Allen's case, the other woman was his long-term lover's adopted daughter, the antithesis of the mature woman. Mia Farrow's realization that she had become Woody Allen's "Medusa" occurred on the day she found nude photos of Soon-Yi Previn in Allen's apartment. Further humiliation was to follow later in court when Allen testified that he had "not slept with Farrow in five years" before he took up with her college-student daughter. "She was raging, angry, beside herself with rage and anger," Allen recalled as he recounted Farrow's fury and suicide threats when she discovered the betrayal. Why was she so enraged? It's not clear whether he understands it to this day.

Allen's film *Husbands and Wives,* made at the time when his affair with Soon-Yi was just starting, is a tour de force about the illusions of love that pits older women against their younger rivals. Farrow plays a forty-something, whiny, manipulative magazine editor married to Allen, a college professor, and Judy Davis plays a middle-aged compulsive-hysteric whose husband leaves her for a brainless aerobics instructor. Not surprisingly, considering his preferences in real life, it is Allen's film fling, the teenaged Rain (Juliette Lewis), who is the movie's most appealing female. Allen's character, Gabe, is struck by Rain's college term paper, "Oral Sex in the Age of Deconstruction." As one of his students, Rain feeds his narcissistic needs with undergraduate adulation—for his teaching, his brilliant insights, and his writing. During a particularly romantic moment when the lights go out during a thunderstorm, Gabe and Rain share a passionate kiss. Gabe hears his "fifty thousand dollars' worth of psychotherapy dialing nine-one-one."

Farrow leveled her full fury at Allen in print and through the comments her friends made on her behalf. Yet what she did not do was more notable. Her legal and ethical strategy never included demonizing her adopted daughter Soon-Yi. She didn't try to obliterate the other woman. Carefully treading around the girl's part in the betrayal, she blamed the perpetrator, not the victim.

Rage at the other woman is natural, but it is used too often in the place of rage that should be directed at a husband or a partner. Most women find it easier to blame the female as seducer than to face the reality of a partner's rejection. Camilla Parker-Bowles, the woman the Princess of Wales "contemptuously calls 'the rotweiler,' " is perhaps the most famous other woman as "dog." But when women turn against one another and compete for the male prize, the entire sex is weakened and dehumanized.

Hagar and Her Sisters: The Rage of Jealousy

The moment a woman gets power, she loses the solidarity she had with other women. She will want to be equal in a man's world and will become ambitious for her own sake.
— Simone de Beauvoir, *The Second Sex*

Envy and jealousy, the twin sisters of female rage, are at the source of friction between females. Envy, as Peter Van Sommers put it in *Jealousy,* "concerns what you would like to have" and jealousy "concerns what you have and don't wish to lose."[5] The envious woman lacks self-esteem and tries to deal with her feelings of inadequacy by hating or denigrating another woman who has what she desires. In some cases, as in the biblical story of Sarah and Hagar, the woman who feels deficient and envious will actually set up a situation in which rage, jealousy, and feelings of inferiority can surface.

Female rage is an integral part of the Old Testament. Biblical females experience rage at God, at their fathers, at husbands, and at other women. Delilah cuts Samson's hair along with his manhood; Jezebel was wanton and committed murder. Rachel was so furious when her father, Laban, excluded her from his inheritance in favor of his sons that she stole his idols. But Sarah's rage is most instructive, illustrating an important dynamic of modern rage among females.

Sarah was thought of as the mother of her ancient people, and God assured her that she and Abraham would produce a male child to fulfill the promise of the Israelites. Yet the couple remained childless for so many years that Sarah, in desperation, suggested that

Abraham have their slave girl, Hagar, bear a child for them. In due course, a son was born: Ishmael. Naturally enough, friction developed between Sarah and Hagar and when, at ninety, Sarah finally gave birth to Isaac, she convinced Abraham to drive Hagar and her son out of the household and into the desert. Ishmael grew up to be a fiery desert dweller, and today many Arab peoples claim their descent from him and the exiled Hagar.

In the story, Sarah makes Hagar a participant in her emotional drama, using her not only as a surrogate but as the object of her rage. Although Hagar has acted out Sarah's own wishes and desires, she must be punished for her deeds. Sarah displaces her anger on the slave girl rather than directing it at her husband or herself. Hagar becomes a living testament to Sarah's barrenness and the embodiment of the woman she would like to be. When Sarah bears her own son and fulfills the promise of her people, her feelings of empowerment and status are restored; now she can banish Hagar, the reminder of her past inadequacy. Thousands of years later, modern women employ this piggybacking dynamic with other females, turning them into enemies without understanding why or how.

Jill, one of the women we interviewed, experienced firsthand how poisonous and punishing another woman's envy can be. Jill met Annie, the director of a community center, when she was a graduate student at Berkeley, and Annie became a mentor as well as an older and wiser friend. Annie was lamed by a congenital hip problem, and she appreciated Jill's attention and eagerness to run errands for her. Sometimes Jill and Annie went shopping on weekends. But one excursion revealed a disturbing dimension of their relationship. As Jill tried on a dress in their favorite boutique, the store owner turned to Annie and said, "That dress looks terrific on your daughter." Instead of calmly and politely correcting the woman's misunderstanding, Annie grabbed the woman by the arm and said in a low voice, "Don't you ever *dare* to suggest that she's my daughter again." Jill was stunned by Annie's feeling but said no more about it.

Their friendship continued without incident until some months later when Annie and her husband asked Jill to help them celebrate their twenty-fifth wedding anniversary. For that occasion, Annie also invited Paul, a handsome young man in his thirties who sometimes escorted Annie to plays and concerts in San Francisco when her husband was unable to attend. Annie, who was helping her husband through a depression, enjoyed this mild form of "vicarious dating"; it enabled her to get out of the house and participate in the cultural life of the city.

The night of the anniversary dinner, Jill and Paul left together, had a nightcap in Jill's living room, and stayed up all night talking; they discovered common themes in their lives and a clear mutual attraction. "It seemed to me that Annie had deliberately set us up," Jill recalls. "We hit it off right away. I was a little older than Paul, but the age difference didn't seem to matter. When he asked me if he could call, I told him that I had just gotten out of another relationship and he should look me up in six months."

Six months later, Annie called Jill for Paul and asked her whether she was ready to see him again. "She encouraged me to invite him for the holidays and seemed enthusiastic when I agreed." But Annie was not about to let Paul out of her life. On New Year's Eve, she called Jill's house, asked to speak to Paul, and inquired about how their romance was progressing.

When Jill and Paul did become lovers, Annie began to behave as if she was Jill's rival. "She called Paul constantly and asked him for the intimate details of our relationship. She developed intentional conflicts so he would have to choose between us. If I were going to meet him in the city, she would decide to make plans with him for the same weekend." After a year of this triangular jockeying, Jill met Jason, who was her own age, attractive, and mature. "I broke off with Paul and felt relieved to be out of that uncomfortable position. Unfortunately, Paul had a difficult time with the breakup; he later confessed that in his hurt he had told Annie some of my deepest fears and confidences, as well as every detail of our sex life. I felt as if I'd been body-snatched."

Jill was everything Annie was not—physically able, sexually appealing, and free to enter a new relationship. Annie's rage was the result of long-term frustrations, a need for attention and for the sexual gratification she wasn't getting in her marriage. Jill threatened Annie's claim on Paul by becoming romantically involved with him, yet perversely Annie had set them up together. Annie's behavior reflects the Sarah and Hagar dynamic of female rage in which one woman feels deprived and tries to fill that void by finding a surrogate female to compensate for her shortcomings, a form of emotional piggybacking. Women who have such deep-seated unresolved problems can't maintain genuine friendships for long.

Snow White and the Poison Apple

. . . they didn't seem to have what we had with each other, a kind of ongoing narrative about what was happening that grew out of our conversations, our rolled eyes, our sighs and jokes and irritated remarks.

—Jane Smiley, *A Thousand Acres*

Women can recognize the blood bonds between each other and among all others of their gender. There may be a tie of kinship, a union not only of friendship and creative sisterhood but of cycles that are mysterious and enduring. When women live and work together, not only are they likely to become psychologically attuned; they may find their monthly cycles have synchronized.

Male bonding centers around sports or intellectual interests, while women make connections by exchanging life experiences. Women cherish their relationships with other women with whom they share so many intimacies. It is precisely because of this closeness and these bonds that women are so enraged when other women betray them.

Women betray other women in small ways—a disapproving glance, a petty remark behind a friend's back—and in big ways—by stealing jobs or spouses. When a woman is betrayed by her close friend, her sister, or her mother, she feels, at least temporarily, as if her entire support system has crumbled and she's without recourse. Betrayal by other women is a thread that runs through the fabric of women's lives, though as a source of rage it is not always acknowledged.

Women often show a disturbing ambivalence in their feelings about other women. As we have seen, these attitudes begin during infancy; a woman develops them naturally in relation to her mother and her mother's body as she competes with her mother for her father. Ambivalence toward other women is nurtured throughout a girl's formative years. She learns from books and films and from her aunts, mothers, sisters, and friends that other women are the competition and not to be trusted.

During adolescence, the needs for inclusion and approval experienced in the formative years come flooding back into a young woman's consciousness. This time, the stakes are higher. She is still vying for the approval, love, and admiration of her parents or girlfriends, but now there are boys to win over, as well. In their study of young girls, Lyn Brown and Carol Gilligan observe the dynamic of popularity among adolescents, when "jealousies and rivalries break out. . . . Divisions and cliques are visible reminders of the potential hazards of being too different, not pretty enough, not nice enough, subtle enough, smart enough."[6]

Adolescent women walk an emotional minefield in all their relationships—with their parents and with both sexes. There is also an ambivalent and a polymorphous quality to their sexuality, as they may experience erotic feelings toward other women as well as toward men. Then, as the majority of young women begin to focus their attention on males, they enter the competitive feminine world. Many adolescent females experience rage with every type of status seeking among their peers: competition over boyfriends, grades, places on the cheerleading squad; comparisons of developing bustlines and designer labels. As junior versions of label-conscious parents, some feel rage because their parents' car or house address isn't fashionable enough.

In *Kiss Sleeping Beauty Good-Bye,* Dr. Madonna Kolbenschlag concludes that the effects of female socialization "considerably diminish our capacity for authentic sisterhood."[7] Subtly and surely, she says, we are taught that "relationships between women are bound to be trivial, inconstant, shallow, and insincere."[8] Little girls listen to the story of Cinderella and hear the scoffing laugh of the stepmother and sisters when she tells them she would like to attend the ball or try on the glass slipper. In the story of Snow White, they observe the rage and jealous vanity of the wicked Queen who banishes Snow White, decides she must die, and makes her a gift of a poisoned apple. Adult fiction, from Hawthorne's *The Scarlet Letter* to Mary McCarthy's *The Group* or John Updike's *The Witches of Eastwick*, features Puritan matrons, Vassar coeds, suburban housewives, all betraying other women. In *Gone With the Wind*, Scarlett O'Hara chirps sweetly, "Oh, Mellie" to the good-hearted woman whose husband she is trying to steal.

If a woman has not had a strong, healthy female role model in her life, the problem is compounded. If she learns early on that women are weaker, less intelligent, more impractical, or even more difficult than men, she will subconsciously project these images onto other women, and she is likely to undervalue or disparage their achievements.

For years, African-American women have been drawing strength and solace from one another. Frequently the sole head of her household, the black woman has turned to her solitary sisters for comfort, understanding, and help. "African women have a sense of female bonding that no other race can share," one of our students said to us. This unique female bonding is clearly seen in *The Color Purple*. Celie is an enraged black Medusa until healed by the love of her husband's beautiful mistress, Shug.

In Alice Walker's novel, it is Shug who imparts wisdom about rage, female sexuality, and redemption after Celie complains that she cannot get sexually aroused because she is so enraged. Shug replies, ". . . just being mad, grief, wanting to kill somebody will make you feel this way. Nothing to worry about. Titties gonna perk up, button gonna rise again."

Clytemnestra *by John Collier.*
Clytemnestra epitomizes
murderous female rage.
Incensed by her husband
Agamemnon's sacrifice of
their daughter Iphigenia and
his return from the war with
a Trojan mistress, she stabs
him in an embrace and
murders his lover.

Crimes of the Heart:
Female Family Rage

Lord help the mister who comes between me and my sister.
And Lord help the sister who comes between me and my man.
                              —"Sisters," from White Christmas

Females in a family form natural alliances; sameness in gender and psychology draw them close. Despite ambivalent feelings, mothers and daughters are natural allies, especially in times of crisis, when a mother's love can be fierce and protective.

Clytemnestra's fury over Agamemnon's sacrifice of their daughter, Iphigenia, who gave her life for fair sailing winds so that the Greek armies might reach Troy, is a classical example of a mother's rage. In his ancient drama *The Agamemnon*, Aeschylus sees her rage as monumental:

Here she waits
the terror raging back and back in the future
the stealth, the law of the hearth, the mother—
    Memory womb of Fury child-avenging
    Fury!

After ten years, the Trojan War is over, and Clytemnestra greets her king and husband by spreading crimson tapestries on the threshold of their palace. Agamemnon arrives, standing in his warrior's chariot with the Trojan princess Cassandra in tow. Inflamed by the memory of Iphigenia and further enraged at the sight of Cassandra, Clytemnestra feigns the loving and faithful wife until she takes him inside and stabs him as they embrace. In her triumph, she revels in "the great sprays of blood" and "murderous shower" she's produced. When the curtain opens on the bloody scene, Clytemnestra stands over the bodies of her husband and his Trojan concubine, Agamemnon's sword in her hand. "Here he lies," she says. "He brutalized me. The darling of all the golden girls who spread the gates of Troy."

Any mother's rage at a violation of her son or daughter evokes primitive calls for retribution. One of the earliest interviews we conducted involved a case of a "double rape." An exceptionally beautiful young woman named Tama was physically violated and her mother, Sarah, experienced the rape secondhand. Sarah's rage was more intense and powerful than Tama's.

"Tama always had a good sense of herself. She was a great believer in fairness and equality," Sarah told us, her voice catching before she went on. "It was the beginning of second semester of her freshman year in college when it happened. Tama's best friend set her up on a date. It was a setup all right. Sally told Tama to meet her at the fraternity house—the Betas were having a party. When Tama got there, her girlfriend had gone off, and she was left alone with twenty guys. They shoved her against the wall, then pushed her into a bedroom while she struggled and screamed for help. She tried to huddle under the bed, but they yanked her out and ripped off her clothes, and then all twenty raped her—one at a time."

When Tama got back to her dorm, she was in hysterics. She managed to call her mother and tell her what had happened. Sarah knew the primal mother-lioness rage of a parent whose offspring is attacked. She wanted to slit the throats of each and every violator; she wanted to castrate them. Instead, she screamed for hours in the shower.

Sarah's rage intensified as university officials thwarted her efforts to obtain justice for her daughter and attempted to silence her outrage at every turn. Sarah persisted and her grievances resulted in disciplinary action against the perpetrators' fraternity, as well as in a new university policy regarding victims of rape. In the end, her rage helped her daughter through the trauma.

In Sarah and Tama's case, their double rage was a powerful force to effect change. But sometimes these open emotional channels between mothers and their daughters carry intergenerational female rage back and forth, well into the child's adult years.

In *Fierce Attachments,* her intimate and at times brutal memoir of her relationship with her mother, Vivian Gornick describes the complexity of the bond as an extended prize fight: "For years at a time there is an exhaustion, a kind of softening between us. Then the rage comes up again, hot and clear, erotic in its power to compel attention."

Beth told us her mother was an angry woman whose own mother had neglected her. The result was a family of enraged women. At ages three and four, feeling she could never satisfy her mother, Beth remembers going into the bathroom and chewing on the rim of a glass. "I couldn't wait for the relief—to crunch the little pieces in my baby teeth. I would think of my mother breaking into a thousand parts." During her later childhood, Beth dealt with her intense rage at her mother's inattention by cutting holes in her clothes, destroying photographs and dolls, and developing food phobias and having tantrums. She also cultivated what she calls "my poker face," a permanent pouty expression.

She describes her rage at her mother as "mythic" or "biblical." "There was so much energy connected with it, I felt I could destroy cities or worlds, push over the pillars of the temple, and put Samson in chains," she told us. Beth's mother played a game of favorites with her three daughters; she discounted Beth's achievements and never gave her the approval she needed. Beth's wounds were deep. But her rage was caught in a psychological time warp; she was captive to the feelings of the past. Since her mother's death almost a year ago, Beth has finally begun to understand the sources of her tantrums. "As an adult, my rage was so disproportionate to minor slights or injuries," she now admits, "if someone treated me only a little badly, I'd fly into a state of fury; I couldn't tolerate disapproval of any kind." After many years of therapy, hard work in groups, and peer counseling, Beth has come to understand not only her own rage but its origins in a family where the mother saw her daughters as reflections of herself rather than as individuals. Today, she smiles and says she channels her rage into her radio show, where she plays jazz and reads poetry. In extreme situations, she gets out the baseball bat and hits her ironing board.

The legacy of rage passed from mother to daughter is at the center of Laura Esquivel's novel and screenplay, *Like Water for Chocolate*. According to Esquivel and her husband, the film's director, Alfonso Arau, the title is a Mexican expression for the boiling point: the temperature water must reach to make chocolate. Mama Elena forbids Tita, her youngest daughter, to marry Pedro, the man she loves, since tradition demands that the youngest girl remain single and take care of her mother until the day of her death. Elena convinces Pedro to marry Tita's sister. As baker of the household, Tita bakes her rage into their wedding cake, causing all the guests to vomit and wail all night over their own lost loves. She spends years tormented by the closeness but unavailability of Pedro, and she pours her passion into cooking. At one point, enraged by her mother, Tita "felt a violent agitation take hold of her. Still fingering the sausage, she calmly met her mother's gaze and then, instead of obeying her order, she started to tear apart all the sausages she could reach, screaming wildly."

When Elena dies, Tita reads her diary and finds out that she, too, spent her adult life in a rage because she had to give up the man she loved.

Many mothers whose lives are painful or who feel deprived create daughter surrogates to bear their rage. Instead of confiding in their daughters and sharing, these mothers use excessive discipline, anger, and criticism to express their pain. When it is too late, many daughters discover their mothers' secrets, and wish their mothers had been more open about their problems and pain. When the women in a family disclose their secrets, many times there is a chance for healing long-term rage and resentments.

Rivalries and emotional battles among sisters are almost as bruising as those between mother and daughter. The three McGrath sisters in Beth Henley's play and movie *Crimes of the Heart* are typical of many sisterly combinations: One minute, they're screaming at one another and inflicting any hurt they can; the next, they're poring over photo albums, sharing popcorn and funny childhood memories.

One woman we interviewed remembers her rage as an eighteen-year-old when she was dating the older man she would eventually marry. On a hot summer afternoon, she arrived back from a swim a few minutes early and found her older sister perched on her boyfriend's lap, kissing him tenderly. The scene is as vivid today as when it happened fifty years ago. One woman remembers how hurt she was when her younger sister, who had been her attendant at both of her weddings, chose another woman friend to be her maid of honor. "To me, it was like a slap in the face," she told us. "I felt betrayed until I realized that my sister was extremely enraged at me. She used this other woman as an irritant to express her hostile feelings and punish and hurt me at the same time."

In *Mixed Feelings,* her book about sibling rivalries, Francine Klagsbrun says that closeness among sisters is what causes so much competition, anger, and rage.[9] The relationship between sisters is the most volatile of the sibling relationships. Unlike brothers, who act out their anger physically, sisters express their aggression as "pulls and tugs about beauty and body images, weight, clothes, and family matters—the stuff of women's identities assigned to them by society and instilled in them in the family early in life."[10] Sisters set up all kinds of Olympic competitions and win points from each other over boyfriends, fathers, mothers, grades, and, in later life, jobs.

Christine Alt, sister of supermodel Carol Alt, tells in *Glamour* how, under pressure from family and friends, she attempted to follow her sister as a successful model and in the process developed anorexia. "I started blaming Carol for everything. I blamed her for my having to go into modeling . . . I blamed her for my having to lose weight."[11] Recalling how competition with her sister distorted her perceptions, Christine describes seeing a picture of Karen Carpenter on the cover of *People* and thinking "how lucky she was she died so skinny." Christine sees her anorexia as an expression of the rage that developed when she began to follow the dictates of others instead of her own inclinations. As she became aware that the path she was on didn't suit her, she subconsciously set her sister, Carol, up as the villain and began to starve herself to death. Only when she recognized that she, not her sister, was responsible for her own feelings of envy could she move on and create a life for herself.

Rage and the Working Girl

I did all the work, and she took all the credit.
                                        —*Single White Female*

Many of our interviews focused on rage at other women in the workplace; women, our interviewees said, were often insensitive to other women's boundaries, their sense of dignity, their position in the business hierarchy.

"If a woman is strong and on a career track, riding the wave of accomplishment with the doors opening, then other women on her level will start questioning how she got there," said Claire, a senior manager in the hotel and restaurant industry who is an effective administrator and high-level negotiator. Claire finds it enraging to hear other women undervalue the hard work of their female colleagues. She recognizes that successful working women are likely to incite envy in other women who haven't yet made it, and she stresses the need to support the strength and daring of those who do. Women often persevere against difficult odds in a world that is still male-centered and dominated by patriarchal rules.

When Supreme Court Judge Ruth Bader Ginsburg was graduated from Columbia Law School in the 1950s, all the firms recruiting the best and the brightest ignored her. Even today, she meets up with other women who rebuke her rather than rejoicing in her accomplishments; they carp about the political correctness of her friendships or her modulated and subtle views on women's issues instead of seeing her life as a testament to the women's movement and its causes.

Our working First Lady is another case in point. No sooner had she left the reviewing stand after the inaugural parade than the forces of pettiness and envy attacked her hat, her hairdo, and the choice of her Hollywood friends as overnight guests at the White House. Hillary Rodham Clinton was too smart, too competent, and too powerful for many people. More vicious speculations surfaced when her real power was seen to threaten the status quo. There were rumors of separate bedrooms, lesbian leanings, an affair with suicide Vincent Foster, and comments about the "unelected co-President." The First Lady has continued to demonstrate her skills in the halls of Congress and as a hostess, refusing to muffle her voice or disparage her own intellect. She has also been photographed for *Vogue*. Unlike Hillary Rodham Clinton, too many women in the workplace betray themselves by playing dumb, for fear of being shot down if they bring their full talents to their tasks.

Some women who achieve success become queen bees, actively working to keep other women down. In the film *Working Girl*, Tess McGill, played by Melanie Griffith, lands a job on Wall Street, working for queen bee Katherine Parker, played by Sigourney

Weaver. Parker encourages Tess to bring her ideas to her for development. Tess's enthusiasm and creativity soar, but she finds that nothing really changes when she goes to work for a woman. She still must take her boss coffee, water the plants, and call the caterers.

Then Parker breaks her leg in a skiing accident and Tess discovers Parker has stolen her ideas and presented them to influential clients as her own. In her rage, Tess undergoes a transformation: she puts on power suits from Parker's wardrobe, tames her hair, and, most importantly, dons a new attitude. "I can make it happen," she declares, "I'm not the same pathetic fool I was a couple of days ago." Masquerading as Parker, Tess becomes a player. The ideas she pitches meet with the approval of the savvy men at the boardroom table.

The showdown comes at a meeting where Tess is about to sign an agreement and Parker bursts in and exposes her as an impostor. Tess reasserts herself, using rage as her powerful catalyst. She receives her due recognition and gets a new executive job. *Working Girl* is a modern fairy tale; this kind of easy ascent doesn't happen for most women, whose bosses thwart their progress, usurp their ideas, and undermine their confidence. But the film makes the point about using aggression and rage to push forward—a message women responded to.

Who's Afraid of Naomi Wolf?
Rage and Feminism

Originally, collective rage propelled the feminist movement. But as the sisterhood accomplished some of its aims, the question of what would happen next generated a profusion of answers and ideologies. Family feuds developed. At the same time, there were always many women who distanced themselves from feminism, not wishing to stray too far from male power. Since Anita Hill stood up to the senators on the Judiciary Committee and Hillary Clinton transformed the role of First Lady, collective female rage has been reignited. This feminist revival has been bolstered by a handful of groundbreaking third-wave books that offer women new models for expressing rage.

Naomi Wolf tells women in a readable, upbeat way that they can have it all—"both breasts and footnotes," as she puts it, convincingly advocating "power" feminism. She even omits the *F* word, *Fight,* from her second book title, *Fire with Fire,* and the words *anger* and *rage* are not found in her index. Her main premise—that females should think like powerful human beings instead of victims—touches many mainstream women.

Centrist Susan Faludi is assertive and logical rather than aggressive. Her well-argued and well-researched book, *Backlash,* defines the forces marshaled against women's advancement and dispels the illusion that our society is no longer sexist. Faludi feels male images of women are motivated by fear of female power.

Camille Paglia, the feminist other feminists love to hate, entered the scene with the publication of *Sexual Personae,* a brilliant survey of Western culture that shook up the smug, complacent academic and feminist worlds. Her combination of pop- and high-culture criticism of art, literature, and society injected new life into both ancient and postmodern works. She uses rage to power her intellect and direct her acerbic wit.

When she appeared in photos in *Vanity Fair,* pouring out of an academic gray bodice, with two black Nubian slaves at each side, many criticized her as a publicity seeker. Feminists feel she's betrayed the sisterhood by calling it "an ideology that attracts weak personalities" and its founders "eccentric individuals." And when she entered the date-rape debate, her rage turned venomous against "boring, uptight academic feminists" and "the deep manipulativeness of rich students" who love to "turn the campus into hysterical psychodramas of sexual transgression."[12]

Betty Friedan's *The Feminine Mystique* was a necessarily strident call to action. Her latest book, *The Fountain of Age,* is a mature work, almost cosmic in the depths of its compassion for the human condition. *Revolution from Within,* Gloria Steinem's latest book, is meditative and confessional. The fiery rhetoric of her early *Ms.* articles is gone, replaced by a more tempered but still-passionate style that allows her to express her personal rage and connect it to the rage of all women as they learn to develop their self-esteem.

But it can take decades for theories to trickle down and reshape the daily lives of the population. Masses of women have to deal every day with the sexism of both men and women. Johanna Zel, a Framingham, Massachusetts, dental assistant and mother, frames the questions of her feminist predicament this way: "I live in a country where women are still treated as sex objects and disposable toys for men in beer commercials and music videos . . . yet when I call myself a feminist I'm pegged as some kind of man-hating cyborg-ette."[13] Many women we interviewed expressed anger at this dilemma; they felt caught in limbo between men who stared at their legs when they walked by and women who snickered if they shaved them.

Women will not be truly potent until they learn to keep their power in the first place in solidarity with other women. Other women are not, as the poet Audre Lorde wrote, "the root cause" of a woman's rage. "I know this, no matter what the particular situation may be between me and another Black woman at the moment."[14] What lies behind women's rage at other women is "the face of my own self, unaccepted," the image we must change before claiming our power.

Now with the cap and pouch and Hermes' sword,
Perseus wearing the winged shoes flew to Medusa's
   island.
There, as her two Gorgon sisters slept,
Medusa beat the air with her hideous wings
and pierced the sky with her pitiful screeches
as her snakes hissed and her brass claws clacked.
But Perseus making great circles in the sky,
looking into the mirroring shield, wearing
the cap of invisibility, swooped down to his destiny.
Slashing backwards he beheaded the dread Medusa
slicing through skin and bone and sinew.
Then, seizing the trophy by its snaky curls,
he flew off with his swarming pouch.
Medusa's suffering was over.
The only protest was the serpents' hiss.

Off with Her Head!

Whoever fights monsters should see to it in the process he does not become a monster.

—Nietzsche

By the fifth century B.C., the Medusa myth had been used by Ovid and others to symbolize the historic moment when the Hellenes swept across ancient Greece and patriarchy triumphed over goddess worship. Medusa represents those aspects of the female that pose a threat to male culture: her sexuality and her rage. With her head of writhing snakes, Medusa is the ultimate femme fatale, suggestive of all that is alluring and dangerous in women. The myth reaches its climax when Perseus in a single stroke beheads Medusa. By vanquishing her, he is not only conquering the matriarchal ruling powers; he is subduing female sexual potency, as well. On a conscious level, a woman with such a sexual charge can bring out a man's basest instincts; in his dreams, he may wonder whether he can satisfy her.

Perseus arrives at the Gorgon's isle well armed, only to find the woman he would slay is sleeping. The sleeping Medusa is our meta-

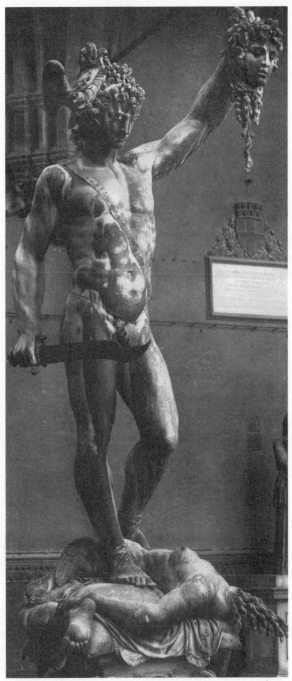

Perseus with Head of Medusa *by Benvenuto Cellini*
Perseus exploits the enormous powers of Medusa's head, which has
both deadly and magical powers. Like rage, the Gorgon head can
spawn a desert of poisonous vipers or turn weeds into filigrees of coral.

phor for the enraged woman in her unconscious state; such a woman is off her guard, vulnerable to any strike, and she passively allows others to control her fate. Such a woman is frightened by powerful emotions; she fears change, public scrutiny, and disruptions in her life. It is less frightening for her to continue in the numbness of a familiar misery than to face the challenges of shaping an active existence.

The Escape of Perseus *by Sir Edward Burne-Jones*
Using Athena's shield as a mirror, Perseus sliced off Medusa's head. He lifted the head, its snakes limp, put it in the magical pouch, and fled from the screeching Gorgons.

Unconscious women are not on guard; their eyes are closed to the dangers of exploitation and the signs of manipulation. Women who don't want to see the reality of their condition trade their insight, intuition, and imagination for naïveté, gullibility, and denial. To shield themselves from confrontations or to avoid disturbing the peace, many women boost the egos of others—usually men—at the expense of their own power and identity. Many women unconsciously repeat these patterns in every aspect of their lives. They don't learn about the intricacies of finance; they follow others' leads in forming their ideas about the world; they depend on someone else to fix things—their cars, their drainpipes, even their sexuality. Sleeping Beauty doesn't climb out of her casket and blaze a trail through the briars back to the castle by herself. What if her knight hadn't come? Women who wait for the enlivening kiss may remain asleep in the forest forever.

Sandra, for example, was a superb hostess; she prided herself on her cooking and her ability to create a warm, convivial atmosphere at home. For ten years, she entertained her husband's partners and business associates, never realizing that some of the clients were really his mistresses, who'd come to compare the wife with themselves. Sandra didn't learn until much later that she had been a partner in a sadistic and manipulative house of games; the clues had been there—the looks exchanged between her husband and each of these women, his lingering good-byes at a car window—but she didn't want to see. Not seeing allowed her to hide her rage from herself.

When a woman chooses not to know, her cognitive systems shut down and she becomes prey to fear, insecurity, and depression. Her rage, prevented from reaching the cognitive part of the brain, the cerebral cortex, gets buried in the brain stem. There it lodges like a time bomb waiting to explode.

In order to avoid her rage, a woman may have to numb herself to all feelings: She may not know whom she likes and whom she doesn't; she may distance herself from her sexuality, burying it in fat or fantasies. Some women retreat from life to keep their rage at bay or, like one woman we interviewed, they may operate on an infantile level. "It's as though you're doing great for a two-year-old," she told us, "and then a six-year-old comes along and knocks you down." They may retire to the bedroom, pull the shades down, and assume the fetal position; some of the women we interviewed said they stay in bed for days.

Psychologist Jeanne Shub believes that the mechanism by which women withdraw from rage "is connected with lack of both identity and a strong ego. Girls are encouraged not to fight it out, and tend not to try." A woman in denial, her head under the covers, allows her rage to ferment and actually increases her long-term vulnerability. The more she doesn't confront it, the more intimidating it becomes. Instead of resolving issues and surviving as capable and knowing adults, some women cling to self-defeating patterns learned in childhood. Many fail to create an identity they feel good about and others respect; they forfeit strength and independence and, according to Shub, get "entwined in this web of fury."

Such a woman falls into deep sleeps of denial, anxiety, and pain, living in a dazed stupor of repressed rage. She may smile and assure everyone that everything's just fine, or she may move about like a zombie whose only goal is making it through the day. She surrenders her voice, her choices, her dreams, passively waiting for some miracle cure.

Medusa the Victim

The story of Hedda Nussbaum dramatically captures the model of behavior in which a woman, cut off from her rage, becomes the perfect victim. Nussbaum's is the story of a woman's slavish devotion to a man who systematically destroyed her. Hedda, whose very name evokes Medusa's beheading, was once a bright, attractive, and statuesque brunette; she graduated from Hunter College and was hired as a children's book editor in a large publishing house. In the spring of 1972, she met Joel Steinberg at a party. Steinberg, a lawyer, would become her mentor, psychological guru, and live-in lover. "She was lovely," Steinberg recalled, "smart, beautiful. All the things a man could ask for." Hedda also remembered those first days with nostalgia: "Everything was so wonderful then. . . . He had these bright sparkling eyes and was very outgoing. We had a kind of ESP."[1]

Although she came from an intact immigrant Jewish family and had a relatively normal childhood, Hedda developed as a child lacking self-esteem. When she was two years old, her grandmother Rachel, to whom she was very close, suffered a nervous breakdown, was hospitalized, and returned to Hedda's parents' house, where she retreated to her room. There she remained as a recluse until her death twenty years later, Hedda recalled: "and I lived with that rejection every single day."[2] To compensate for the loss of her beloved grandmother, Hedda formed an intense bond with her older sister Judy and seems to have lived in her shadow. "I was always trying to be a good girl, so I would be left alone," she said, "And I never showed my anger."

Nussbaum, with her low self-esteem and diminished ego, was the perfect foil for the high-powered, narcissistic Steinberg. She thought he was the most wonderful man she had ever met and that he had godlike supernatural powers. But Steinberg's behavior toward Nussbaum was not so godlike. His live-in lover before Nussbaum told *New York* magazine that he would fly into rages, lunge at her, throw her to the floor, and continue to beat her as she cowered between his legs. He achieved sexual highs during these attacks; he would become "more aroused with every blow."[3]

In 1976, four years after their meeting, Nussbaum moved into Steinberg's Greenwich Village apartment and he began beating her. At first, the batterings were occasional, but soon they were occurring weekly. One day, his punches sent her to the operating room with a ruptured spleen. Eventually, the black eyes and missed days caused Hedda's dismissal from her job and she became more dependent than ever on this abusive man.

In 1986, after Joel Steinberg beat their adopted daughter Lisa to death, Hedda Nussbaum emerged from her underworld looking like the reincarnation of Medusa. Her flattened nose and distorted eyes told a monstrous story of abuse. She was permanently disfigured. From her own accounts, Steinberg had strangled her, beaten her breasts and genitals, urinated on her, lacerated a tear duct by poking a finger in her eye, and burned her with a propane torch. She had been controlled in mind and body and believed herself powerless to act.

As if those years of physical and mental abuse weren't enough, Steinberg's defense attorneys called her allegations "inconsistent, delusional, and unreliable" and blamed her for the fall of the family. It was the classic blame-the-victim strategy and an attempt to deflect scrutiny away from the victimizer.

Hedda Nussbaum's story publicly challenged our ideas about battered women and the degree to which they participate and collude in their abuse. Was Hedda the ultimate victim or the lamb who arranged for her own slaughter? Did she consciously relinquish her responsibility and enable Lisa's death or was she so cognitively and emotionally debilitated that she couldn't see or think straight?

Feminists were divided. Gloria Steinem recognized the "Hedda" in all women; Susan Brownmiller insisted on Hedda's participation in the tragedy. Marilyn French has suggested that Hedda was a "slave" in bondage, while Ann Jones sees her as a classic case of battered-woman syndrome. Naomi Wolf comes down on the side of Hedda's culpability, holding her responsible for destroying her own life and, in the process, that of an innocent child.[4]

Whatever her culpability, Nussbaum presented herself to the public as a helpless victim. She was clearly out of touch with her rage and had obviously been unaware throughout her years with Steinberg that there was power in her dark side. Many women fall victim to the insidious traps of learned helplessness, covering up intense rage with a childlike paralysis. There are certain tasks they think they cannot perform, ways of asserting themselves they can't imagine, and options they refuse to see. By the time a woman understands the dangers of her conditioned immobility, the neurological patterns are set, and anyone with sufficient psychic or physical strength can overwhelm her.

Learned helplessness robs women of their options, their opinions, and their ability to function as adults. Even if there are choices, as many believe there were for Nussbaum, a woman who believes herself to be helpless is too deluded to see them. A woman who denies her core self and her feelings eventually becomes depressed; her brain chemistry changes in a measurable way as her natural optimism and determination shut down.

But to cast any woman as a helpless victim is to undermine female power and perpetuate this model of behavior. Naomi Wolf is on the right track when she says "it's crucial to understand how low self-esteem, drug addiction, lack of institutional support, the pressures of destructive ideals, the unwillingness to go outside because of a battered face, and the psychological effects of battering all conspire to erode the choices of a woman like Nussbaum."[5]

Modern feminism began when victims stood up and wouldn't take it anymore. Reclaimed, rage transforms a woman's way of thinking and burns through the fog of depression and learned helplessness and the pattern of inaction. A woman aware of her rage can act and do something, perhaps even save her child's or her own life.

Medusa the Vigilante

If a fellow insists on using his penis as a weapon, I say that, one way or another, he ought to be swiftly disarmed.
—Barbara Ehrenreich

Hedda Nussbaum is an icon of the provictim feminists; Anita Hill is an empowering image for the female power elite; while Lorena Bobbitt became a folk hero of the nineties for women outside the loop of the feminist establishment.

Aside from stirring up what Katie Roiphe in *The New York Times* called "deep revenge fantasies," Lorena Bobbitt's act of penile mutilation was a watershed dividing men and women. Dr. Joyce Brothers commented at the time that men laughed nervously at the Bobbitt situation because it terrified them. Women, on the other hand, laughed because they felt empowered. For women, John Wayne Bobbitt, a macho marine whose wife said he subjected her to painful rapes and verbal abuse, became a symbol of male oppression and dominance. For men, Lorena's action summoned their worst archetypal nightmares of castrating women and phallic mothers wielding knives.

Underneath the snickers, the groin holding, and the jokes about Lorena's "performing brain surgery" on her mate, there are serious issues at work. Like *Thelma and Louise* on-screen and Anita Hill in the hearing room, Lorena Bobbitt's bedroom surgery entered popular folklore as a symbolic reinstatement of female power. It said "The bitch is back," and she's going for his lifeblood.

Women at the grass roots clapped as Lorena left the courtroom each day and applauded the decision that found her not guilty because of an "irresistible impulse." Feminists who were battered-woman advocates saw Lorena Bobbitt as a trauma victim, the Hedda Nussbaum of the nineties. "Power feminists" such as lawyer Susan Estrich and social critic Camille Paglia distanced themselves from Lorena's act of vigilantism; both urged women to grapple with the psychological complexities in relationships and cautioned them against acting out their rage. Paglia went as far as to label the Bobbitt marriage a sadomasochistic affair, but she also acknowledged that the cutting showed that women are at least as vengeful, dark, and aggressive as men.[6] Barbara Ehrenreich noticed that "the feminist intellectuals seemed slightly out of touch" with the proceedings in Manassas, "preoccupied these days with their own factional matters, such as the great stand-off over the subject of victimhood."[7]

When Lorena became a vigilante taking up Perseus's sword, there was a dramatic turnabout in the old story. In the patriarchal myth, Medusa is a victim; in Lorena Bobbitt's case, it was the victim who claimed Medusa's terrible powers.

The Bobbitt decision validated the reality of a battered woman's life and exposed the violence and sexual abuse in her marriage. By identifying with Lorena, women around the world vicariously released their personal fury at husbands, lovers, bosses, and boy-friends. A collective catharsis had occurred that left men sleeping on their stomachs.

Hell Hath No Fury

But Lorena Bobbitt, so powerful as a symbol for many women, turned her own rage into a nightmare. If she doesn't understand its energy and self-destructive power, rage can destroy any woman's life.

Psychologists tell us that all wounds to the core of the self—both emotional and physical—evoke one of the most terrifying feelings a human can experience: the threat of annihilation. Some women ex-perience this existential terror during panic attacks. Battered women suffer chronic feelings of annihilation and bury their accumulated rage under passivity and silence. These women are engaging in what battered-women's advocate Michael Dowd calls "the zombie's waltz," a dance of the living dead.

A woman who feels threatened with annihilation eventually ex-plodes to preserve her sense of self. She experiences what Vermont psychotherapist Jilisa Snyder describes as "an intense pressure, a ten-sion, a muscle constriction . . . a panic sensation . . . our sense of self is about to fragment. Rage is then compounded by anxiety; the woman becomes frightened by the emotion she experiences. The panic on top of the initial emotion can snowball . . . and we become overwhelmed." Without knowledge and understanding of rage, a fu-rious and threatened woman feels helpless and powerless. Lacking the skills she needs to use her rage, she strikes out impulsively.

Medusa's beheading resonates for modern women caught up in uncontrollable feelings of vengeance. Suddenly bolted into con-sciousness by some last straw she cannot tolerate, her impulse for revenge takes over, usually in response to a humiliating experience— the shame of berating, betrayal, or battering. An attack may be unex-pected, like the sudden knifing of tennis player Monica Seles or the surprise bludgeoning of skater Nancy Kerrigan's knee. The humiliation may go on for years and end in a moment of climax. The camel's back broke for Lorena Bobbitt that last time when her husband John Wayne forced her into violent sex.

After suffering years of her husband's beatings and infidelities and listening to his recitation of the names of all the women he had slept with, the steam building up in Lorena's pressure cooker finally blew. When, using a Marine Corps pinioning technique, John Wayne plunged his elbow into her chest, pulled down her underpants, and raped her, it was the last straw; she felt reduced to the status of a helpless child.

As she walked into the kitchen for a glass of water, the knife lying on the counter caught her eye. That knife literally became the wounding phallus: It was both the symbol of her oppressor and the instrument to cut him down. Lorena's account and the testimony of the expert witnesses at the trial confirm that from the moment she picked up the knife to the time she reported what she had done, rage usurped her reason. She operated on her primitive impulses, before her conscious mind could process her actions. Her reasoning powers only kicked in after she had disposed of the penis in the field and traveled to the beauty shop to alert the police. She acted out of blind fury, or an "irresistible impulse," as the condition is called in Virginia courts of law. By taking her revenge in the heat of rage, she injured herself as well as her sleeping husband and became, temporarily, the madwoman of myth and literature.

This fusion of identity and emotion, when the person becomes the feeling itself, is peculiar to women, according to Jeanne Shub, Albany child and family therapist. She says:

> Women get stuck in the feeling, in contrast to men who can think more dispassionately about the situation; they can compartmentalize their rage. Women get obsessed and caught up in the wounding, the rejection, the abandonment, and the rage of separation, while the men I treat can be coldly rational and self-protective. They are better able to focus on cleaning out the bank account,

signing up at the dating service, or maintaining a routine with the children.

Even mainstream feminists retreat at the mention of revenge and shy away from explaining basic instincts like vengeance. Anna Quindlen, writing in *The New York Times,* reassured part of her audience during the Bobbitt affair: "never fear, gentlemen; castration was really not the point of feminism." But the average woman in the United States is far more in touch with her fantasies of revenge than columnists will ever guess.

Women are more likely than men to seek revenge, probably because their rage hibernates longer and is therefore more intense and harder to control. As Anne Campbell in *Men, Women, and Aggression* learned from her research: "Women had cornered the market on the seething, unspoken fury that was always threatening to explode."[8]

Like rage, the issue of female revenge was taboo until recently, when the media began playing up angry women in graphic and dramatic ways. In a satiric piece in *Mirabella,* Anne Beatts envisions a posh Manhattan tea party with Lorena Bobbitt, Jean Harris, Amy Fisher, Sylvia Plath, and Mary Jo Buttafuoco as her guests. While they wait for Lorena, who had to "go back for something she accidentally threw out of her car window," the others pussyfoot around the issue of revenge—the "dish best tasted cold," as Sylvia Plath put it.

To strike out with a low-level prank may temporarily restore a woman's equilibrium as well as her sense of humor after a betrayal. June called her ex-husband and his mistress every hour throughout the night and relished the disturbance of their sleep. Andrea, when she found out about her husband's affair, put dried dog turds in the drawer with his jockey shorts; when Sandy's boss, Evelyn, ran for local office, Sandy told every voter she could what Evelyn was like to work for. While these responses may provide temporary relief, they do nothing to help a woman acknowledge and process her rage. And these acts may lead to feelings of shame.

Revenge is also a way of asserting power, and it may easily get out of hand: The more powerful a woman feels in pulling off an act of revenge, the more tempted she may become to escalate the fight instead of letting what goes around come back to her oppressor over time. What began as a low-level tit for tat may suddenly turn into a more dangerous game. Several women have told us about feel-good revenges that started rather innocently and ended in foreclosures on their houses, calls to their employers, and legal and libel suits against them.

Hazardous to a woman's psyche, revenge can threaten her entire life. Beyond the obvious risks of job loss, financial penalties, and, in extreme cases, imprisonment, there is a social censure women who take revenge are likely to suffer. The teenaged Amy Fisher marked herself for life when her rage exploded and she attacked her lover's wife, Mary Jo Buttafuoco. In *My Story,* written with Sheila Weller, Amy describes her feelings and thoughts during the final seconds before her emotional time bomb went off.[9]

> She turned around and said, "Get the fuck off my property." . . .
> What you're feeling, what you know, it doesn't count. I had felt
> that from people for so long, and the only way I could triumph
> over it was to become tougher, much tougher, than they. . . . All
> those years of being terrified to be alone with my father, and my
> grandmother dying in the middle of rescuing me. . . . Being raped
> by that creepy workman and thinking it was my fault. . . . Being
> told that I was just going out to dinner with my escort clients—and
> then having to have sex with them. . . .

Amy's thoughts during the shooting and her graphic compression of incidents that triggered her rage go far toward explaining what makes enraged women take action. Amy felt invalidated; her instinct told her that Mary Jo, like all other adults in her life, not only doubted her veracity but wished to dismiss and erase her. After Mary Jo's nonrecognition ignited Amy's fury, other rage-producing incidents in her personal history kicked in (her father's abuse, her grandmother's death, a rape, other betrayals) and she struck out. "I had been fiddling with the gun in my pocket the whole time we were talking," Amy remembers. "I took the gun out. I hit her on the back of the head. Then I hit her a second time. Harder than I thought I could. This second time the gun went off."

As Dr. Teresa Bonesatti points out, vengeance against men is considered unfeminine and a betrayal of a woman's loyal bond to remain docile with the opposite sex. Caught in a bind between a rage that cries out for vengeance and a culture that threatens punishment, shame, and loss of sexual appeal, women still take their revenge.

Two models of female revenge course through Western culture and remain the dominant stereotypes today. The first is Medea's solution, taking out her vengeance on others; the second is the revenge of self-destruction. In either case, revenge becomes a woman's way to reassert herself and reclaim her waning powers in the world. It says, "I am here; look at me; I am alive." If a woman has been feeling powerless, passive, and unable to act, revenge also verifies the presence of her authentic self that she has felt stirring in her subconscious.

The Medea Solution

The fiercest anger of all, the most incurable,
Is that which rages in the place of dearest love.
—Euripides, *Medea*

Medea, the subject of one of Euripides's greatest tragedies, is a woman of intense passions whose lust for vengeance and retribution has made her an emblem of female rage.[10] Like countless women since ancient times, Medea experiences cataclysmically her husband's abandonment after many years of their being together; his preference for a younger woman galls her.

Born as a barbarian princess with powers of sorcery, Medea as a young girl fell madly in love with the handsome argonaut Jason and helped him procure his first million, the famous Golden Fleece. "I'll

Jason and Medea, *by Gustave Moreau (1865) Jason, the leader of the Argonauts, and Medea, the barbarian princess, in happier times after she used her powers of sorcery to help him capture the Golden Fleece and aid in their escape.*

begin at the beginning," Medea says, launching a verbal attack on her departing husband and counting the many ways she has come to his aid. "I helped you catch the fire-breathing oxen / And harness them, and sow the fatal field / I killed the dragon, the sleepless senti-nel / That wound its coils around the Golden Fleece."[11] In choosing to desert her father and her home for Jason, she even murdered her own brother, littering the sea with his body pieces to impede the pursuit of her father's fleet.

"Full of love and empty of thought in those days," Medea recalls how as an exile from her country she even killed King Pelias, "using his own daughters' hands / For the unkindest death, to wipe his blood-line out." Her deeds secured Jason's wealth and power, and they finally came to live in the city of Corinth, where she was loved and admired by its people.

As the play opens, it is several years later. Medea is the mother of two sons, and the upwardly mobile Jason has rejected his barbarian wife and married Glauce, a young princess and the daughter of Corinth's king. Medea is furious and tells him, "I did all that for you, and now you drop me." Her power stripped away, Medea plots to take revenge, the only weapon besides angry words a powerless woman possesses:

> For in other ways a woman
> Is full of fear, defenseless, dreads the sight of cold
> Steel; but, when once she is wronged in the matter of love,
> No other soul can hold so many thoughts of blood.

Granted one full day to leave Corinth by King Creon, Medea's fury turns to pure energy as she secures safe passage for herself and her sons and she plots to "make dead bodies of three of my enemies—father, the girl, and my husband." Should she set fire to the palace and burn the bridal chamber? Or creep up to their bedside and murder them in cold blood? Medea settles on poison, the art in which she is most skilled. Her rage, fueled by Jason's power in the world, by his disregard for all she has done for him, and by the thought of his lovemaking with the virginal princess, grows monumental when she contemplates her future:

> Where am I to go? To my father's?
> Him I betrayed and his land when I came to you.
> For this is my position—hated by friends
> At home, I have in kindness to you, made enemies
> Of others whom there was no need to have injured.

Medea sends her two sons to Creon's palace bearing for the princess a finely woven dress and a golden crown that she has anointed with deadly poison. Glauce can't resist the gorgeous robe and puts the crown on her curly head. Then the young princess's legs begin to tremble; she staggers about as a devouring fire of deadly acid begins to ooze out of her head and while the flesh from her bones drops away, torn by the hidden fang of poison that also consumes her father, Creon, as he tries to save her.

Despairing for the safety of her two sons, who will be the victims of her enemies, and spurred on to wound Jason even more, Medea brings her children to her to feel their "soft, soft skin . . . the gentle smell of childhood" of her sons one last time. "I know what I intend to do is wrong," she says, "But the rage of my heart is stronger than my reason— That is the cause of all man's foulest crimes." Trying not to think how sweet they are, Medea stabs her children, spending all her rage at Jason on their slaughter.

By acting to avenge her wounded pride, she gains a momentary illusion of power and the satisfaction she has once more made her presence felt. "Call me savage, call me a tigress, call me what you like. But I have reached you. I have struck your heart." But the cost to Medea is her loss of humanity—her acts place her beyond redemption.

"Pulling a Butterfly"

> This *is how I have my say. This is how I say*
> *what I thought about it* all *and I say* No.
> —Marsha Norman, *'night, Mother*

Medea acts out her rage; other women turn their fury back on themselves. *M. Butterfly* playwright David Henry Hwang calls committing suicide "pulling a butterfly." When she learns that her beloved Pinkerton has betrayed her and married an American wife, Madama Butterfly of the Puccini opera can't bear the reality that all her hopes were illusions and her years and years of waiting were in vain. She stabs herself behind a rice-paper screen.

Once awakened to their rage, many women want to die. Myth,

Medea Premeditating the
Murder of Her Children, *a
Roman wall painting (1st century)*
In a rage because he has
left her for a younger, wealthier
princess, Medea plots her
revenge against Jason. She
sends his new wife a tiara and
bridal robe coated with deadly
poison and she then contemplates killing the two others he
loves best—his sons.

history, literature, opera, popular culture, and the evening news are strewn with the bodies of women who killed themselves rather than face the anxiety, fear, and enormous challenge of dealing with abandonment. Unable to confront their fury in a fully conscious and deliberate way, they panicked when emotional pain and financial difficulties overwhelmed them. They were lured by the seduction of death, wanting it to be all over. Jean Harris, Betty Broderick, and Lorena Bobbitt all testified that their initial response to rage was the desire to kill themselves.

Anna Karenina throws herself under a train rather than face protracted rejection by her lover, Count Vronsky, or remain trapped in the lifeless marriage from which she has fled. Hedda Gabler, unable to go on with her claustrophobic life, in which she plays the part of the perfect lady and perfect mother while she lacks the instinct and inclination to do either, uses her father's pistols to put herself out of her misery. Edna Pontellier, the heroine of Kate Chopin's novel *The Awakening*, sees no way in the end to pursue her desires within the rigid Creole society of turn-of-the-century New Orleans. Unable to break with convention, she swims out into the Gulf of Mexico, past the point of no return. Surrendering herself to the sea, the oceanic mother, she remembers the days of her sun-filled childhood as she drowns.

Writers like Virginia Woolf, Sylvia Plath, and Anne Sexton expressed their "divine madness" in fiction and poetry but couldn't sustain a balance between mind and body in their daily lives. Highly sensitized to the particular rages and agonies women contend with in relationships with mothers, husbands, sisters, children, themselves, each chose suicide. Plath, in her poem "Komino," sees herself as a modern Clytemnestra whose fury is unleashed at an overprotective husband.

> I shall unloose—
> From the small jeweled
> Doll he guards like a heart—
> The lioness

The shriek in the bath
The cloak of holes.

The summer before she killed herself, Plath had been so enraged by
the infidelity of her husband, the poet Ted Hughes, that she built a
bonfire and burned an accumulation of his letters and drafts of
poems. As biographer Paul Alexander tells it: ". . . as she threw hand-
fuls of letters onto the flames, she began to dance around the bonfire.
She did this for two reasons: to exorcise Ted from her system and to
seek an omen in the form of a signal."[12] Her omen arrived when the
ritual ended and a piece of unburned paper sailed to her feet. On that
paper, the word *Dido* was written: Plath took it as her signal to
follow in the path of Vergil's queen of Carthage, who immolated
herself on a pyre after she was abandoned by Aeneas. A month later,
Plath was dead.

When love turns to resentment, as in cases of rejection, obsessive
rage can stoke the flames of both love and hatred at once. After his
betrayal, Sylvia Plath couldn't tolerate the sound of her husband's
name, yet she would watch out the window for a glimpse of him as
he arrived to pick up the children. Desire and longing combine with
pain and rage in such situations; the ultimate punishment the woman
can imagine is her own death and her betrayer attending the funeral.

On October 8, 1991, Ann Humphrey, wife of Hemlock society
founder Derek Humphrey, rode her horse into the woods, turned
him loose, and administered to herself a fatal dose of barbiturates
and alcohol.[13] According to her biographer, Rita Marker, her rage at
Derek had a long history. It began when he used her to persuade her
terminally ill parents to submit to an assisted suicide; when knockout
pills didn't work, Derek slipped pillowcases over Ann's parents'
heads and suffocated them while Ann stood by and watched. Then in
1989, when Derek found out that Ann had breast cancer, the same
disease that had taken the life of his first wife, he left her a message
on their answering machine telling her he was leaving her. Subsequently, he discredited her in public as "crazy," a "borderline personality," and "unstable."

Ann struggled with Derek's accusations, reunited with an adopted son and found friends to help her through her illness, but her pain and increasing guilt about her part in her parents' suicide drove her over the edge. In her suicide note, addressed to Derek, Ann began, "There. You got what you wanted." Her statement expressed not only rage but self-hatred and the ultimate surrender of her power.

Having taken out their vengeance on every species of sexist male, Thelma and Louise end their road trip with a plunge into the canyon. One image stayed in the minds of the women seated in the movie theater: the Thunderbird poised over the abyss. Callie Khouri's screenplay advanced the cause of females by putting pretty faces on Medusa's fury and providing a vicarious outlet to release fantasies of revenge. But in the end, her heroines chose a traditional solution to their dilemma, pulling a butterfly instead of facing the music.

Waking to the Realities of Rage

Something's crossed over in me. I can't go back.
—Thelma and Louise

To reverse the effects of sleep and become fully conscious, women must open their eyes to reality. A vigilant woman is aware of what is best for her, and she guards against anything or anyone who would interfere with her ability to live a full and responsible life. She recognizes which of her friends are nurturing and which she should let go. She acknowledges and pursues her interests and seeks out others who would expand her horizons. Accepting responsibility for rescuing herself, she can reclaim her power and repossess her life. In touch with her rage, she is not asleep, but on guard. She knows how to monitor threats, she distinguishes between anger and rage, and, if necessary, she fights back.

When a woman awakens, it is with a flood of comprehension: Recognition bathes the hemispheres of the brain. Finally she gets it, the pieces of the puzzle all fit together, and there is no more guessing or confusion. She sees the whole picture and cannot feed the mechanisms of her repression any longer.

In her autobiography, *I, Tina,* Tina Turner reflects upon her long, unhappy relationship with Ike: "So this was my life, and I was starting to see it real clearly now."[14] Her young girl's need for love and acceptance had turned into the grown woman's fear of a violent and abusive man. It had taken years to develop the strength and courage to know what she must do next.

Tina Turner, christened Anna Mae Bullock, was abandoned in childhood both emotionally and physically, first by her mother and then by her father. When, as a teenager, she was hired by Ike Turner to be the singer with his popular band, she was dazzled. At first, their relationship was platonic, and it gave the young woman confidence: "that kind of confidence was a foundation for me, for the first time in my life—a kind of family love." But eventually she and Ike became lovers, and "from there it just sort of went on and on. . . . Yes, I fell

Tina Turner, whose open mouth and moussed-up hair suggest a modern Medusa, screams her rage into rock songs like "What's Love Got to Do With It?"

in love. Became addicted to it. . . . I would have been lost in my life at that point without him." As his control over her increased, Ike renamed her Tina and created her wild-woman persona.

But once they were married, he began to show his ugly, violent side, beating her with shoe stretchers, wire hangers, and his fists, burning her with lighted cigarettes. Nevertheless, she had two children with him. Like so many women, she felt she should "stay put" and "just try to make things better." As the beatings became more severe and visits to the emergency room more frequent, she feared for her life, and fear kept her immobilized.

It wasn't until she caught him in their bed with another woman that she snapped: "there they were, Ike and Ann. *Aaah!*" At this point, she began the process of disengaging from Ike and planning her escape. In a dark moment, she took a nearly fatal dose of Valium and learned just how little she meant to him. "That's when I started to hate Ike Turner." Tina had awakened to her rage.

As all of the pieces fit into place, Tina faced the truth of her life. She determined that the future would not be a repetition of the past. She began by channeling her rage into strategies for self-empowerment. A friend taught her Buddhist chanting, which calmed her down and centered her energies. She stopped deceiving herself and came to terms with her denial.

Some women, like Tina Turner, are capable of waking themselves up. Others require help. As professors in a large university, we have seen women awakened from their slumbers by classroom discussions, reading groups, and community seminars. Books, films, and educational consciousness-raising have profound effects, particularly on returning female students.

Novels that have an awakening effect on women include *Tess of the D'Urbervilles, Orlando, Lady Chatterley's Lover, Tender Is the Night, Small Changes, Their Eyes Were Watching God, The Color Purple, Fear of Flying,* and *Rubyfruit Jungle.* The publishing explosion of nonfiction books dealing with women's issues and psychology—such as *Women Who Love Too Much; My Mother, Myself; The Erotic Silence of the American Wife; Backlash; The Dance of*

Anger; The Beauty Myth; and *Women Who Run with the Wolves*—has created a semantic network in which women can situate their problems, their common pain, and their rage. For others, awakening can come from films like *The Good Mother, The Accused, The Prince of Tides, Beaches, The Piano, Scenes from a Marriage,* and *Camille Claudel.* Each time a woman witnesses another's coming to consciousness, she comes closer to her own awakening.

Some women are awakened suddenly, in a face-to-face encounter with a startling truth that confounds all understanding. When Mia Farrow saw Woody Allen's erotic photographs of the naked Soon-Yi Previn, she experienced the psychological equivalent of electric shock. There could be no mistake about what she was looking at; it was prima facie evidence that the man she loved desired her adopted teenaged daughter. What was once inconceivable was now irrevocably true.

With this kind of revelation, there is no time to become gradually accustomed to the facts. Before it can be repressed, rage rushes to the surface. When women talk about these moments, they're filled with rage anew. Until she puts her rage behind her, this kind of shock to a woman's system leaves her stunned and obsessed over the incident.

Victoria had just returned from a two-day visit with her ailing mother. Tired and soaked from an afternoon rainstorm, she entered her house, hoping her husband would be a little late from his university classes so she could have a soothing bath. She put her key into the front door lock, only to discover the door was open. Puzzled and a little frightened, she crept silently through the foyer and the living room. In the hall, she froze. She could hear moans of ecstasy coming from the bedroom. "I don't know how I did it," she told us, "but I walked into that room. There was my husband, in bed with one of his graduate students. I made sure they saw me and then I walked out. I was too shocked to scream at them, and the girl had the sense to leave quickly. There was nothing my husband could say—he was caught in the proverbial act. Very calmly, I told him to get a suitcase together and leave, and when he was gone, I literally fell apart and started gasping for air. I spent hours after that crying and staring into space. As soon as I could, I got a divorce."

Victoria got through the explosive moment by meditating at intervals throughout the day, using techniques she had learned at a yoga center. Other women find refuge in the sympathy of friends; taking some action is a woman's first solution.

What is common to these awakenings is the burst of energy women feel as they come out of their sleep; one woman called it "jet fuel in my veins." The question becomes, How is the energy of rage to be channeled? Into revenge? Into power? Or both?

The Collective Awakening

Millions of women felt the scales fall from their eyes in 1963 as they read Betty Friedan's *The Feminine Mystique,* in which Friedan identified "the problem that has no name." As she explored and exploded the myth of the "happy housewife," Friedan electrified generations of females who instinctively knew there was more to life than what had been passed down to them. Women sighed with relief that someone was giving their discontent a voice, that they were not alone in their feelings. In her chapter "The Forfeited Self," Friedan wrote:

> If women do not put forth, finally, that effort to become all that they have it in them to become, they will forfeit their own humanity. A woman today who has no goal, no purpose, no ambition patterning her days into the future, making her stretch and grow beyond that small score of years in which her body can fulfill its biological function, is committing a kind of suicide.[15]

As women flocked to universities and into the labor force, they encountered resistance to their power and growth, but among them there was solidarity. They had a sense that a national voice was speaking their language and elucidating their plight as women. Friedan's work sent shock waves around the world, serving notice that the flimflam of past centuries wasn't going to work on the women of the 1960s. In speaking out, she set the stage for Gloria Steinem and other second-wave feminists, and later for Susan Faludi's explication of the politics of backlash.

Bella Abzug and Shirley Chisholm accomplished a collective female political awakening in the 1960s. Fearless in the face of criticism, they won seats in Congress and refused to keep their mouths shut. They served as pioneers and made a path for Dianne Feinstein, Barbara Boxer, and Carol Moseley-Braun to follow. Many women who watch these models will be encouraged to follow their lead and enter politics.

There are more women in Congress than ever before, in part because of the collective fallout of the Anita Hill hearings. In their aftermath, Joey Buttafuoco was sentenced to prison after finally admitting he had had sex with a minor; heavyweight champion Mike Tyson went to jail for raping Desiree Washington; and former Judge Sol Wachler was convicted of harassing his former lover Joy Silverman and her daughter. More and more women have begun to challenge the social norms, the ideological underpinnings of the culture. Rage used well can change all women's lives.

It has been told that when Medusa was beheaded
the blood spurting from the artery in her neck
gave birth to Pegasus, the winged horse of creativity,
and to Chrysador of the golden sword.
From her snakes' blood came healing fluids
as well as the venom that causes war;
even on Athena's shield, Medusa's emblem frightens
*   all enemies.*
When Perseus rested Medusa's head at the water's
*   edge*
the soft ferns and sea grasses felt her power
and became hard filigree of precious coral.
And some poets tell how Athena, listening to the hiss
in Medusa's hair, invented the art of music.

Medusa's Magical Fluids

Ovid and other poets tell us about the magical properties of Medusa's bodily fluids. Some say that once she was beheaded, her bloodstream divided in two: Blood that came from her right side brought sadness and death to anything it touched, but the blood that flowed from the left was a fluid that restored life.

The magical properties of Medusa's blood can be seen as the negative and positive qualities of the energies of rage: From this enormous storehouse can spring a desert of poisonous serpents or an abundance of supercharged energy.

Rage can consume a woman. We watched this phenomenon on the evening news at the time the cannibalistic serial killer Jeffrey Dahmer was being sentenced. Before his final pronouncement, the judge allowed the victims' relatives to speak to Dahmer directly and express their outrage at his vicious and bestial acts. An African-American woman spoke for her brother, who had been mutilated. Her anger seared the courtroom and then turned to fury. Her arms flailed as if she could not control them; she bellowed; her face contorted as if she had been possessed by rage's swirling demonic energy. She had to be dragged from the courtroom.

For many women, rage is like a foreign language over which they have no control. To master rage, a woman needs to study it and learn its grammar, its syntax and vocabulary. Feelings of rage usually arise with a precipitating incident and there are two ways a woman may respond: impulsively or with insight.

Fire in the Body

To translate the fire of her rage and change it into positive energy, a woman needs to learn how to control and direct the flames. Leslie, one of the women we interviewed, told us that her newfound energy came in the moments after an emotional shock and it jolted her into action. In the ensuing months, she learned how to harness that energy and produce results that worked for her instead of against her.

For years, Leslie was emotionally and financially dependent on her husband. During this period, anxiety, chronic fatigue, and depression cloaked her rage and depleted her energy. She behaved like a zombie; afraid of striking out and leaving a dysfunctional marriage, she was even too frightened to leave the house. At times she wouldn't drive to the supermarket without company. Panic attacks—during which her heart would race and she would imagine her imminent death—were becoming a daily occurrence. While her mind and body were speaking to her eloquently, telling her something was wrong, Leslie wouldn't entertain the possibility that her fifteen-year marriage to Dick was falling apart.

She had just returned from a two-week vacation at her summer home and was on the porch with her sister, having iced tea, when her cleaning woman told her there was something she ought to know. While she and her son had been away, her husband, Dick, had been living in their home with his mistress of four years and her thirteen-year-old daughter. On hearing the news, an enormous surge of energy rushed through Leslie's system. Her vision got blurry, then it cleared and she actually felt relieved. Miraculously, she told us, all her former fears seemed to disappear from that moment on.

She sprang into action, called the number of a prominent divorce lawyer in another city, and made an appointment for the very next day. After her rage finally surfaced, she accomplished more in those first few hours than she had during years of procrastination. The next day, she traveled three hours by train in ninety-five-degree heat to consult with her attorney about the kind of settlement she wanted from her husband. "I felt effective for the first time in years," she said, describing the issues they discussed.

With the help of a therapist, Leslie learned visualization techniques that transformed her rage and focused its energy.

In one of the exercises Leslie learned how to visualize the expulsion of her rage. She would lie on her bed, count backward from one hundred until she was relaxed, and then begin to acknowledge the intensity of her feelings. She would imagine she was in a large humid room where there was an empty swimming pool. Standing in it were all the people who had hurt and betrayed her. Her husband was there, his mistress and her child, and those friends who had lied to her and covered up her husband's affair. Once she had a clear picture of the scene in the pool house, she would visualize herself turning on a spigot; excrement would pour out, filling the pool and overflowing until all of her enemies were drowned in it. She visualized the excrement oozing into their noses, mouths, and ears. As the last one sank into the muck, she viewed the scene with satisfaction, and it slowly receded from her mind. Then she visualized the energy that propelled her rage. It was like the flame of a Bunsen burner, with a neon glow, and she imagined it flooding every part of her body.

Leslie used this technique every time her rage threatened to overwhelm her and she felt tempted to seek revenge against her husband. She began to condition her response to rage. Eventually, it became automatic; when an incident produced rage, she would first indulge her fantasies of revenge; she would visualize herself throwing muriatic acid in the face of the man who had infuriated her; she would imagine the woman who had crossed her falling off a ski lift into a bottomless chasm. Once her aggressive impulses were eventually satisfied, she could relax and visualize the neon blue flame. When she did so, she would be flooded with energy. Combining the visualization technique with in-depth psychotherapy, strenuous lap swimming, and workouts on a rowing machine, Leslie was able to emerge from her divorce proceedings two years later with her rage under management and with the desired financial settlement.

Rage in Public

Once rage is harnessed, it can be used as a catalyst for change not only in the personal life of a woman but in the public sphere. The 1992 elections brought a record number of women to Congress. As Victoria Secunda put it in *New Woman* shortly after the elections, "None of this could have happened without rank and file women putting their non-stop energies where their rage was last fall."[1]

Carol Moseley-Braun of Illinois, the first black female senator from any state, was elected during the Year of the Woman. She ran, she said, because of her outrage after the Hill-Thomas hearings, but her personal rage only ignited on the Senate floor when her colleagues voted to renew the patent on the insignia for the United Daughters of the Confederacy, which consisted of the Confederate flag encased in a wreath. Visibly stirred by rage and empowered by its energy, Moseley-Braun stood up and turned her fury into an eloquent speech. She argued that the vote was not about the insignia itself, but about race and the memory of slavery, which she called the single-most-painful episode in American history. Her words so moved the senators that in a second roll call, the Senate reversed itself, voting against the insignia seventy-five to twenty-five. Even Senator Howell T. Heflin, a white southern Democrat remembered from the Anita Hill hearings as the man with the slowest drawl in the Senate, could not put "his stamp of approval on a symbolism that was offensive to a large segment of the American people."

When rage turns into energy, as it does when a woman begins to claim her power, she can feel magically alive. Morning talk-show host Joan Lunden knows the feeling: "Sometimes my outrage at what's going on [in her personal life] turns into energy—and I'm actually great on the air."[2] During her widely publicized divorce from Michael Krauss, Lunden said, she experienced bouts of rage that threatened her TV persona. For years, she had educated Americans about bringing up children; she greeted viewers every morning as the most wholesome mom on TV, but in fact she was a master of "keeping up appearances." Her marriage was really a mess. Once she started divorce proceedings and stopped pretending she was a perfect anything, Lunden found that all the energy she had used to maintain her false image was now available to her. Joan Lunden began her transformation when she told her story; as soon as she shattered her image of perfection, she began to change her life.

Where the Gorgons Live: Finding Our Rage

> And I will flee to the place where the Gorgons live,
>
> And I will touch the snakes in my sisters' hair
> And the snakes will be rainbows. . . .
> —Karen Lindsey

Each woman deals with her rage in a manner unique to herself. Some are able to do so without professional help, but for many women outside intervention is needed, and often psychotherapy is the tool of choice. Sandra Cross Strawbridge, an MSW, has practiced psychotherapy for many years. She has also conducted workshops on rage and self-assertion and is part of a growing number of male and female therapists who are beginning to work with rage as a pivotal issue in women's lives. "I see rage as a very positive emotion," she told us. "Rage tells us who we are, how really big we are, how really huge we are on the whole planet."

In working with women and their rage—through dreams, body

work, and in group sessions, Strawbridge has them first talk out their rage in order to open up areas of repression and touch into those buried feelings at the core. "Rage usually first comes out as anger," she says. "The rage is more difficult to get to; it is buried underneath the anger and has seeped into the tissues because it is imbedded in the human survival system. There are exercises and ways to bring the rage up in a therapeutic situation. But normally, we hit rage in therapy by surprise."

A therapist probes for rage the way a dentist probes for cavities. When the patient cries out, the therapist knows she or he has hit a nerve. A reaction that is out of proportion to the stimulus is always a sign of a tender spot. Resistance is also a clue to unresolved unconscious feelings. The intensity of a reaction may prompt some therapists to use age regression, in which they hypnotize a patient and return her to the childhood time when a trauma occurred. When she reexperiences the original psychic pain, toxic energy is released, freeing her for more productive activity.

"When rage comes out," Strawbridge told us, "a woman starts to breathe more easily; she can feel her own heart beat again; she smiles and her skin looks better; her eyes are clearer; and she is more the woman she should be."

In *Women Who Run with the Wolves,* Clarissa Pinkola Estés invites her readers to "make rage into a fire that cooks things rather than a fire of conflagration."[3] It is rage, she believes, that lies buried beneath the pain and anger of traumatic memories. When untransformed, Estés says, "rage can become a constant mantra about how oppressed, hurt, and tortured we were. . . . Rage corrodes our trust that anything good can occur."[4]

When they prepare to "cook" over the powerful fire of rage, women must first find the pieces of their lives that have caused them to become so incensed. To gather these memories together, Estés prescribes a ritual she calls "descansos." "To make descansos means taking a look at your life and marking where the small deaths, *las muertes chichitas,* and the big deaths, *las muertes grandotas,* have taken place."[5] She suggests drawing a time line of one's life on a piece of paper, marking out the crossroads and the paths not taken over the years. For many women, the "big deaths" are memories of traumas: betrayal, harassment, sexual abuse, or rape. The "little deaths" are more subtle misdemeanors—wounding slights, belittling comments, and painful rejections.

Every woman who has been interviewed for this book has made a kind of descansos. To tell and learn of her psychic injuries, a woman must go to the place where her own Gorgons live. Plumbing the depths of her psyche and unearthing the layers of sedimental pain is a ritual that can lead her to cleansing of the spirit.

The Shadow Piece: Claiming Aggression

In the myth, Medusa's final transformation occurs when her head becomes an emblem on Athena's shield. Painted in miniature as part of the goddess's armor, Medusa's head symbolizes the proper place of rage in a woman's life and validates the dark, aggressive side of the female nature.

Pearl Mindell is a Jungian analyst working on a new paradigm of female development; her research on rage led her to the Medusa myth and particularly to the emblem on the shield. "This Medusan remnant means many things," says Mindell, "but it is particularly that part of the feminine that the patriarchal world is so frightened of—the cycles of life, sex, and nature. It is the piece of rage we must redeem." Medusan rage is Athena's secret weapon; it guards her boundaries and links her to the passions at her core. When a woman accepts her capacity for rage and aggression, she also lays claim to her own power.

Many women can't identify what rage actually feels like, and they are also afraid that if they allowed it to surface, its power would destroy them; as a consequence, they are unable to use its energy. Dr. Jilisa Snyder says that each woman has a different bodily sense of what rage is, but many of them mistake their rage and aggression for fear. Those women who don't express their needs directly or know how to assert themselves are prone to panic attacks.

"The goal of therapy," Snyder says, "is to learn not to stop the emotion because it feels uncomfortable but to reframe it as a positive experience. Therapy provides a safe and neutral environment for expelling these primal emotions. Once a woman sees that her rage doesn't kill her or anyone else and that she doesn't fall apart when she lets it out, it becomes a tool rather than a cause of anxiety."

Pearl Mindell starts her therapeutic work with the woman's unique imagery and fantasies, her dreamworld, where repressed rage hides out. "The rage characters come through dreams as persecutors, rapists, terrorists, and Nazis," Mindell says, "people who are after them. These figures are pieces of their own assertiveness and aggression turned against them—and projections of the ways in which they've been abused."

Mindell sees rage figures in dreams as externalized and split-off fragments of the self—characters in the drama of a woman's wounded psyche. "You work with the split-off parts," Mindell explains, "and stand together with a woman while she talks to the rapist, who is the rageful part of herself. As she starts to tell the rapist's story, she begins to describe her own life." Once these women look at and question the wounded children from their past, they are able to let them go and allow the adult female to emerge. As the women develop a more conscious relation to the tough, rageful piece of themselves, Mindell says, they learn to use this nugget of psychic energy, the enraged piece of the self, as the building block or foundation for the adult personality.

Mindell calls rage "the unattended warrior in ourselves." In Jungian terms, rage is part of the shadow side of the psyche and is bound up with a woman's animus, or the male within. In many females, the animus has been repressed. Women's task now is to find feminine ways of using the warrior's masculine skills—his power of reason combined with feminine powers of intuition. "We need both skills to know and say, 'My husband's been fucking around, and I will not take any more of his lies and abuse,' " Mindell says, or "That's a great job opportunity and I'm not going to let it get away from me."

Using images from mythology and the terminology of Jung, Mindell describes the woman warrior as a passionate seeker who knows her own mind and psychological makeup and is on good terms with her dark, aggressive side. Unlike Persephone, who enters the underworld as the vanquished bride of Pluto each winter, the female warrior descends to the underworld in order to explore its depths, and she does so on her own timetable. "Warriors have gotten a bad press in the past," says Mindell, "but women need to perform these incredible heroics just as men do."

Through a combination of intuition and self-knowledge, women who are warriors know instinctively when the "last straw" is broken, when someone has tested their personal limits, and rage is the only appropriate response. As Clarissa Pinkola Estés says in *Women Who Run with the Wolves:*

> There are times when it becomes imperative to release a rage that shakes the skies. There is a time—even though these times are very rare, there is definitely a time—to let loose all the firepower one has. It has to be in response to a serious offense; the offense has to be big and against the soul or spirit. All other reasonable avenues for change have to be attempted first. If these fail, then we have to choose the right time. There is definitely a right time for full-borne rage.[3]

In seeking her aggression, the female warrior needs a companion, Mindell says, a spiritual adviser, a women's group, a therapist who is familiar with his or her own dark places. This companion should be there to navigate and witness a woman's descent and must also be acquainted with the "luminous quality of the dark." When she comes face-to-face with Medusa, the aggression in herself, a companion can dry up her tears.

Eight years ago Sylvia's marriage was falling apart; she was attending Al-Anon meetings for codependent spouses of alcoholics and was filled with rage. She loved her job as a sales rep, traveling around her region for a major publishing house, and she adored her infant son. Yet Sylvia's anger at her lawyer husband was increasing daily as his bouts with alcoholism and his concurrent promises to stop drinking became more frequent. "I was enraged at the disease, at his deterioration, and his moral and psychological breakdown," she says. And she was also frightened by his violent outbursts. He would yell at her, slam doors, and even sweep the dishes off the table. Most of the time Sylvia was able to control her own rage through her dedication to work. And when her son was born, she was so happy, she says, "I put my rage on the back burner."

Three years later, her immune system weakened and, suffering from a painful case of shingles, Sylvia realized that her husband, still drinking, could never be there for her emotionally and that he might actually become violent with their son. "At that point I consciously began to rewrite my future. I reasoned and raged to myself. I love publishing, I love the book business, and I love my son. I thought to myself: Create a life from these loves; put your blinders on and go for it, honey."

After six years of marriage, Sylvia left her husband and moved in with her family. She felt she was progressing until a few months later when she returned to the house she had shared with her husband for a few of her things. On the floor were used condoms; sneaking out the side door were her husband and his secretary, the woman he had installed as Sylvia's live-in replacement a few days after she had moved out. Sylvia was furious.

"I come from a good WASP family that laughed a lot," Sylvia said. "Anger was never condoned; my family's formula was always to turn anger into parody. This time when I came home to my parents I was so enraged I was catatonic for about twenty-four hours. I remember sitting out on my parents' lawn and looking at the clouds and concocting revenges. I wanted to pile all her things, including the condoms, on a dolly and roll it into the middle of his law firm. What made me so mad was that he had taken away all my good memories of our relationship, and all I could think of were those condoms— reminders of their lovemaking.

"My family was great. They just bundled me and my son up in rain slickers and drove us to Niagara Falls. My sister took me down the side of the falls to a secluded grotto called the Bridge of Rainbows. She stuck me under a miniwaterfall and told me to sit there," Sylvia says. "I let the water beat the hell out of me for what seemed hours. Then I looked up and saw zillions of rainbows. It was my baptism. All the rage, the catatonia, and self-inflicted illnesses seemed to wash away. It was a turning point."

After that incident Sylvia felt more in control and determined to make a good life for herself. "I felt I had to make up for all those years of rage that had deprived me of being happy. I really learned how to take care of myself. Now I think of my rage as a positive emotion. It is a tremendous ball of fiery solar plexus energy. When I first experienced rage," Sylvia says, "I thought it was something negative—an emotion corroding my gut that was destroying me. Then I realized something else was also happening. I had to stop and ask myself, Is this thing really eating away at my insides, or is this the furnace that is stoking my energy?"

Using rage as her catalyst and her knowledge of the book business as her base, Sylvia bought a bookstore in an upscale shopping plaza near a large university. After four years, it was thriving, and Sylvia began to expand; she remodeled and then bought an adjoining space and created a children's bookstore. It was her second "baby," the one conceived on her own.

Then, two years ago, "two big guys" moved in on the block; these large book superstores threatened her business. "What enraged me most of all," Sylvia says, "was that the playing field was so unequal. Here I had struggled to create my store and now these corporate giants were turning me into the little guy. I'm a good capitalist and I needed to even out the playing field. After three months of sleepless nights, I decided to turn my rage into something productive. I empowered myself, using my frustration and fury, by coming up with new marketing strategies and getting the message out to the public. I wrote an open letter to all my customers, telling them frankly about the plight of small bookstores, asking for their continued support, and offering special discounts. I also began networking with small bookstore-owner colleagues. The results have been gratifying. Most of my customers have remained loyal, while the small booksellers in the area are banding together, taking out mutual advertising, planning signings, and fighting to survive."

Sylvia turned her rage into determination, persistent goal setting, and creative solutions for solving problems. She was also able to reach out to her family for support, understanding, and help when she needed it.

There was a time in her twenties and thirties when Deborah was consumed with fury. "For me rage had always been like an amoeba, a primitive substance coursing through my body that took many shapes and forms," she says. "When I was younger, it was the alien being that ruled my life. Now it's the signal that something's wrong." Deborah carried the rage accumulated during her difficult childhood into an early marriage. A series of miscarriages, followed by a doctor's warning not to try to get pregnant again, left her feeling cheated out of her dream; like many women of that fifties generation, she had envisioned being a wife and mother, and that was that. Now she felt useless, and her grief, fueled by her rage, took on a life of its own. Although friends urged her to adopt, she felt she could never love a child who wasn't her own flesh and blood. Eventually, her patient husband suggested therapy.

Educating herself about her rage is the first step in any woman's journey toward managing and understanding her feelings. Deborah learned that depression, accompanied by tantrums directed at her husband, was her way of expressing shameful or unacceptable feelings. "The way I reclaimed myself was to bring my rage into focus during this early period," she told us. "It was no longer vague and amorphous—it was rage in concentrated and very focused form. I deliberately placed my rage at the foreground of my life, got in touch with why I was so enraged at myself and my husband."

Deborah had two companions on her journey: One was her therapist; the other was her husband, who encouraged her to return to school and held her hand through the forward movements and backsliding of the therapeutic process.

It was during classes on "The Self in Romantic Poetry" and "The Mythic Journey of the Hero" that she saw the parallels between her own search for fulfillment and other famous quests; she identified with Odysseus's lust for adventure and his ingenuity in the face of adversity; she heard the measured sounds of her own voice making sense of Milton's *Paradise Regained*.

"There was nothing actually heroic about my returning to school," she told us. "It was the necessary step I took to survive. What I learned from literature and mythology was that the hero's quest is an archetype that women can use as their model just as men can. Women can participate in deep spiritual transformations and journeys to the underworld. My own archetypal journey began as a way of coming to terms with my inability to bear children and turned into a doctorate and then a job as a professor teaching young adults about comparative mythologies. My aim now is to teach college students about finding personal myths that work for them," she says. "Oh yes! And last year I became a mother. Last year I adopted a little girl from Peru."

The woman warrior, the way the patriarchy defines her, is a sexy Amazon, a Barbarella, a kitten with a whip. But when a woman creates and gets to know the warrior within herself, it doesn't matter what she looks like. Her inner life is what guides her quest.

Rage as Radar and Guardian of the Boundaries

Circumstances force some women to confront their rage without benefit of therapy, but all women can exploit and claim its beneficial properties. By becoming aware of her unconscious patterns and by looking at her self-destructive behavior, any woman can use rage as radar. It will tell her where her boundaries are and signal when someone has trespassed against her.

. . .

At forty-five, Irene's fury literally exploded when a duodenal ulcer burst open and threatened her life. "I realized I'd had the same pain in my stomach from the time I was twelve," she told us, "but I always thought it didn't matter. I guess I thought *I* didn't matter. All I cared about was pleasing other people by being good. Lying in the intensive-care unit with all those tubes and machines hooked up to my body was when I realized that no one else was going to take care of me. I had to do it myself.

"My doctor told me I had to stop swallowing my anger. I didn't even realize I was angry, but now I started to think about it. I thought about all the roles I'd invented for myself—I was the perfect daughter, the superteacher, and the benevolent caretaker; I was the glue that held my dysfunctional family together."

Irene's had been a childhood of mixed blessings. Her father drank and her parents were always fighting, and so she became the "savior" in the family. At Catholic school, the nuns provided her with some structure and the calm love she never found at home. "These women were my role models," she remembers fondly, "and they encouraged me to develop a relationship with God that has sustained me."

After high school, she chose to enter a convent, where her goodness could be expressed through religious life and she could escape from the turmoil at home. But in this setting, her anger surfaced for the first time and was directed at the mistress novice. Appalled and terrified by her rebellious emotions, Irene left the convent and became a junior high school teacher.

She excelled as a teacher-administrator in a big-city school system, but she had never acknowledged her rage, and again and again she found herself filled with righteous indignation. "I didn't think it was fair for administrators to take credit for teachers' work. It tore me apart when my brother took my alcoholic father for a model. I thought I could keep my own life in order by being absolutely neat. When my ulcer burst and I survived, I learned about caring on a whole new level. But this time, it was caring for myself."

Three years ago at age forty-seven, Irene resigned from her teaching job and moved to a Northeast coastal island and established a tutoring service and counseling bureau for college-bound juniors and seniors. In getting to know the local residents, she's been able to allow herself to have too many beers once in a while, to flirt with men at parties, to curse the winter weather with the fishermen at the dock. "I live now where I want to live, in a place where you can see the stars at night. On this island, I love the fierceness of the winter storms and taking my dog for a walk on the beach. I like the way the beach changes with the quietness of spring, the bustle of summer, and the golden lapse into fall. I feel at peace now. My rage is almost entirely gone. I used to think I had to control my world or I would fall apart. Now I can see that God is in control."

Rage and Body Work

In recent years, more and more physicians, psychotherapists, and body workers have been acknowledging and exploring the mind/body connection. Deepak Chopra, M.D., tells us in his books that every single thought or emotion registers in our cells; the energies of the body and the energies of the mind are constantly interacting. "With even the slightest change of awareness, energy and information move in new patterns. The reason old habits are so destructive is that new patterns aren't allowed to spring into existence," he writes in *Ageless Body, Timeless Mind.*[5]

When we are angry, we are conscious of being angry, but rage operates in the darkness of the unconscious mind and the unconscious body and has to be brought to light. One of the most powerful ways to exhume rage and release its toxic energy is through body work. Practitioner-assisted techniques include massage, acupuncture, shiatsu, and chiropractic. On her own or in classes, a woman can do aerobics, weight training, martial arts, yoga; she can play tennis, run, swim, bike, hike; the possibilities are practically endless. Body work releases tensions and alters emotional states. It should be practiced in conjunction with psychotherapy, meditation, or other forms of self-analysis, since the emotions it releases still must be dealt with and their sources understood. However, for a woman stuck in rage, body work can be a first step in giving her relief and providing a gateway to the issues with which she must contend.

Betsy, a comedian, had always felt rage as an intense body experience and entered therapy because of sporadic tantrums that were interfering with her relationships. In one dramatic incident after a fight with her ex-boyfriend, she destroyed her canopy bed and took her plants and threw them out a fifth-story window.

"For me, rage is always connected with lots of energy and power," she told us. "When I'm enraged, I want to kick, pound, and break things." She can remember being filled with rage from the time she was four. "As a child, I used to bang my head against the wall or hit my head with a tennis racket. I would jolt my whole body around on the bed and bounce on it endlessly." She attributes her feelings of rage and powerlessness to lack of attention from her high-powered father. "He had no interest in me and nothing I was going to do would please him. Even when the whole family went to the beach, he'd be sitting there talking on a cellular phone. I'd come out of the water and drip on his papers.

"But mostly I took my rage at him out on my mother. I would really get into it, almost as if I was a performance artist. When I was ten, I painted 'I hate you Mom' in maple syrup across the kitchen floor. My mother would enrage me even more by not acknowledging my anger; she would grow calmer and calmer the more rage that I expressed. By the time I entered adolescence, I was freaking out. Sports saved me. My tantrums would have controlled my life if it hadn't been for the concentration and refocusing techniques I learned from gymnastics. My work on the balance beam helped me to steady my emotional life," she told us. "I put rage into back handsprings. I played field hockey with a vengeance. On the tennis court, I *had* to win. I would grunt out my rage on my serves, like Monica Seles."

Betsy and the professionals we've interviewed agree that sports are a positive way of releasing rage but that this kind of anger management can only go so far. At twenty-three, Betsy continues to utilize sports; she is now playing squash and learning karate for self-defense; she also recently enrolled in a nine-week program of intense psychotherapy, where she learned to participate in psychodrama as a way of working through her rage. After leaving the program, she refined her comic psychodrama skits and began performing them onstage; in one of them, she mimics her father talking on the phone at the beach.

Comedy and satire are time-honored ways of transforming rage. Until recently, men dominated the field. In the 1950s and 1960s, Phyllis Diller, Lucille Ball, and Martha Raye became stars, but they used themselves as the butt of their jokes: Lucille Ball, the ditzy housewife; Martha Raye, the loudmouth; Phyllis Diller, the harridan. The newer generation of comics—Lily Tomlin, Whoopi Goldberg, and Roseanne Arnold—take the rage-producing scenarios of our culture for their material. These comics have put female rage into the mainstream and given it a healthy outlet.

Journalist Elizabeth Hilts sees comedy as a way to "get in touch with the Inner Bitch," which she describes as "the Bette Davis in all of us," the powerful and true part of every woman that "serves as an absolute defender of the boundaries." Comedy is the bridge between rage and self that helps a woman to listen and laugh it off.

Chrysador and Pegasus

When Medusa's head is cut off, according to Ovid's version of the myth, two offspring come forth from the blood of her headless trunk. The first is Chrysador, a mighty warrior and symbol of strength, and the other is Pegasus, the winged horse and spirit of creativity. Chrysador represents a woman's inner strength, from which she may gather the courage to face her rage and understand its enormous power as a catalyst for change. The winged horse Pegasus symbolizes flight into the imaginative and spiritual realms. In the encoded language of myths and religion, the birth of Pegasus signals a higher level of consciousness. As Thomas Moore puts it in *Soul Mates:*

> Anger may provide an opportunity to establish firmness and strength in one's own character, and in that way, at least, prepare for a relationship that will be well grounded. Taking anger deep within, making its qualities of strength and intensity a constant element of character, a steeling of one's heart, constitutes significant initiation of the soul, one that is necessary for an intimate relationship with another.[8]

The Gorgon Powers of Art and Writing

Guided by my heritage of a love of beauty and a respect for strength—in search of my mother's garden, I found my own.
—Alice Walker

Perseus set down Medusa's head in a bed of seaweed and sweet ferns and the dark grasses drank in the Gorgons' magic fluids. "Stems, leaves, and tendrils hardened into semi-precious stones," Ovid wrote, "while wilted greens changed into filigrees of coral." This other aspect of the myth tells us that rage is mutable. It can turn raw nature into something precious and permanent, just as artists do when they create paintings, poems, and music.

As Jane Marcus observes, "rage and savage indignation sear the hearts of female poets and female critics."[9] Rage has inflamed the hearts of female novelists like George Eliot and Emily Brontë, and of essayists, as well. Although some creative women, like poets Sylvia Plath and Anne Sexton, were ultimately not able to transcend the immensity of their rage, their poems are part of a long literary and artistic tradition that links art and anger.

Virginia Woolf, for example, habitually recorded intense feelings
of rage in the pages of her diaries. Later, after "melting it down,"
sifting the feelings through her imagination by a process she called
"incandescence," she transformed her rage into the finely honed
prose of novels such as *Mrs. Dalloway* and *To the Lighthouse*. Emily
Dickinson's rage was an integral part of her identity, her life, and her
poetry. In one of her most famous and mysterious poems, she imagines her life as "a loaded gun," its passions ready to explode. In another, she describes her face as volcanic, or "Vesuvian." More than a
century later, the poet Adrienne Rich was able to express the guilt-
ridden rage of motherhood in more direct language. Totally unaware
of how common and prosaic her "selfish" resentment of her young
babies is, she envisions herself as a monster in their eyes. Imagining
how her rage looks to them as she checks on them in sleep, she
writes:

> You blurt a cry. Your eyes
> spring open, still filmed in dream.
> Wider they fix me—
> death's head, sphinx, Medusa.[10]

Rage has always been a source of creative power and energy in
women's fiction. In the past five years, young American women have
begun publishing detective novels, and in the process they have created a new version of the female warrior. The writer Sue Grafton was
so enraged during brutal custody battles that she plotted to kill her
ex-husband—in a book. "I really did think about killing him," she
says. "I knew I'd bungle it and get caught, so I wrote a book instead.
I didn't really relish the idea of spending the rest of my life in a shape-
less prison dress."[11] Instead, she embarked on the now-famous series
of detective novels, each of which begins with a different letter in the
alphabet. In *A Is for Alibi,* she turned her scheme to murder her
enraging ex-spouse—filling antihistamine capsules with the poisonous leaves from a common evergreen—into the first Kinsey Millhone
story and "murdered him on paper."

Grafton had worked for fifteen years as a professional writer before rechanneled rage propelled her to the top of the mystery-detective field. "Women mystery writers are at an advantage," she believes. "Women do not have any macho tradition to uphold. We are socialized to be nurturing and nice. Beneath those feelings, however, has always beat an icy rage. When you ask a woman to focus her imagination toward murder, she treats it as fresh turf and brings to it an enthusiasm that may not be that naturally shared by a man, exposed as he is to violent moments all his life."

Kinsey Millhone, Grafton's creation, has a "very sassy nature" and "views the world with a cold eye and will say things people only think." Grafton says that although Kinsey is thinner, braver, and younger than her creator, she is perhaps the woman she might have been if "I had not married young and had children." Grafton is one of a trio of writers of mysteries—Sara Paretsky and Linda Barnes are the others—whose detective heroines know how to manage rage and, unlike many women in real life, are able to express it through their work.

Filigrees of Coral: The Art of Frida Kahlo

Mexican painter Frida Kahlo, born in 1907, channeled the energy of rage into self-portraits the author Martha Zamora calls "brushed with anguish."[12] Her paintings are beautifully mythic and fascinating yet energized by unspeakable suffering and devastating pain. She painted herself cracked open and weeping beside her extracted heart, hemorrhaging during a miscarriage, anesthetized on a hospital trolley, sleeping with a skeleton.

In 1932, when Kahlo set out to make a painting of every year in her tortured life, she began by envisioning her own birth. *My Birth* is a surreal canvas that incorporates rage at her mother and rage at her own recent miscarriage with the stark yet poignant message: Through pain and rage, we give birth to ourselves. The large-headed baby who emerges from the outspread legs of its shrouded mother in the painting is both Frida herself and the dead baby she has just lost. Literally a still life of female grief, Kahlo's birth image reminds us of Medusa—a mother whose progeny are death, courage, and art.

Kahlo believed she first experienced rage with the birth of her sister Christina eleven months after her own birth, when she felt abandoned by both her mother and her nurse Nana, who was banished from the household for drinking. Kahlo's sense of loss is vividly depicted in *My Nurse and I*. In this painting, which her biographer, Hayden Herrera, calls a "double self-portrait," she suckles at the breast of a dark creative muse.

The two figures here are the strong, fertile muse as wet nurse,

My Nurse and I *by Frida Kahlo (1937)*
In this painting, Kahlo imagines herself with the head of a grown woman and the body of an infant sucking at the breast of a majestic wet nurse. The nurse, a Mexican earth mother, wears a death mask while her breast is a network of plants feeding the artist's imagination.

whose identity is disguised behind a dark pre-Columbian mask, and the emotionally vulnerable Frida with the head of an adult woman and the body of an infant girl. Kahlo seems to be saying that a woman must feed her vulnerable little girl from the sources of female creativity: her dark primitive side, her dreams, her history, and her cultural roots.

At twenty-two, she married the Mexican painter Diego Rivera, who was then forty-three and a muralist of world renown. Their marriage was passionate, comradely, and tempestuous, punctuated by their mutual infidelities. Frida had affairs with such men as the sculptor Isamu Noguchi and the exiled revolutionary Leon Trotsky, as well as with other women, yet she experienced intense rage over one particular adultery of Diego's. "I suffered two accidents in my life," Kahlo once said. "One in which a streetcar knocked me down . . . the other was Diego."[13] She was referring to his affair with her younger sister, Christina. This deep betrayal led to the breakup of the marriage in 1939 and to a startling painting called *Memory*.

Frida is depicted as a wounded woman; hanging at her sides are the costumes of her former identities. To the left, a hanger holds the girlish white dress of an innocence now discarded. To the right is her Tehunana costume with one arm of flesh. As a memento of her desirability and feminine powers, each empty dress represents a separate death.

Memory is also Frida's expression of rage and pain at Diego's betrayal. "As always," Herrera comments, "she used bodily wounds to suggest psychic injury." At the center of this painting stands a desexualized Frida with cropped hair and wearing conservative clothes that cover up her sensuality. Her disembodied heart pumps rage as blood into the world around her. A sword balanced like two careless Cupids pierces the empty space where her heart was; her arms are severed like Venus's, while the foot injured in the streetcar accident is bloated and swathed in bandages.

In self-portrait after self-portrait, Frida Kahlo's outraged gaze assaults the viewer. Yet unlike many women whose fury tortures them, Frida was able, in the words of her beloved Diego, "to open her chest and heart to reveal the biological truth of her feelings." Although Kahlo's works might seem to be the ultimate in self-indulgence, she painted them in order to transcend her personal torment. The two hundred works she produced before she died at the age of forty-seven compel us to look at her beauty, pain, and rage and to examine and acknowledge the darkness in ourselves.

Medusa's magical fluid is already in women's veins. It is the rocket fuel that can take them wherever they want to go. Rage transmuted into energy is a powerful weapon for change but must be guided by forgiveness, the final stage in a woman's transformation of her anger. Bitterness and cravings for personal vengeance are natural responses to betrayals, particularly following those falls from innocence that leave us staggering. When a woman holds on to her rage, it becomes a poison circulating in her bloodstream; when she transforms it, rage can become determination, creativity, courage, and passion.

In his book *Real Magic,* Wayne Dyer writes that it is useful to think of betrayals and trespasses as snake bites: "When you are bitten by a snake there are two sources of pain. One is the bite itself, which cannot be unbitten. It happened, it hurt, and you have the mark to prove it. You then go on from there and learn how to avoid snakes in your life. The second source of pain is the venom that is now circulating through you. No one has ever died from a snake bite—it is the aftershock of the venom circulating through the body that is fatal."[14]

Letting go of rage begins when a woman defangs the snakes in her life by seeing them as flawed human beings sent to teach her important lessons. Perceiving enemies as mere mortals and not as mythic monsters allows her to see herself more accurately as an autonomous human being distinct from friend and foe alike. Separating and forgiving create a climate for the assimilation of rage and the possibility of love where Medusa's coils are "not snakes but rainbows." The opposite sides of rage are love and compassion—love of self, love for and from others. Forgiveness follows when we choose to close those painful episodes in our lives and slip off rage like a dress that doesn't fit us anymore.

The Medusa Myth

Retold by Arnold Weinstein

Medusa was Athena's loveliest handmaiden;
golden strands of hair capturing the sunlight
crowned the rare fairness of her face.
She was the human granddaughter of Gaea,
goddess of Earth. Many hopeful young men
   pursued her.
But she was wary of their ways.
And when the sea god Poseidon wanted her
she refused him too. Some say
he came to her as a sinewy stallion
and turning her into a mare took her
in Athena's sacred grove.
Others tell simply of the rape of a maiden
by a relentless god, in a goddess's temple.

Athena, goddess of wisdom and war, was a virgin;
she watched the violation of her temple
hiding her divine disgust behind her shield.
Then fury swept her godly reason away,
she transformed the ravaged girl into a dragon;
Medusa's soft shoulders sprouted hideous wings,
the delicate hands became bronze claws,
fangs hung where her teeth had gleamed,
and a long tongue lapped her chin.
In place of Medusa's soft bright hair,
asps and vipers writhed from the roots
encircling her once lovely features. Finally

the goddess put a stare in Medusa's eyes—
a stare that turned men to stone.

Medusa was helpless, bewildered, ashamed
of what she did not commit, repulsed
by her own grotesquery, terrified
of petrifying her loved ones with a look.
She flew to exile on her loathesome wings
and marooned her horrific self on a dismal island,
hideously, piteously, wailing to the winds
mourning her torn innocence, her beauty, her
    sanctity.
Debauched by a god, deformed by a goddess,
she turned the sailors to stone who sailed by
to stare upon her hideous form, and they sank
into the sea, their own tombstones.
Then, looking into the inky water she saw the ugly
reflection of her pain. She seemed at times
to frighten even herself.

Perseus was a brash and brave young man
whose mother was Danaë; Zeus his father
had come to her bed as a shower of gold,
Perseus was born of this sly union.
The son and mother, abandoned by the god,
wandered until they came to a land
ruled by the evil tyrant Polydectes,
who wanted Danaë for his wife.
He offered them uncharitable hospitality,
hating the boy for his kinship to the gods.
To appease Polydectes, Perseus promised him
a prize: the famed Medusa's head as trophy.

The tyrant urged the boy on,
to die among the rocks that once were men
who dared glimpse Medusa's snaky head.
But the gods are a close family: Wise Athena
gave her father's child her mirrored shield
to deflect Medusa's deadly gaze.
Wily Hermes gave him an unbreakable sword
and told him how to find the Grey Ladies,
strange wrinkled crones who knew the whereabouts
of the monstrous Medusa.

Perseus came to the dismal cave of the Grey Ladies
and asked them how to slay Medusa.
The ancient hags said no one could slay Medusa
without the helmet that could make him invisible
and the winged sandals that could make him fly,
and the magic pouch that could hold Medusa's head.
When Perseus asked for the magic objects,
The three hags refused to tell where he could find
    them.
The Grey Ladies had among them only one tooth
and a single eye to share among them.
So they were passing them one to the other.
Perseus snatched the eye and tooth
and in so doing, forced the Grey Ladies
to reveal their secret.

The Grey Ladies told Perseus of the Stygian Nymphs
who were the keepers of the winged shoes,
the magic pouch, and the cap of invisibility.
Perseus sailed to the home of these nymphs,
glad place of joy and revelry,

and told them of his tyrannized mother
and his need of the treasures in their keeping.
His sorrowful voice enchanted the nymphs;
they put into his hands the magical things.
He promised to return. They're waiting still.

Now with the cap and pouch and Hermes' sword,
Perseus wearing the winged shoes flew to Medusa's
    island.
There, as her two Gorgon sisters slept,
Medusa beat the air with her hideous wings
and pierced the sky with her pitiful screeches
as her snakes hissed and her brass claws clacked.
But Perseus making great circles in the sky,
looking into the mirroring shield, wearing
the cap of invisibility, swooped down to his destiny.
Slashing backwards he beheaded the dread Medusa
slicing through skin and bone and sinew.
Then, seizing the trophy by its snaky curls,
he flew off with his swarming pouch.
Medusa's suffering was over.
The only protest was the serpents' hiss.

It has been told that when Medusa was beheaded
the blood spurting from the artery in her neck
gave birth to Pegasus, the winged horse of creativity,
and to Chrysador of the golden sword.
From her snakes' blood came healing fluids
as well as the venom that causes war;
even on Athena's shield, Medusa's emblem frightens
    all enemies.

When Perseus rested Medusa's head at the water's
  edge
the soft ferns and sea grasses felt her power
and became hard filigree of precious coral.
And some poets tell how Athena, listening to the hiss
in Medusa's hair, invented the art of music.

Workshop: How Enraged Are You?

Although one woman we interviewed was convinced that all women are enraged, others were unsure how to name their constellation of feelings. The following can serve as a guide and reference to determine your rage quotient.

For each of the questions, give yourself two points for often, one point for sometimes, and zero for never. After completing the test, add up your score and compare your results with our table at the end.

One: General	Often	Some-times	Never
1. I believe that I'm at a disadvantage because I'm female.	___	___	___
2. I think men as a group "just don't get it."	___	___	___
3. I'm uncomfortable expressing my anger and rage openly.	___	___	___
4. I don't seem to be able to communicate my needs.	___	___	___
5. I continually try to please people.	___	___	___
6. I seek approval for most of my actions.	___	___	___
7. I feel like a doormat most of the time.	___	___	___
8. I hide my real self and my feelings.	___	___	___
9. People are always disappointing me.	___	___	___
10. I often get into arguments.	___	___	___
11. People think of me as a bitch.	___	___	___

	Often	Some-times	Never
12. I am highly competitive.	_____	_____	_____
13. I lack assertiveness.	_____	_____	_____
14. I am easily victimized.	_____	_____	_____

Two: Family and Childhood

	Often	Some-times	Never
1. My parents let me know they were unhappy I was a girl.	_____	_____	_____
2. My parents discouraged me from doing things because I was a girl.	_____	_____	_____
3. My family members didn't respect my need for privacy at home.	_____	_____	_____
4. My mother didn't prepare me for the physical changes of adolescence.	_____	_____	_____
5. One or both of my parents were alcoholic.	_____	_____	_____
6. I was sexually abused as a child.	_____	_____	_____
7. There are long periods of time when I have no communication with my mother.	_____	_____	_____
8. My parents never paid attention to what I had to say.	_____	_____	_____
9. I was physically abused as a child.	_____	_____	_____
10. My family didn't allow me to voice my anger.	_____	_____	_____
11. My brother/sister was the favorite.	_____	_____	_____
12. My parents fought.	_____	_____	_____

Three: Relationships with Men

	Often	Some-times	Never
1. I'm always the one to give the strokes.	_____	_____	_____

	Often	Some-times	Never
2. I always say "I love you" before a man does.	____	____	____
3. I can be pressured into going to bed with a man earlier in a relationship than I want to.	____	____	____
4. If a man doesn't call the next day, I spend hours wondering what I did wrong.	____	____	____
5. I will change my style, hair color, tone of voice, shoe height—you name it—for a man I'm interested in, even though it's not me.	____	____	____
6. I work harder on our relationship than he does.	____	____	____
7. I'm uncomfortable asking for what I want in bed.	____	____	____
8. I'm financially dependent on him.	____	____	____
9. I'm emotionally dependent on him.	____	____	____
10. I'm easily swept away and then disappointed.	____	____	____
11. I put all my eggs in the relationship basket.	____	____	____
12. I'm never the one to choose the movie or the restaurant.	____	____	____
13. I feel furious when my man talks to another woman for any length of time at a party.	____	____	____
14. I'm never the one to hang up first from a phone call.	____	____	____

	Often	Some-times	Never
Four: Rage at the Workplace			
1. My work environment is anxiety producing.	____	____	____
2. I have seen or felt sexual harassment at work.	____	____	____
3. I have felt gender discrimination while applying for a job.	____	____	____
4. I do not feel I can talk openly with my employer about problems I encounter at work.	____	____	____
5. I do not receive an appropriate salary for the work I do.	____	____	____
6. Women do not have equal opportunities in my field.	____	____	____
7. My coworkers are extremely competitive with me.	____	____	____
8. I always feel I am being undermined by others who want my job.	____	____	____
9. Others take credit for work that I have done.	____	____	____
10. I never openly voice my objections if I am asked to take on more work than I'm responsible for or can handle.	____	____	____

Five: Rage and Mind/Body

	Often	Some-times	Never
1. When excessively angry, I feeling a burning sensation or pressure in my head.	____	____	____
2. I experience chronic headaches.	____	____	____
3. I have an overwhelming sense of dread.	____	____	____

	Often	Some-times	Never
4. When I am really angry and there's no one else to blame, I cut myself.	___	___	___
5. I seem to have memory lapses.	___	___	___
6. I drink alcohol to excess.	___	___	___
7. I am a workaholic.	___	___	___
8. I struggle with weight and bingeing.	___	___	___
9. I chain-smoke.	___	___	___
10. I experience panic attacks.	___	___	___
11. I feel depressed.	___	___	___
12. I feel phobic when traveling or meeting people.	___	___	___
13. I have insomnia.	___	___	___
14. I spend money or shop compulsively.	___	___	___
15. I take drugs.	___	___	___
16. I grind or clench my teeth.	___	___	___
17. I have pain in my face and jaws.	___	___	___
18. I have pain in my neck and shoulder area.	___	___	___
19. I experience muscle constriction in my body.	___	___	___
20. When I become very angry, my vision blurs or becomes foggy or dark.	___	___	___

Six: Behaviors and Dealing with Rage

1. I hide my real self and its feelings.	___	___	___
2. I create allies and collude against others.	___	___	___
3. I need to be noticed or to be the center of attention in every conversation or situation.	___	___	___

	Often	Some-times	Never
4. I have feelings of entitlement: "I deserve something just because I exist."	_____	_____	_____
5. I overreact to seemingly trivial events.	_____	_____	_____
6. I suffer from low self-esteem.	_____	_____	_____
7. When I get into an argument, I slam doors, break dishes, throw things.	_____	_____	_____
8. I feel like another person possesses me when I am very angry.	_____	_____	_____
9. Instead of confronting the person I am angry with, I get back at him/her through gossip.	_____	_____	_____
10. I feel powerful expressing rage.	_____	_____	_____
11. Sarcasm is one of my favorite weapons.	_____	_____	_____
12. I will go for long periods not speaking to someone with whom I am furious.	_____	_____	_____
13. I imagine elaborate revenges.	_____	_____	_____
14. I feel guilty and apologize after expressing anger.	_____	_____	_____
15. I routinely say, "I'm premenstrual" or "I'm feeling bitchy."	_____	_____	_____
16. I act impulsively when faced with a rage-inducing situation.	_____	_____	_____

Your Rage Quotient

The maximum score is 186 points:
    Up to 40 points: Low-grade anger
    40 to 80 points: Healthy outrage
    80 to 120 points: Moderately enraged
    120 to 172 points: Filled with rage and unresolved anger

Workshop: Channeling Your Rage

Recognizing the signs and symptoms of rage is the first step in a woman's transformative process. Excavating your rage, reframing the way you think about anger, learning how to assert yourself, and confronting fears can bring the possibility of forgiveness and the promise of renewed energy.

Assessing Your Beliefs About Rage and Anger

What we have learned about anger in our families of origin or from the culture has unconsciously shaped our ways of relating to others and of resolving conflicts. Which of the following beliefs about rage and anger do you hold? Check each true statement.

_____ A woman who is good or feminine does not express rage.

_____ Anger and rage do not belong in a healthy relationship.

_____ People will reject or abandon me if I get angry.

_____ If I become enraged, I will lose all control and go crazy.

_____ Anger is one of the deadliest sins.

_____ When I feel rage, I will throw something, hurt, or even injure.

_____ Rage isn't worth the time.

_____ If people feel anger toward me, it must be my fault.

_____ If someone gets angry at me, he/she doesn't love me anymore.

_____ I deserve to feel guilty if I feel rage.

_____ If I get angry, I am a selfish person.

_____ Rage is frightening.

Yes, rage can be frightening. But none of the other statements listed here are true. If you have checked any one other than the last, you need to reevaluate these beliefs. Becoming aware of your false beliefs and deciding which myths you can discard are the first steps in dealing constructively with rage. Challenge these false beliefs by examining and absorbing the following realities:

Rage is a basic instinct; it serves to protect us.

Anger and rage are normal and healthy emotions.

Rage is a feeling that affects the whole body and must be examined.

I can feel rage without expressing it directly.

It is okay for me to experience feelings of rage throughout my body.

I can work with my rage and turn it into positive energy.

It is better for me to feel rage, then take the appropriate actions and steps.

My rage tells me when someone has crossed me or is exploiting me.

My rage tells me what my beliefs and values are.

My rage tells me I am alive; that I am a healthy, feeling person.

Conducting an Inner Dialogue

One of the ways of accessing rage is to meditate, delve into past memories, and put your feelings on paper in a rage journal. Find a quiet place and lie or sit in a relaxed, comfortable position. Close your eyes and take ten deep breaths, counting to six on each inhalation. When you have finished your breathing and with your eyes closed, try to think of your earliest memory of your own rage. Recall the experience. What did you feel? How did those closest to you react? Was it a personal frustration or did someone else provoke you in some way? Describe the most recent incident when you felt the same way.

Next, think back to your family of origin. How did people handle their anger? How did members of your family handle differences of opinion or conflicts? How did they resolve problems? What did they look like when they were enraged? Were they silent? Was there physical or emotional abuse? What tone of voice did they use when angry? How were problems resolved in your family of origin? Were you allowed to express angry feelings? Were you punished if you did? What were the punishments?

When you have completed this meditation exercise, record your memories and the feelings invoked in your journal.

Writing Your Rage History

Write out your rage history, logging major incidents, betrayals, and circumstances that incensed you in the past. For each incident, describe your feelings at the time, the result of your actions, and whether it was effective.

You may want to tape several pieces of paper together and create a time line to go with your rage history. Ruling off your paper vertically, allowing one-half inch per year, you can then write in the significant incidents with dates.

Identifying Your Rage Triggers

Rage is rooted in a woman's fears and individual insecurities and is stirred up when she feels threatened or under stress. What makes your blood boil will depend on your personal rage triggers: that person, that frustrating situation, or that outrageous injustice that makes you see red.

Make a list of all your fears. Compare them with the feelings and emotions collected from your rage history; they may include fears of abandonment, economic insecurity, lack of power, imperfection, falling apart. Are these themes and constants in your life? To find out what threatens you and under what conditions, ask yourself the following questions each time you are upset.

What is threatening me? A look? A comment? A criticism? Social inequality?

Do I feel threatened by an individual? an individual's action? feelings within?

How does this person, action, or feeling threaten me?
    Does it insult my intelligence?
    Does it question my skills or competency?
    Does it undermine my reputation or character?
    Does it humiliate or dismiss me because of my gender?
    Does it go against what I believe?

Sometimes when we begin to explore our own rage triggers, we discover a long history of the same problem. We might ask:

Is my present reaction part of a pattern? Have I reacted similarly in another situation?
Is this threatening occasion like one I experienced in childhood? in adolescence?
Has my reaction to this type of threat always been the same?

By identifying your fears and behavior, finding rage triggers and patterns, you can begin to work alone or with a therapist to understand them and overcome them.

Identifying Addiction to Rage

Rage is a conditioned response ingrained from past hurts. Many women have told us they feel "powerful" when expressing rage, and sometimes this sense of power increases in proportion to the intensity of the reaction. If expressions of rage are chronic or the only means a woman has in order to feel powerful and in control, expressing rage can become an actual addiction, becoming her habitual way of relating to others, meeting inner needs, or feeling validated. To check for symptoms of rage addiction, consider the following questions:

Do I use rage to punish others? Whom do I punish? My partner or
spouse? My children? My parents? Intimate friends? Coworkers?
Myself?

Where do I express my rage? At home? At work? At a friend's?
Alone?

Do I distance others with my rage to avoid conflicts or hurt?

Do I become enraged so I do not have to face tough personal
issues?

Do I project my rage on others, blaming them for my
shortcomings?

If you find that you abuse rage or are addicted to using rage for
feeling powerful or expressing real needs, keep a journal of incidents
and angry outbursts. This will help you track your self-destructive habits and bring your impulsive behavior under conscious control.

Making Amends and Forgiveness

List and identify all the people who have been hurt by your rage and
tell them in your journal that you are sorry. List and identify all the
people who have hurt and betrayed you and forgive them. In forgiving them, you don't need to love or even like them. Just let them go
with your blessings. Perhaps write or telephone a friend or family
member you haven't spoken with in months or years; holding on
to grudges only empowers the other person. Hostility breeds more
anger, and revenge can backfire; forgiveness restores balance, inner
harmony, and a sense of well-being.

Imaging

Some therapists suggest that their patients engage in imaging, asking
them to picture an ideal or workable resolution to a rage-producing

problem. To practice imaging, you might try one or more of the following exercises:

Form an image of how you would feel empowered.

Picture yourself responding in a way that would make you proud.

Remember a time in your past when you handled a rageful incident well. What did you do? Could you use that technique in this situation?

Think of someone whom you think handles situations well. What would she do?

Can you adopt any of those techniques to the present situation?

You may also use these imaging techniques to learn from negative experiences, reframing them into positive behaviors.

Think of a time when you were enraged and weren't pleased with your response.

In retrospect, how do you wish you had handled it?

Form an image of yourself handling it differently.

What, specifically, would you have done?

Can you incorporate any of that more ideal behavior into the present situation?

Learning to Be Assertive

Assertiveness is an antidote to rage. When women are assertive, they abandon their position of helplessness by creating an equal playing field on which to face others as equals. They stand up for themselves and are able to set limits. Assertive women can say no, set and realize goals, and express what they really think and believe themselves. Being assertive means declaring who you really are without trampling on the territory or feelings of others; it also means listening and empathizing with other people; it means picking fights wisely and stating your ideas and rights in a noncombative, direct but forceful way. Asserting and declaring your rights moves you out of the role of the victim and teaches others that you are unwilling to be victimized. Small acts, such speaking up when someone cuts in line, telling a caller that Sunday morning before nine o'clock is off-limits, and asking a restaurant hostess for a more comfortable table are incremental steps toward learning self-assertion.

Immediate Relief for Runaway Rage

Sometimes there's a crisis. Emergency measures are needed. The following quick fixes will provide immediate relief when rage takes over mind and body.

Do something physical. Tai chi and yoga require deep breathing and muscle extension, which calm the body and mind. Aerobics, running, pace walking, StairMaster, dance, whatever your body work of choice is, will serve you well to defuse rage and quiet the adrenaline rush to your system.

Take a time-out. If possible, visit a park, an art museum, or a church for half an hour to divert your focus and calm your senses. Or lie down and play a relaxation tape or pleasant, uplifting music.

Try Progressive Muscle Relaxation (PMR). Lie down in a peaceful room where there will be no interruptions or distracting noises, take ten deep breaths, and visualize, in your mind's eye, a favorite spot where you feel warm and secure. It may be a sunlit beach or a forest with dappled light. Imagine the warm sun penetrating every inch of your body as you relax each part, starting with the top of your head, moving to the eyelids, ears, jaws, neck, and shoulders, and then relaxing your arms, hips, thighs, calves, feet, toes.

Try Rescue Remedy. A Bach's flower remedy, this is an herbal for frayed nerves and out-of-control feelings. Six to ten drops of Rescue Remedy will calm you and allow you to examine the source of your rage and to consider what to do about it in a calm and more objective manner. (The herb valerian, available from health food stores in liquid form, is also effective.)

Meditate. Any number of books will describe how to meditate, a process where your heart rate slows and your breath becomes quieter. Concentrating on the breath or a specific word or mantra will lead the mind away from obsessive thoughts and into stillness, that calm place at the center of being.

When to Seek Professional Help

Rage is just one symptom in the complex psychology of human beings, but when tantrums, bitterness, or sarcasm define a woman's personality, interfere with her interpersonal relationships, disrupt her work, or affect the quality of her life, then professional intervention may be indicated. Rage may disguise itself as depression, may underlie phobias and panic reactions, or may cloak itself behind compulsive eating disorders. You need to find a qualified professional knowledgeable in women's issues who can assess your situation, discuss appropriate approaches, and develop a treatment plan with and for you.

Notes

Introduction: Rage Comes of Age

1. May Sarton, *Selected Poems,* eds. Serena Sue Hilsinger and Lois Byrnes (New York: W. W. Norton, 1978), p. 160.

Chapter 1. The Birth of Female Rage

1. Debbie Reynolds and David Patrick Columbia, *Debbie* (New York: Pocket Books, 1988), p. 28.
2. Andrew Morton, *Diana: Her True Story* (New York: Pocket Books, 1992), p. 95.
3. Michael Lewis, M.D., "The Development of Anger and Rage," in *Rage, Power, and Aggression: The Role of Affect in Motivation, Development, and Adaptation,* eds. Robert A. Glock, M.D., and Steven P. Roose, M.D. (New Haven: Yale University Press, 1993), p. 151.
4. Henri Parens, M.D., "Rage Towards Self and Others in Early Childhood," in *Rage, Power, and Aggression.*
5. Lucy Lafarge, M.D., "The Early Determinants of Penis Envy," in *Rage, Power, and Aggression,* p. 85.
6. Camille Paglia, *Sexual Personae* (New Haven: Yale University Press, 1990), p. 110.
7. Louise J. Kaplan, *Female Perversions: The Temptations of Emma Bovary* (New York: Doubleday, 1991), pp. 92–93.
8. Ibid., p. 99.
9. Ibid.
10. Dorothy Dinnerstein, *The Mermaid and the Minotaur: Sexual Arrangements and Human Malaise* (New York: Harper Perennial, 1976), p. 47.
11. Milan Kundera, *The Unbearable Lightness of Being* (New York: Harper & Row, 1984), p. 61.
12. Elizabeth Debold, Marie Wilson, and Idelisse Malave, *Mother-Daughter Revolution: From Betrayal to Power* (New York: Addison-Wesley, 1993), p. 234.

13. Ibid., p. 231.
14. Judith Levine, *My Enemy, My Love: Man-Hating and Ambivalence in Women's Lives* (New York: Doubleday, 1992), p. 200.
15. Elizabeth Cady Stanton, "Eighty Years and More" in *Growing Up Female in America,* ed. Eve Merriman (Boston: Beacon Press, 1971), pp. 54–55.
16. Debold, Wilson, and Malave, p. 232.
17. Linda Schierse Leonard, *The Wounded Woman: Healing the Father-Daughter Relationship* (Boston: Shambala, 1983), p. 11.
18. Jane Smiley, *A Thousand Acres* (New York: Fawcett Columbine, 1991).
19. Robert Bly, *Iron John* (New York: Vintage Books, 1990), p. 92.
20. Ibid., p. 97.

Chapter 2. The Face of Rage

1. Naomi Wolf, *The Beauty Myth: How Images of Beauty Are Used Against Women* (New York: Anchor-Doubleday, 1991), p. 69.
2. Harriet Goldhor Lerner, *Women in Therapy* (New York: Harper & Row, 1988), p. 54.
3. Aeschylus, *The Oresteia,* trans. Robert Fagles (New York: Penguin, 1975), p. 233.
4. The source for this description of the Bacchae is Euripides, *The Bacchae,* trans. Michael Cacoyannis (New York: Penguin, 1982), pp. 40–41.
5. Jamake Highwater, *Myth and Sexuality* (New York: American Library, 1990), p. 64.
6. John Updike, *The Witches of Eastwick* (New York: Alfred A. Knopf, 1984), p. 75.
7. Teresa Bernardez-Bonesatti, M.D., "Women and Anger: Conflicts with Aggression in Contemporary Women," *Journal of the American Medical Women's Association* 33: 1978, 215–219.
8. Sigmund Freud, "Medusa's Head," in *Sexuality and the Psychology of Love,* ed. Philip Reiff (New York: Collier, 1963), pp. 212–213.
9. Philip E. Slater, *The Glory of Hera: Greek Mythology and the Greek Family* (Princeton: Princeton University Press, 1992), pp. 14–23.
10. Ovid, *The Metamorphoses,* trans. Horace Gregory (New York: Penguin, 1960), pp. 384–385.

11. Edith Hamilton, *Mythology: Timeless Tales of Gods and Heroes* (New York: Signet NAL, 1969), p. 284.

12. Hélène Cixous, "The Laugh of Medusa," in *Critical Theory Since 1965,* eds. Hazard Adams and Roy Searle (Tallahassee: Florida State University Press, 1986), p. 315.

13. Judith Levine, *My Enemy, My Love: Man-Hating and Ambivalence in Women's Lives* (New York: Doubleday, 1992), p. 163.

14. Bram Dijkstra, *Idols of Perversity: Fantasies of Feminine Evil in Fin-de-Siècle Culture* (New York: Oxford University Press, 1986), p. 309.

15. Bram Stoker, *Dracula* (New York: Signet, 1992).

16. Anne Roiphe, "The Hatred Behind Sexual Aggression in *Hers,*" *Glamour,* April 1993, p. 262.

17. "Report Documents Tailhook Debauchery," *Albany Times-Union,* April 4, 1993, p. A-4.

18. Ethel Pearson, *Dreams of Love and Fateful Encounters: The Power of Romantic Passion* (New York: Penguin, 1988), p. 92.

19. Jon Tevlin, "Why Women Are Mad as Hell," *Glamour,* March 1992, p. 206; Richard Schickel, "Gender Bender," *Time,* June 24, 1991, pp. 52–57; Richard Alleva, "Over the Edge," *Commonweal,* September 13, 1991, pp. 513–515.

20. Nancy Friday, *Women on Top: How Real Life Has Changed Women's Sexual Fantasies* (New York: Pocket Books, 1991), p. 170.

Chapter 3. The Inner World of Rage

1. Gerrald F. Rosenbaum, M.D., *The Menninger Letter* (Topeka, Kansas: Menninger Foundation, March 1994), p. 7.

2. Dana Crowley Jack, *Silencing the Self: Women and Depression* (Cambridge, Massachusetts: Harvard University Press, 1991), pp. 141, 168–169.

3. Roy Schafer, "Women in the Maze of Power and Rage," in *Rage, Power, and Aggression: The Role of Affect in Motivation, Development, and Adaptation,* eds. Robert A. Glock, M.D., and Steven P. Roose, M.D. (New Haven: Yale University Press, 1993), p. 18.

4. Ibid., p. 28.

5. Linda Schierse Leonard, *The Wounded Woman: Healing the Father-Daughter Relationship* (Boston: Shambala, 1983), p. 119.

6. H. P. Laughlin, *The Ego and Its Defenses* (New York: Jacob Aronson, 1979), p. 114.

7. Ibid.

8. Naomi Wolf, *The Beauty Myth: How Images of Beauty Are Used Against Women* (New York: Anchor-Doubleday, 1991), p. 31.

9. Ellyn Kaschak, *Engendered Lives* (New York: Basic Books, 1992), p. 192.

10. Ibid., p. 205.

11. Heidi Waldrop, *Showing Up for Life: A Recovering Overeater's Triumph Over Compulsion* (New York: Ballantine, 1990).

12. Ibid., p. 63.

13. Marion Woodman, *The Owl Was a Baker's Daughter: Obesity, Anorexia Nervosa and the Repressed Feminine* (Toronto: Inner City, 1980), p. 57.

14. Judith Brisman, "Di's Private Battle," *People*, August 3, 1992, p. 61.

15. Ibid.

16. Geneen Roth, *Breaking Free from Compulsive Eating* (New York: Signet, 1986), p. 159.

17. Elizabeth Sporkin, Joyce Wagner, Craig Tomashoff, "A Terrible Hunger," *People*, February 17, 1992, pp. 92–95.

18. Ann Landers, "Self-Mutilators Stop Cutting Themselves," *Albany Times-Union*, February 24, 1993.

19. Louise Kaplan, *Female Perversions* (New York: Doubleday, 1992), p. 372.

20. Ibid., p. 373.

21. Ibid., p. 385.

22. Ibid.

23. This definition is taken from the *Diagnostic and Statistical Manual of Mental Disorders (DSM III)*, Robert L. Spitzer, M.D., ed., The American Psychiatric Association, 1980, p. 253.

24. Kaschak, p. 246.

Chapter 4. Rage and Relationships

1. "Sleepless in Seattle's Nora Ephron," *Glamour*, August 1993, p. 148.

2. Charles Whitfield, M.D., *Boundaries and Relationships: Knowing, Protecting, and Enjoying the Self* (Deerfield Beach, Florida: Health Communications, 1993), p. 126.

3. Harriet Goldhor Lerner, *Women in Therapy* (New York: Harper & Row, 1988), p. 158.

4. Gloria Steinem, *Revolution from Within* (Boston: Little, Brown, 1992), p. 266.

5. Barry Dym, Ph.D., and Michael L. Glenn, M.D., *Couples: Exploring and Understanding the Cycles of Intimate Relationships* (New York: HarperCollins, 1993), p. 85.

6. Frank Pittman, M.D., "The Nineties Man: Why Is He So Scared of Us?" *Glamour,* April 15, 1993, pp. 199–201.

7. Dalma Heyn, *The Erotic Silence of the American Wife* (New York: Signet, 1992), p. 65.

8. See "What Is Love?" *Time,* February 15, 1993, pp. 47–52, and "Love: Have We Learned Anything Yet?" *Psychology Today,* April 27, 1993, pp. 56–60.

9. Anastasia Toufexis, "The Right Chemistry," *Time,* February 15, 1993, p. 50.

10. Ibid., pp. 50–51.

11. Dym and Glenn, p. 85.

12. Quoted in "What Is Love?" *Time,* February 15, 1993, p. 51.

13. Dym and Glenn, pp. 86–87.

14. Ethel Pearson, *Dreams of Love and Fateful Encounters: The Power of Romantic Passion* (New York: Penguin, 1988), p. 331.

Chapter 5. The Rage of Age

1. Barbara Walker, *The Crone: Woman of Age, Wisdom, and Power* (New York: Harper & Row, 1985), p. 100.

2. Images of three wise women who act in unison are familiar from fairy tales, myths, and drama. There are the ancient Fates who spun and cut the thread of life; the three witches in *Macbeth;* and fairy-tale godmothers who always come in groups of threes. These females appear in stories of significant life passages: birth, puberty, marriage, and death. Their gifts, prophecies, and curses establish them as women of power and insight, and vessels of truth.

3. "Images of Age," *Psychology Today,* November-December 1993, p. 74.

4. Information from Madeline Bennett is taken from an extensive interview and sections from *Sudden Endings: Why Husbands, Wives, and Lovers Walk Out on Long, Loving Relationships* (New York: Pinnacle, 1991).

5. Germaine Greer, *The Change* (New York: Alfred A. Knopf, 1992), pp. 118–119.

6. Gail Sheehy, *The Silent Passage* (New York: Pocket Books, 1993), p. 81.

7. Robert Bly, *Iron John* (New York: Vintage Books, 1990), pp. 11–12.

8. Jean Harris, *Stranger in Two Worlds* (New York: Zebra Books, 1986), p. 197.

9. Diane Wood Middlebrook, *Anne Sexton: A Biography* (Boston: Houghton-Mifflin, 1991), p. 16.

10. Alice Walker, *Possessing the Secret of Joy* (New York: Pocket Books, 1993).

11. Because this altering of female genitals makes sexual intercourse difficult and painful, the procedure serves in tribal life to keep women in their place as childbearers and nurturers rather than as pleasure-seeking autonomous adults.

Chapter 6. Rage at Other Women

1. "Attitudes," *New Woman,* April 1993, p. 52.

2. Jean Shinoda Bolen, *The Goddesses in Every Women: A New Psychology of Women* (New York: Harper & Row), p. 81.

3. Quoted in "A Thump on the Head to . . . ," *New Woman,* September 1992, p. 168.

4. Quoted in "Attitudes," *New Woman,* July 1993, p. 152.

5. Peter Van Sommers, *Jealousy: What It Is and Who Feels It* (New York: Penguin, 1988), p. 86.

6. Lyn Brown and Carol Gilligan, *Meeting at the Crossroads* (Cambridge, Massachusetts: Harvard University Press, 1992), pp. 100–101.

7. Madonna Kolbenschlag, *Kiss Sleeping Beauty Good-Bye, Breaking the Spell of Feminine Myths and Models* (New York: Harper & Row, 1988), p. 43.

8. Ibid., p. 34.

9. Francine Klagsbrun, *Mixed Feelings: Love, Hate, Rivalry, and Reconciliation Among Brothers and Sisters* (New York: Bantam, 1992).

10. Ibid., p. 99.

11. Christine Alt, "Viewpoint," *Glamour,* March 1992, p. 150.

12. Camille Paglia, *Sex, Art and American Culture* (New York: Vintage, 1992), p. 53.

13. "Why Women Are Angry: Enough Is Enough, They Say," *Boston Globe*, April 29, 1992, p. 43.

14. Audre Lorde, *Sister Outsider: Essays and Speeches* (Freedom, Col.: The Crossing Press, 1984), p. 145.

Chapter 7. Awakenings

1. "A Tale of Abuse," *Newsweek*, December 12, 1988, p. 56.

2. "The Saga of Hedda Nussbaum," *People*, December 5, 1988, p. 34.

3. "A Tale of Abuse," *Newsweek*, December 12, 1988, p. 56.

4. Naomi Wolf, *Fire with Fire* (New York: Random House, 1993), p. 135.

5. Ibid., p. 211.

6. Transcript #271: "Day 3 of the Lorena Bobbitt Trial," CNN & Company: January 12, 1994.

7. Barbara Ehrenreich, "Feminism Confronts Bobbittry," *Newsweek*, January 24, 1994, p. 74.

8. Anne Campbell, *Men, Women, and Aggression* (New York: Basic Books, 1993), p. 18.

9. Amy Fisher with Shelia Weller, *My Story* (New York: Pocket Books, 1993), p. 168.

10. Euripides, *Medea and Other Plays*, trans. Philip Vellacott (New York: Penguin, 1963).

11. All quotations are from "The Medea" in *Euripides*, Rex Warner, trans., and Richmond Lattimore, ed. (Chicago: University of Chicago Press, 1955) and from *Medea*, Alistair Elliot, trans. (London: Oberon Books, 1992).

12. Paul Alexander, *Rough Magic: A Biography of Sylvia Plath* (New York: Penguin, 1991), p. 286.

13. Rita Marker, *Deadly Compassion: The Death of Anne Humphrey and the Truth About Euthanasia* (New York: William Morrow, 1993).

14. Tina Turner with Kurt Loder, *I, Tina* (New York: Avon Books, 1987), p. 172.

15. Betty Friedan, *The Feminine Mystique* (New York: W. W. Norton and Co., 1963), p. 336.

Chapter 8. The Energy of Rage

1. Victoria Secunda, "The New Female Activism," *New Woman*, November 1992, pp. 110–116.

2. Janice Kaplan, "Joan Lunden Bounds Back," *TV Guide,* September 5, 1992, pp. 5–10.

3. Clarissa Pinkola Estés, *Women Who Run with the Wolves* (New York: Ballantine Books, 1992), p. 361.

4. Ibid., p. 353.

5. Deepak Chopra, M. D. *Ageless Body, Timeless Mind* (New York: Harmony Books, 1993), p. 14.

6. Estés, p. 353.

7. Estés, p. 365.

8. Thomas Moore, *Soul Mates: Honoring the Mysteries of Love and Relationship* (New York: HarperCollins, 1994), p. 205.

9. Jane Marcus, "Art and Anger," *Feminist Studies* 4 (February 1978): 94.

10. Paula Bennett, *My Life a Loaded Gun: Dickinson, Plath, Rich and Female Creativity* (Urbana: University of Illinois Press, 1990), pp. 6, 185.

11. This account of Grafton's story is culled from Lorenzo Carcaterra, "B Is for Bestseller," *Writer's Digest,* January 1991, pp. 43–45, and Susan Morgan, "Female Dick," *Interview,* May 1990, pp. 152–154.

12. Martha Zamora, *Frida Kahlo: The Brush of Anguish*, trans. Marilyn Zone Smith (San Francisco: Chronicle, 1990).

13. Hayden Herrera, *Frida Kahlo: The Paintings* (New York: HarperCollins, 1991), p. 55.

14. Dr. Wayne W. Dyer. *Real Magic* (New York: Harper Paperbacks, 1992), pp. 70–71.

Further Reading

Atwood, Margaret. *The Robber Bride*. New York: Nan Talese Doubleday, 1993.

Atwood's suspenseful, topical novel penetrates the dark side of being female and shows how three women allow a psychopathic woman named Zenia into their lives. Zenia is our worst nightmare of a friend and the embodiment of female treachery—she steals husbands, corrupts sons, and embezzles funds. Atwood's trio of friends are bonded not only in their rage toward Zenia but also through childhood rage that has produced dual personalities and passive-aggressive behavior and that sets them up for exploitation.

Bennett, Madeline. *Sudden Endings: Why Husbands, Wives, and Lovers Walk Out on Long, Loving Relationships*. New York: Pinnacle, 1992.

Using her own experience—the discovery that her husband has left her for a man—Bennett explores the sudden-ending syndrome, when a lover or marriage partner abruptly exits a long-standing relationship. This kind of abandonment stirs up powerful emotions such as shame, rage, and rejection as well as mutual fault-finding, legal entanglements, and "bad object rage." Bennett covers the warning signs, what to do if it happens, what to tell the children, and where to get legal and financial advice.

Bepko, Claudia and Jo-Ann Krestan. *Too Good for Her Own Good: Searching for Self and Intimacy in Important Relationships.* New York: HarperPerennial, 1991.

This book is about women trying too hard to be good, and how they feel anger because their own needs are not being met. Often, emotionally overresponsible women feel worthless and unable to live up to their own impossible standards. Bepko and Krestan offer a new "Code of Balance" that tells women how they can nurture themselves as well as take care of others in more healthy ways.

Campbell, Anne. *Men, Women, and Aggression.* New York: Basic Books, 1993.

Criminologist Anne Campbell contends that biology, nurturing, and particularly the opinions women and men hold about aggression determine the patterns of rage in marriages and how couples communicate. Men, she believes, use aggression for control and to compensate for feeling vulnerable, while women think aggression means losing self-control and rely on tears to respond to the stresses of intimate family life.

Chicago, Judy. *Through the Flower: My Struggle as a Woman Artist,* Introduction by Anaïs Nin. New York: Penguin, 1993.

Author, feminist, and artist Judy Chicago interweaves her personal history of marriage, betrayals, sexual awakening, and ostracism as a woman artist with the universal issues of gender, art, and power. Chicago includes a capsule history of female portrait artists, her blueprint for creating a community of women artists, and a description of how rage inspired her to create a uniquely feminine idiom—a woman's body and its sensations. Inspiring for both the nonartist and artist.

Conde, Maryse. *I, Tituba, Black Witch of Salem,* translated by Richard Philcox. New York: Ballantine Books, 1992.

The black witch of Salem, Tituba, looked for her story in the town
records and could not find it. Her story, just like the stories of
other African-American men and women, was missing from history until Caribbean writer Maryse Conde gave her a voice and a
history. Tituba's rage was born at age seven as she watched her
mother hang for daring to injure a plantation owner who was
raping her. Instead of seeking revenge, she learns the powers of
healing and magic; instead of hating men, Tituba finds a rich
erotic life and powerful love.

Debold, Elizabeth, Marie Wilson, and Idelisse Malave. *Mother-
Daughter Revolution: From Betrayal to Power.* New York: Addison-Wesley, 1993.

These authors expose the way mothers often betray their daughters
by leaving them powerless, passive, and silent. Well researched and
filled with sound advice on how to form a revolutionary mother-
daughter alliance, this book shows women how they can reclaim
their mothers' courage, how to give their daughters voice lessons,
and how to join with other women to seek the truth.

Dym, Barry, Ph.D., and Michael L. Glenn, M.D. *Couples: Exploring
and Understanding the Cycles of Intimate Relationships.* New
York: HarperCollins, 1993.

Dym and Glenn map out the cycles of intimate relationships and
tell us what to expect at each stage in a couple's drama. The authors guide their readers through each transition and suggest ways
to deal with Expansion, the period of getting to know each other
when partners feel terrific about themselves and each other, with
Contraction, as partners pull back and revert to stereotyped gender roles, and finally with Resolution, when a couple renews their
love in a more realistic way.

Esquivel, Laura. *Like Water for Chocolate: A Novel in Monthly Installments with Recipes, Romances and Home Remedies.* New York: Doubleday, 1992.

This novel is about passions and food, rage and romance, and how all of these ingredients get mixed together at meals and in marriage beds in Mexican family life at the turn of the century. It is a love story with recipes and an oral fantasy about food and family romance. The rage of women is passed down from one generation to the next and is folded into wedding cakes, squeezed into spicy sausage, and transmuted into fiery passion.

Euripides. *Medea,* translated by Alistair Elliot. London: Oberon Books, 1992.

This new translation by Alistair Elliot captures Medea's colossal rage and makes it contemporary for women who also feel like poisoning their husbands' mistresses and punishing the husbands who reject them. Her words are ancient but resound today—I sacrificed so much for you, I put you through medical school and raised your children; how can you leave me after all these years for a younger woman, a "trophy wife"? This translation was the book for the 1993–94 London and Broadway stagings of the play starring Diana Rigg.

Faludi, Susan. *Backlash: The Undeclared War Against American Women.* New York: Crown, 1991.

"Backlash" has become part of the national vocabulary since the publication of Faludi's book. She makes the case that the struggle for women's independence and equality has caused a backlash in the media. Her exhaustive research encompasses every aspect of popular culture and "trend journalism" that plants ideas which work against women's progress.

Friday, Nancy. *My Mother, Myself: The Daughter's Search for Identity*. New York: Laurel, 1987.

This book, a classic in the seventies, is still relevant today. Friday understands and articulates the ambivalence, intense love, hate, and rage that many woman feel toward their mothers, the first love in their lives. Friday examines the impact of this relationship on our self-esteem, identity, romantic relationships, and the paths we take through life to become ourselves and mirrors of our mothers.

Gornick, Vivian. *Fierce Attachments: A Memoir*. New York: Simon and Schuster, 1987.

Gornick's intense and intimate autobiography is about the complex relationship she has with her mother. She directs her readers to those startling moments of being—the times when a mother discloses a dark family secret or a friend tells us that our lover has invited her to have an affair with him. Gornick accurately describes the attendant rage—the feeling that she would like "to put her sneakers on and walk across the world."

Gray, John, Ph.D. *Men Are from Mars; Women Are from Venus: A Practical Guide to Improving Communication and Getting What You Want in Your Relationships*. New York: HarperCollins, 1992.

Using the metaphor that men and women are from different planets, John Gray explains why it's so difficult to talk to and understand the other sex. Although somewhat problematic in the reduction of the sexes to their essential natures, Gray's insights are helpful in telling us why men are so sensitive, how to listen without getting angry, why men pull away, and why women pressure them not to.

Heyn, Dalma. *The Erotic Silence of the American Wife.* New York: Signet, 1992.

Too often, American women enter marriage sexy and filled with vitality, but then lose their sexuality and sense of selves in trying to be perfect wives. Dalma Heyn's book breaks the silence about this loss of sexual identity and investigates why married women turn to infidelity to feel alive again and to alleviate depression.

Jack, Dana Crowley. *Silencing the Self: Women and Depression.* Cambridge, Massachusetts: Harvard University Press, 1991.

As a therapist, Dana Crowley Jack listened to many depressed women and found that they had silenced or disguised their real selves. To hold on to relationships, they pleased, stifled anger, censored their thoughts, or created false, secret selves that eventually erupted into hostility and angry explosions. According to Jack, the movement out of depression begins with acknowledging anger: "Women can use anger to disarm the inner tyrant and free the inauthentic self."

Lerner, Harriet Goldhor, Ph.D. *The Dance of Anger: A Woman's Guide to Changing Patterns in Intimate Relationships.* New York: Harper & Row, 1985.

Lerner, whose books *The Dance of Deception* and *Women in Therapy* are also extremely clear and helpful, takes a cognitive approach to anger. She provides women with ways to express anger that don't make them feel helpless, ashamed, or powerless. She explores anger at impossible mothers and how the dance of anger is based on triangles. Her do's and don't's show how to avoid triangle traps and how to deal directly with the person who has angered you.

Middlebrook, Diane Wood. *Anne Sexton: A Biography*. Boston: Houghton-Mifflin, 1991.

This biography stirred up tremendous controversy at the time it was published, because Sexton's family allowed Middlebrook to use tapes of the poet speaking to her psychiatrist under hypnosis. Sexton's life, those tapes, and Middlebrook's exhaustive research reveal a woman coming apart at the seams, enraged by her childhood, and courageously surviving by writing her poems. Rage is Sexton's inheritance which she passes down to her daughter in ways that will both intrigue and appall the reader.

Roth, Geneen. *Feeding the Hungry Heart: The Experience of Compulsive Eating*. New York: Signet, 1983.

Geneen Roth understands the emotional issues that lie behind compulsive eating and offers solutions on how to differentiate between physiological hunger and what she calls "the hungry heart." Many compulsive eaters binge, she writes, because they are angry and can't express it; learning to express anger directly is one of the first steps in her program for disconnecting food from emotions.

Schlessinger, Laura. *Ten Stupid Things Women Do to Mess Up Their Lives*. New York: Villard Books, 1994.

Dr. Laura Schlessinger, psychotherapist and host of an enormously popular radio talk show in Los Angeles, tells her readers to take responsibility for their problems. Pinpointing those passive and victimizing behaviors many women employ (being the nice gal, iron-fisted denial, desperate attachment, invalid anger, and many others), she offers practical advice on how to get smart and how to make real changes in your life.

Smiley, Jane. *A Thousand Acres.* New York: Fawcett Columbine, 1991.

This Pulitzer Prize–winning novel about three daughters, their father, and rage on a farm in Iowa traces the intertwining of generations and the burden of guilt from incest. The dynamics of family life, sibling rivalry, infidelity, divorce, and the shattering of men's and women's dreams are powerfully evoked.

Steinem, Gloria. *Revolution from Within: A Book of Self-Esteem.* Boston: Little, Brown, 1992.

After years of leading revolutions against the oppression of women, Gloria Steinem looks inward at those internal barriers and feelings of emptiness that keep both sexes from discovering their true selves. Her focus is self-esteem—how it develops, the current research, and ways to improve it. This book blends her personal reminiscences and crises with solid commentary on how to tap into personal power and growth.

Tannen, Deborah. *You Just Don't Understand: Women and Men in Conversation.* New York: Ballantine Books, 1991.

Deborah Tannen believes that each gender has much to learn from the other's style as she lays out the differences between the ways men and women talk. She pinpoints a major source of female rage, showing how avoiding confrontation sets up women for exploitation. This best-seller also looks at dialogue patterns and the kinds of words women use to placate others rather than to admit they're angry.

Tavris, Carol. *Anger: The Misunderstood Emotion,* revised edition. New York: Simon and Schuster, 1989.

Carol Tavris's study was the first to suggest that venting and angry outbursts are not necessarily healthy for human beings. This updated version of her comprehensive study asks whether

PMS and testosterone are excuses for anger and aggression and provides useful strategies for dealing with rage, with family battles, with chronically angry people, and with anger resulting from divorce, abuse, and even difficult children.

Whitfield, Charles, M.D. *Boundaries and Relationships: Knowing, Protecting, and Enjoying the Self.* Deerfield Beach, Florida: Health Communications, 1993.

Whitfield clarifies what boundaries are and explains why a lack of clear personal boundaries or too rigid parameters around the self set up women for unhappiness in relationships. Through charts, tests, and lucid prose, he touches on such issues as dependency and the need to control or being controlled by others.

Wolf, Naomi. *Fire with Fire: The New Female Power and How It Will Change the 21st Century.* New York: Random House, 1993.

Naomi Wolf follows up *The Beauty Myth* with this lively and readable investigation of nineties' feminism that asks why so many women eschew the feminist label. Wolf distinguishes between the victim feminism of the past few decades and challenges women with a manifesto for claiming power in the future. She also tells women to embrace their dark sides.

Credits

Grateful acknowledgment is made for permission to reprint the following text: lines from "Visions," in *Falling Off the Roof*, copyright © 1975 by Karen Lindsey, by permission of the author; lines from "The Muse as Medusa," reprinted from *Collected Poems of May Sarton 1930–1993*, with the permission of W.W. Norton & Company, Inc., originally published in *A Grain of Mustard Seed*, copyright © 1971, 1993 by May Sarton; an excerpt from "Eye to Eye: Black Women, Hatred, and Anger," in *Sister Outsider* by Audre Lord, copyright © 1984 by permission of The Crossing Press, Freedom, California.

Grateful acknowledgment is also made for permission to reproduce the following illustrations:

Chapter 1. The Birth of Female Rage

Woman in Yellow by Dante Gabriel Rossetti (1863), courtesy Tate Gallery, London/Art Resource, New York.
American Athena by Audrey Flack (1989), photo by Steve Lopez, courtesy Louis K. Meisel Gallery, New York.

Chapter 2. The Face of Rage

Head of Medusa by Caravaggio, courtesy Uffizi, Florence/Alinari/Art Resource/New York.
A Bacchante by Annibale Carracci, courtesy Uffizi, Florence/Alinari/Art Resource, New York.
Circe (or Song of Circe) by Alice Pike Barney (ca. 1895), courtesy National Museum of American Art, Washington, D.C./Art Resource, New York.
Le Viol (The Rape) by René Magritte (1945), courtesy of a private collection/Giraudon/Art Resource, New York.

The Vampire by Edvard Munch (1895/1902), courtesy Munch Museum, Oslo/Scala/Art Resource, New York.

Chapter 3. The Inner World of Rage

Medusa by Carlos Schwabe (1895), courtesy Barry Friedman, Ltd., New York.

Ophelia by Sir John Everett Millais (1851), courtesy Tate Gallery, London/Art Resource, New York.

Chapter 4. Rage and Relationships

Terra-cotta frieze of Perseus and Medusa. Artist unknown. Courtesy Acropolis Museum, Athens/Alinari/Art Resource, New York.

Danaë by Titian (c. 1554), courtesy Kunsthistorisches Museum, Vienna/ Foto Marburg/Art Resource, New York.

Chapter 5. The Rage of Age

Medusa mask. Artist unknown. Courtesy Acropolis Museum, Athens/ Alinari/Art Resource, New York.

Destiny (The Three Fates) by Goya, courtesy Prado, Madrid/Alinari/Art Resource, New York.

Chapter 6. Rage at Other Women

Clay relief of a Gorgon. Artist unknown. Courtesy Museo Archeologico, Syracuse, Sicily/Alinari/Art Resource, New York.

The Three Graces, courtesy Museo Archeologico Nazionale, Naples/ Giraudon/Art Resource, New York.

Clytemnestra by John Collier, courtesy Guildhall Art Gallery, London/ Bridgeman/Art Resource, New York.

Chapter 7. Awakenings

Head of Medusa by Antonio Canoca, courtesy Museo Archeologico Nazionale, Naples/Alinari/Art Resource, New York.

Perseus with Head of Medusa by Benvenuto Cellini, courtesy Loggia dei Lanzi, Florence/Alinari/Art Resource, New York.

The Escape of Perseus by Sir Edward Burne-Jones, courtesy Southampton Art Gallery, Hampshire/Bridgeman/Art Resource, New York.

Jason and Medea by Gustave Moreau (1865), courtesy Luxembourg Museum/Giraudon/Art Resource, New York.

Medea Premeditating the Murder of Her Children, courtesy Museo Archeologico Nazionale, Naples/Alinari/Art Resource, New York.

Photo of Tina Turner by Lynn McAfee/Shooting Star International.

Chapter 8. The Energy of Rage

Colossal Head of Medusa by Audrey Flack (1990), photo by Steve Lopez, courtesy Louis K. Meisel Gallery, New York.

My Nurse and I by Frida Kahlo (1937), courtesy Fundacion Dolores Olmedo, Mexico City/Schalkwijk/Art Resource, New York.

Index